POP CULTURE
FOR BEGINNERS

POP
CULTURE
FOR BEGINNERS

JEFFREY ANDREW WEINSTOCK

broadview press

BROADVIEW PRESS – www.broadviewpress.com
Peterborough, Ontario, Canada

Founded in 1985, Broadview Press remains a wholly independent publishing house. Broadview's focus is on academic publishing; our titles are accessible to university and college students as well as scholars and general readers. With 800 titles in print, Broadview has become a leading international publisher in the humanities, with world-wide distribution. Broadview is committed to environmentally responsible publishing and fair business practices.

© 2022 Jeffrey Andrew Weinstock

Library and Archives Canada Cataloguing in Publication

Title: Pop culture for beginners / Jeffrey Andrew Weinstock.
Names: Weinstock, Jeffrey Andrew, author.
Description: Includes bibliographical references and index.
Identifiers: Canadiana (print) 20210221402 | Canadiana (ebook) 20210221429 | ISBN 9781554815654 (softcover) | ISBN 9781770488113 (PDF) | ISBN 9781460407608 (EPUB)
Subjects: LCSH: Popular culture—Study and teaching. | LCSH: Popular culture—Textbooks. | LCGFT: Textbooks.
Classification: LCC HM623 .W45 2021 | DDC 306.07—dc23

Broadview Press handles its own distribution in North America:
PO Box 1243, Peterborough, Ontario K9J 7H5, Canada
555 Riverwalk Parkway, Tonawanda, NY 14150, USA
Tel: (705) 743-8990; Fax: (705) 743-8353
email: customerservice@broadviewpress.com

For all territories outside of North America, distribution is handled by Eurospan Group.

Canada

Broadview Press acknowledges the financial support of the Government of Canada for our publishing activities.

Edited by Tania Therien
Book design by Michel Vrana

PRINTED IN CANADA

CONTENTS

ACKNOWLEDGMENTS

As with my *Mad Scientist's Guide to Composition*, this book is the product of more than a quarter century's worth of experience teaching undergraduates. As such, first and foremost I want to thank the students who have been my guinea pigs over the years as I honed the approach to popular culture outlined in the pages to come. It is absolutely true that I have learned as much from them as they have learned from me—not least because I have depended on them to keep me up to speed on popular culture!

Thanks goes as well to those who supported the construction of this book both indirectly and directly. Of note in this regard are Anirban Baishya, Amanda Firestone, Nicholas Laudadio, Julie Webber, and Justin Wigard, who lent their expertise to the unit sections. Gina Arnold and Konrad Sierzputowski also composed sample essays specifically for this book, while Cait Coker, Kathleen Hudson, and Matthew Payne assisted me in obtaining permission to reprint their works in excerpted form. With that in mind, thanks go to *Refractory: A Journal of Entertainment Media* for permission to reprint Kathleen Hudson's "'Something from Your Life, Something That Angers You ...': Female Rage and Redemption in Netflix's *Stranger Things* (2016–2017)," to Intellect LTD and the journal *Fandom Studies* for allowing the reprinting of Cait Coker's "Everybody's Bi in the Future: Constructing Sexuality in the *Star Trek* Reboot Fandom," and to New York University Press for granting permission to reprint Matthew Thomas Payne and Michael Fleisch's chapter "Borderlands" from the edited collection, *How to Play Video Games*.

Heidi Lyn provided many of the amazing cosplay images sprinkled throughout the book and assisted me with obtaining permission to reprint the ones she herself didn't take, while the wonderful fan art in chapter 10 came directly from the artist, Kate Carleton. Among the many people who answered questions and directed me to resources to assist with chapters was Robin Reid, whose scholarly knowledge about science fiction fandom is unsurpassed.

ACKNOWLEDGMENTS

And a final thank you to Marjorie Mather and all the delightful people at Broadview Press for their assistance and support.

INTRODUCTION

Want to hear a secret?

There Are No Pop Culture Beginners

This book is titled *Pop Culture for Beginners*, but unless you've either been raised by wolves or grew up on a desert island with no contact with the outside world, you're no pop culture beginner. Indeed, you've been steeped in it your whole life. Have you seen any superhero or *Star Wars* movie? Pop culture. Do you stream programming on Netflix, Hulu, or Amazon? Pop culture. Do you participate on social media platforms such as Instagram or Snapchat or TikTok? Pop culture. Have you read a *Harry Potter* book? Own a smart phone, tablet, e-reader, or iPod? Did you watch the Super Bowl? Have you been to a Disney theme park or a Starbucks or a McDonalds? Do you listen to rock, hip-hop, or country music? Do you have a tattoo or piercing? Do you own a pair of jeans or sneakers? What would you do if you saw a single red balloon hovering strangely in place? Pop culture, pop culture, pop culture all the way down. You get the idea.

There are lots of different ways to define what is and isn't popular culture—and we'll get into the nitty-gritty in a little while in chapter 1—but, to get us going here, we can start to think of popular culture broadly as referring to widely shared beliefs, practices, and objects in a given time and place. Pop culture is often associated with youth culture and, in particular, with the idea of **subcultures**—groups such as skaters, punks, goths, and bikers with values and norms that differentiate them from the larger culture; this is a part of pop culture, but pop culture is more expansive than this—fast food and the Super Bowl are parts of popular culture without being restricted to a particular age or social group. Pop culture is also often thought of as being what's trendy or in fashion—and fads certainly are part of popular culture—but, again, it doesn't have to be the case: not only can we discuss the popular culture of bygone eras, but things like Disney and rock music and blue jeans remain popular culture even if they've been around for a long time.

Incredibly Important and Totally Meaningless

So you know popular culture. Indeed, you're an expert on it—at least, on some parts of it—and that's a real strength when it comes to thinking and writing about pop culture. Maybe you know all the lyrics to every Billie Eilish song ever or can quote freely from *Rick and Morty* or your fantasy football team just killed it because you know the ins and outs of fantasy draft day or you can't wait for the next season of *Stranger Things*—or maybe all these references are already outdated, so substitute your own, because pop culture changes quickly! We all live popular culture on a daily basis (well, except those who become hermits) and it is central to our lives—and our personal preferences and activities and hobbies can serve as a starting point for investigation. While there is some danger in writing about something you know and love—this can make it hard to be unbiased and objective in your evaluation—you can also draw upon your personal experience and expertise.

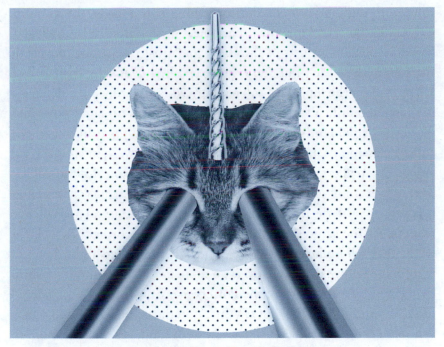

Laser Cat is Pop Culture

The irony of popular culture studies, however, is that these same activities and beliefs and things that are so central to people's lives are at the same time also frequently regarded by them as meaningless or trivial. This is what I call the **Pop Culture Paradox**. On the one hand, people spend countless hours (and often tons of cash!) enjoying video games or hip-hop or comic books; on the other hand, they often regard these investments of time, energy, and money as "just for fun"—depthless activities that don't really mean anything. We might wonder what there could possibly be to say about Drake or Lady Gaga, *Red Dead Redemption* or *World of Warcraft*, *Game of Thrones* or *The Big Bang Theory*, WWE or college football. It turns out that there is a lot to say, and our goal here is to figure out what that is and how to say it as we move forward.

There are a number of reasons though for this knee-jerk dismissal of the value and complexity of the things we love, and they tend to cluster around the ideas of *labor* and *utility*. First, we tend to associate value with difficulty: the harder something is to master, the more its mastery matters, and the more that object or skill in turn is privileged. For example, lots of lists of the "best" or "most important" novels of the twentieth century put one from 1918 called *Ulysses* by Irish author James Joyce at the top. Have you read it? Odds are probably not. *Ulysses* is a long and difficult work that makes use of experimental prose and places great demands on readers—and it is seldom read outside of college classrooms. J.K. Rowling's *Harry Potter* novels, in contrast, are enjoyed by readers of all ages and have sold over 500 million copies. There is certainly something to be said for literary works that seek to innovate, to push the boundaries of literary expression, and to challenge readers. At the same time, there is something to be said as well for works that sell millions of copies—and, when one gets right down to it, intimate knowledge of *Ulysses* is no more useful in the modern world than extensive knowledge of the Potterverse. So why is one considered more important than the other? What criteria are being used to establish value or merit? At least to some extent (and, yes, there is more to it than just this), *Ulysses* is privileged precisely because it is difficult to master. Getting through *Ulysses*, learning how to read it, understanding its complexities and allusions, is regarded as an accomplishment and a marker of education. The *Harry Potter* novels, in contrast—despite or perhaps even because of their widespread appeal—are considered less complicated, meaningful, and "serious."

Here, however, we need to be wary of the false dichotomy that distinguishes between "simple" and "difficult." To illustrate what I mean, allow me to step back briefly from pop culture and turn to two paintings.

On the left, in Fig. 0.1, we have a portrait (who it is doesn't really matter for our purposes, but it happens to be of Anna Maria Talbot, who was Countess of Shrewsbury, England, from 1659 to 1668. Interestingly, her husband, Francis Talbot, the 11th Earl of Shrewsbury, died from wounds he received from her lover ... but I digress). On the right, in Fig. 0.2, we have Marcel Duchamp's 1912 *Nude Descending a Staircase*. Unless you have a background in art history, you probably find the portrait of the woman on the left easier to make sense of than the Duchamp on the

Figures 0.1 and 0.2

right. Why? Because portraiture is familiar to us and we know how to approach it. When we look at the portrait, we grasp that it is posed, but still regard it as "photographic" in the sense of an "objective" attempt to represent reality. From the woman's luxurious hair and smooth complexion, we understand that she is a relatively young woman and that she is the focus of the picture. We may not be able to date the period, but her clothes mark her as both wealthy and from an earlier time period. Her meeting our gaze and her exposed skin mark her as assertive and a bit daring. Although the portrait seems to "naturally" convey these things, it only seems natural because, over time, we have developed interpretive strategies to make sense of our experience of images such as these. We see the painting and we can instantly categorize it: portrait, realistic, woman, young, rich. Not hard, right?

We don't realize that we are deploying deeply engrained interpretive strategies to make sense of the world until we encounter something— like the Duchamp painting—that those strategies can't accommodate.

Then we are left scratching our heads and wondering (with Homer Simpson-esque inflection), "What the heck is that?!" Learning about the painting, the artist, the intention, and the context can all help—knowing, for example, that the artist's goal was to try to convey a sense of movement though time in a single image gives us a starting point for understanding what we are seeing. Maybe we encounter the painting in an art history course and learn about the early twentieth-century artistic movements known as Cubism and Futurism with which Duchamp was associated. We see other examples. And then the next time we see something like Duchamp's *Nude Descending a Staircase*, we know what's going on. The point here is that we often mistake familiarity for simplicity—because something is familiar to us and we have well-established frameworks for making sense of it, we assume that there isn't much there to interpret. There is nothing natural or simple about interpreting a portrait; we have just learned how to do it, so it seems easy.

Shifting back to popular culture, we can realize the same point by considering what media scholar John Fiske (who we'll be discussing in chapter 5 in particular) refers to as the "**technical codes**" of television and film. How do you know when a character on TV is daydreaming? Because of familiar cues such as gentle harp music, a cloudy effect around the edges, sometimes a brief waviness of the picture. This was something we had to learn, of course. As a consequence of repetition over time, now we "naturally" associate these effects with daydreaming—but there is nothing natural about it. We've been trained to interpret these cues. Similarly, how do you know when a character in a horror film is in danger? Again, we are guided by technical cues that have become familiar over time such as an ominous, plodding soundtrack, dark lighting, sometimes a point-of-view shot with an unsteady handheld feel to it intended to connote the character is being watched. After we've seen a few scary films or TV programs, we understand how to interpret these cues and don't need to think about them anymore. But this is far from simple: we are being guided and manipulated by the producers of the film or program.

A Dream Sequence Beginning

Our considerations of popular culture, therefore, will be attentive to how meaning is created, conveyed, and "naturalized"—made to seem obvious and inevitable—and we won't make the mistake of assuming that just because something is popular and/or familiar to us, it lacks depth or meaning and isn't worth analyzing. Indeed, familiarity and popularity are two compelling reasons precisely *for* analyzing something because, if something is familiar, it is part of our lives, and if something is popular, it is part of many people's lives. So, we need to ask lots of questions: what is this thing before us? What are its qualities? How does it compare and contrast with other similar things? What messages does it seem to convey? How does it convey these messages? What qualities of it guide our interpretation of it? How do we use it? What explains its appeal? What assumptions about the world does it reconfirm or challenge? What explains its popularity? And so on. As you will see, coming up with the questions to ask and the language with which to ask them will be a major component of this book.

Work vs. Fun

The other reason a tendency exists to downplay or dismiss the importance of popular culture is a perceived opposition between fun on the one hand and utility on the other. We have it drilled into us from a young age that mastering academic subjects such as math, science, reading, and writing is essential to success as an adult—with success generally being defined as a job that earns one enough to support oneself and acquire various material objects that confirm one's success—car and home chief among them. We're told we can enjoy academic subjects ("learning is fun, kids!"), but nevertheless we're told at the same time we have to take our studies seriously or we'll never amount to anything. Oh, the places you'll go, right? First, however, you've got to buckle down, put your nose to the grindstone, stop fooling around, get serious, focus, pay attention, commit yourself to your studies, and so on.

Our activities outside of work—including hobbies but extending beyond them—on the other hand are presented precisely as rewards for a job well done: compensation for the important drudgery of labor. In contrast to our "work" (which is serious), the things we do for fun (and this is often where pop culture comes explicitly into the picture) are forms of play, done for relaxation and for amusement. Gaming is something we do (or are supposed to do!) after work or after our homework is done. **Cosplay** at cons is a vacation—an escape from reality. Tailgating before football games is something we do on weekends. Because these activities are categorized as play and contrasted with the "serious work we must do to be successful," there is a curious tendency to regard them as less meaningful. The irony is that there is often an inverse correlation between enjoyment and our perception of value. The more we enjoy it, the less it seems like work, and, as a consequence, the less important or meaningful it seems. When you stop to think about it, it is a very strange phenomenon: the things that mean the most to us are the things we tend to disparage as having the least meaning.

The What and How of Meaning

To take popular culture seriously is to "flip the script," so to speak. Our goal isn't to argue that popular culture is more important or meaningful than academic or professional labor, but rather to regard popular culture as just as meaningful, complex, and worthy of analysis as more "traditional" topics. In part this means bracketing and setting aside judgments about the "value" or "merit" of an object or practice. Our objective isn't to say that PBS's *Masterpiece Theater* is "better" than *Grey's Anatomy* or vice versa (although we can certainly analyze popular culture objects and make arguments about their construction and consistency, and why they succeed or fail at achieving whatever goals we conclude they have). Instead, our project is to consider various kinds of "**texts**"—"text" understood here as anything we interpret or "read"—and to analyze *what* they say and *how* they say it. Once we've done that, then we're in a position to start to speculate about the implications of our findings and what they tell us about ourselves, our moment, and where we might be headed—but we need to start with the object, practice, or belief first.

Put succinctly, we will consider all popular culture practices, beliefs, and objects as meaningful and we will set out to consider *what and how they mean*. The primary approach we will adopt, outlined in chapter 2, is called a **semiotic** one. Semiotics studies how meaning is created and communicated, and focuses on the rules that govern different systems of communication. Spoken and written languages are obviously systems of communication. So are sign language and semaphore (a visual method of signaling often using flags or lights). And, for that matter, so is fashion. A semiotic approach to fashion would consider the rules—learned but often unstated—that allow clothing to communicate meaning. What does it mean if we see a woman in a little black dress? What does it mean if we see a man in the same little black dress? What does it mean if someone is wearing Birkenstock sandals? What if that person is also wearing a tie and jacket? What does it mean if someone wears a black leather jacket to a metal concert? What does it mean if someone wears a black leather jacket to a fancy restaurant? As you've probably already guessed, it gets complicated very quickly. What clothing tells us—how clothing means—depends on many factors: the historical context (yoga pants today are common, something like yoga pants in the 1930s: scandal!), the associations connected to the individual items of clothing (tie-dyed clothing is associated with the hippie movement of the 1960s and 1970s), the combinations of garments (a blue blazer and solid-colored tie signal "conservative"; the blazer and tie together with flip-flops strikes us as eclectic), the body wearing that clothing (in American culture, women wear skirts, men generally don't; in Ireland, the kilt is traditional clothing for men), and the context in which the clothing is worn (a bathing suit at the beach is conventional; a bathing suit to work is unorthodox). Our semiotic analysis of fashion would try to tease out the rules that govern how fashion conveys meaning (and we would probably find rather quickly that we need to get more specific than the broad topic "fashion"—so we might decide to narrow things down to footwear or hats).

Our approach then will be to start with the things—the objects, the practices, the beliefs—and to think about what they are and how they *signify* or convey meaning. This process will involve brainstorming a lot of questions. Let's say our object of focus is a social media app (which we will attend to in much more detail in chapter 9). Among the questions we might consider in relation to the app are:

- What are the stated purposes of the app? What other purposes does it have? How does it seek to achieve its purpose(s)?
- How is the app constructed? What does it look like, what functions does it permit or prohibit, and how does one access and navigate it? What is the "experience" of using the app like?
- How does the app differentiate itself from other similar apps?
- Who are its primary users? In what ways does the app target particular populations? Are particular populations intentionally or unintentionally omitted or excluded?

- What assumptions are built into the app about users, their abilities, and their preferences? What assumptions do users bring to the app?
- How do users interact with each other using the app? Who "talks" to whom, about what, when, and in what ways? How does the app organize, direct, or manipulate users?
- Who generates content? How is content distributed, by whom, and to whom? If some content is user generated, in what ways does the app constrain or influence user-generated content?
- What is content used for and by whom? How long is content available? What makes content on the app more or less valuable or enticing?
- What behaviors does the app reward, permit, discourage, or prohibit? What rules—stated or implicit—govern how users interact with the app and each other?
- How are users rewarded or punished for their ways of using the app? How is power distributed on the app?

These questions ultimately lead us to a final, important one:

- In what ways does the app reconfirm or challenge established ways of thinking?

This final question about how something reconfirms or challenges established ways of thinking makes clear a fundamental premise that will govern the approach to popular culture in this book: popular culture is always **ideological**. What this means is that *popular culture practices, beliefs, and even objects ultimately affirm a particular understanding of the world.* In some cases, the messages are clear—Childish Gambino's 2018 track "This Is America" clearly laments and protests gun violence in the US and racism against African Americans. In other cases, the set of assumptions and values embedded in an object or practice isn't stated directly but is nevertheless present. Consider the orientation of almost every classroom you've ever been in. How is it set up? Who is standing, who is sitting? How is your attention directed? Is it a warm and comfortable space or spartan and cold? Do you have sofas, chairs, or tiny desks? What idea of education—of what learning is and how learning should take place—is communicated to you by the space and orientation of the classroom itself? These things are not stated directly, but are nevertheless built into the organization of the classroom space itself.

The Teacher Stands in Front of the Class

The example of the classroom makes evident a caveat to the "everything's ideological" approach to popular culture to be adopted here—when drawing conclusions about the "meaning" of something, we have to be attentive not only to what something says, but how it says it. Take, for example, a book addressing the dangers of climate change, but published by a major publisher in hardback, softcover, and e-book form. At the same time that the book is telling us we need to change our habits in order to combat global warming, the hard- and softcover versions exacerbate the problem the book seeks to solve by contributing to deforestation and propping up global capitalism, which gobbles up everything in sight. Of course, publishing the book as e-book only might limit the audience for the book as well as any potential income for the author. Nevertheless, the physical forms of the book are at odds with its message—and we, as readers, end up with a conflicted artifact: something that reconfirms ideas about books, publishing, and capitalism even as it seeks to address a problem these ideas feed.

Of Killjoys and Overreading

Before I talk a little bit about how this book is set up, I want to address two other criticisms of popular culture studies: the "you're taking all the fun out of it!" and the "you're reading way too much into this!" responses. The "killjoy" response is voiced by those who either see critical thinking as antithetical to enjoyment or who don't wish their enjoyment of something to be undercut by guilt or shame. To those who say "why do you have to pick it apart? Can't you just enjoy it?" one can respond that not only is there enjoyment in tinkering with something to see how it works, but the tinkering itself is a form of admiration. When you scrutinize something carefully, considering what it is and how it functions, you take that thing seriously, giving it your time and attention. As for selfish enjoyment, all one can say is "I'm sorry"—no one who isn't entirely dead inside likes to be told that the thing they enjoy is implicated in patterns of systemic exploitation and abuse. It's hard to think about factory farming when eating a Big Mac or the forced labor involved in mining rare earth minerals for smart phones when using your iPhone. It's hard to think about sexist representations of women in Bond films in relation to rape culture or the way video games might naturalize gun violence when you are a fan of first-person-shooter video games—but this is part of being a mature critical thinker who acts deliberately rather than simply reacts, and who weighs the costs and benefits of decisions in relation to one's personal ethics: knowing this, I'm still OK with it or I'm not.

As for the concern about overreading, not only does this concern often arise from the mistaken assumption that works of popular culture are simple or depthless, but from an overvaluing of the idea of **authorial intent**. When we refer to authorial intent, we are referring to what an author—and here we can extend this to any creator of a cultural artifact—meant their creation "to say." Of course, when exploring the meanings of a pop culture object or practice, it is reasonable to bear in mind authorial intent to the extent that it can be known. But authorial intent shouldn't unduly constrain interpretation for a number of reasons: first, because creators can be influenced in ways they are not consciously aware of and thus embed meanings they don't consciously intend; second, because all texts are to varying extents ambiguous and thus able to support competing interpretations; and third, because we create our own meanings when we interact with popular culture texts and the world. My experience of Jordan Peele's film *Get Out* isn't your *Get Out* and is different from Jordan Peele's own take on his film by virtue of my background, experiences, and associations.

The question of overreading, finally, is really the question of whether claims made can be supported. Do you have the evidence to back up your assertions? Does your analysis support your conclusions? If the answer to these questions is yes, then you may have a wild idea, but it isn't overreading.

To Infinity and Beyond!

This brings us then to this book, which is set up in two sections. The first section provides context and a set of tools for approaching popular culture with a critical eye. In chapter 1, I provide a fuller discussion of what popular culture is and an overview of how popular culture studies has developed. In chapter 2, I outline various approaches to thinking critically about popular culture. Here is where I explain semiotics in more depth. In chapter 3 then, I offer a consideration of other lenses one can use to focus on what and how popular culture means: **Marxism, feminism and gender studies, ethnic studies, postcolonialism**, and **critical race theory**. In chapter 4, I round out the "toolbox" section with a consideration of a number of key terms or "pivot points" for contemporary discussions of popular culture: **authenticity, convergence culture, intertextuality, structure of feeling**, and subculture.

Section two is set up as a series of units built around particular topics central to popular culture studies: television and film, music, comics, gaming, social media, and fandom. Each of these chapters will suggest a series of enabling questions to facilitate consideration of the topic and introduce key terms and background. There will be stopping points along the way for discussion, and each of the unit chapters will end with one or two sample readings illustrating scholarly approaches to the chapter's focus, suggested larger assignments, a list of works cited in the chapter, and then suggested texts for further reading. Throughout the book, when words are boldfaced, you will find them in the glossary at the end.

The goal of this book on popular culture is not finally to unscrew your head, pour in knowledge, shake you up, and ask you to regurgitate it. Studying pop culture is not like a biology class in which you have to memorize and be able to identify the different parts of the body or the stages of the Krebs citric acid cycle; instead, the purpose here is to prompt reflective engagement with the world around us and provide a set of tools for critical thinking. Put differently, this book is a starting point that provides some background, a set of approaches, and a variety of examples that can serve as templates for future investigation. Once we get past the assumption that pop culture is simple and without depth, a world of meaning opens up for us to investigate—and doing so helps us understand the network of forces that shape our experience and the ways we ourselves are implicated in reinforcing or challenging "the way things are."

And one last thing: pop culture in many cases has a very short shelf life, which creates complications for any textbook like this one seeking to introduce examples. What's hot as I'm writing likely will have cooled considerably by the time the book is published and finds its way into your hot little mitts. What this means is that any attempt to seem especially timely is doomed from the start. (Nothing makes a textbook like this one feel dated more quickly than addressing "flash in the pan" phenomena that sink out of sight before the book is even published!) For that reason, the examples and sample readings provided will tend to focus on more established texts: ones that were extremely important during their moment and that hopefully still have some relevancy. This book is intended, however, to provide a vocabulary and set of approaches that you can then apply to the pop culture phenomena of your choice.

THE POP CULTURE TOOLBOX

WHAT IS POPULAR CULTURE?

Hmmmm.....

Here is a brain teaser to start off chapter 1: when should something be considered "pop culture"? Consider this short list of events, activities, programs, celebrities, and products:

NASCAR. Quilting. Miley Cyrus. Miles Davis. Banksy. Botticelli. *Downton Abbey*. *Family Guy*. Luciano Pavarotti. Public Enemy. Cognac. Coors Lite. Easter. Valentine's Day.

Which of these do you think would qualify as popular culture and why?

In just asking this question, we're entering some surprisingly murky territory because a curious feature of popular culture studies has been the elusiveness of a single, clear definition for popular culture. In part, this has to do with the ambiguities connected to the name itself, especially the "popular" part. Just how popular is popular? Is there some threshold number of people or percentage of the population that divides popular from not popular? And does it matter with whom something is popular? If something is popular mainly with millionaires and billionaires, for example, is it popular culture? What if it is extremely popular only with a particular ethnic group or in a specific geographic region? Does age matter? Is popular culture purely for "the young" (whatever that means)? Or if something is very popular with senior citizens, is it still popular culture? What about something obscure like certain specialized niche sub**genres** of music—say neurofunk or wonky pop or chap hop or psychobilly? (which are 100 per cent real things—google them. Especially chap hop). And if something doesn't actually have to be widely popular to be considered pop culture, then what criteria for designation are in fact being used? Of course, we can take the same question in the other direction: is there a point at which something is so ubiquitous that it stops being popular culture and becomes simply culture? If so, where is that line?

Chap Hop

YOUR TURN: What do you think? How important is "popularity" when evaluating something as a part of popular culture?

The "culture" part of pop culture has its own issues, because it resonates in several different ways and comes with some problematic baggage. For our purposes, we will think of **culture** in terms of **material practices**: the things that people do and make in a particular time and place. These material practices then reflect a more general understanding of culture as a set of shared attitudes, values, and understandings (more about this below). There is, however, also a long history of thinking of "culture" in the sense articulated by precocious nineteenth-century theorist of popular culture Matthew Arnold as "the best which has been thought and said" (Arnold viii). With this in mind, to be "cultured," then, is to possess the ability to distinguish and appreciate intellectual and aesthetic "excellence." This sense of culture aligns with the idea of "good taste." To possess good taste is to have discerning judgment regarding what is artistic, fashionable, or socially appropriate—someone with good taste is someone who recognizes and prefers "quality" in art and literature, who knows how to dress in an appropriate and pleasing way, who acts in accordance with social expectations, and so on. This idea of taste then often goes hand in hand with the idea of "sophistication," which means the ability to appreciate nuance and subtlety. Someone with good taste in wine appreciates the subtle distinctions in vintages of the same type and knows which wine pairs best with a particular meal. Someone with good taste in music knows exactly which composition best suits a given occasion. The "cultured" person of good taste is refined and elegant rather than crude and vulgar—and are frequently found at the center of nineteenth-century "novels of manners" by authors such as Jane Austen and Edith Wharton. Such characters are also frequently lampooned as pompous snobs in modern comedies, such as *Schitt's Creek* or *The Big Bang Theory*, that contrast a down-to-earth protagonist or love interest against someone arrogantly elitist.

According to Whom, Based on What Criteria, and Serving Whose Interests?

You'll notice my use of what are called scare quotes around the words "cultured," "excellence," "good taste," "quality," and "sophistication" to imply some skepticism concerning them. The understanding of culture as "the best which has been thought and said" has been influential—and, as we shall see, still carries some weight. It is, however, also deeply problematic because it enshrines the values, tastes, and opinions of particular groups as uncontested fact—and this deserves a bit of push-back. To the idea of culture as the "best which has been thought and said," we can ask: according to whom, based on what criteria, and serving whose interests? Indeed, these are useful questions to ask any time assertions of quality are made about anything: *according to whom, based on what criteria*, and *serving whose interests*?

In some cases, criteria for evaluating the quality of something are relatively obvious and objective: one important measure of the quality of a sports team is the ratio of wins to losses. One therefore can assert that the more wins a team racks up, the better it is at what it does because winning the game is the primary objective. The football team that wins the Super Bowl, for example, is pronounced "world champion" (although it is remarkable, when you think about it, that an American team wins every year).

> **YOUR TURN:** What other ways could the quality of a sports team be evaluated apart from its win / loss ratio? Why is it that winning is prized most in twenty-first-century American culture?

The quality of a medication can also be evaluated in a straightforward way by considering its success in achieving its intended objective: curing someone who is sick while limiting side effects.

But when it comes to evaluating the "best which has been thought and said" or the quality of a work of literature, art, or music, things aren't quite as straightforward. To return to an example from my introduction to this book: many literary critics consider Irish author James Joyce's 1918 novel *Ulysses*—a complicated, dense work using a variety of different styles including stream-of-consciousness writing to tell a story paralleling Homer's *Odyssey*—as the best novel of the twentieth century. *Ulysses* is a very demanding novel on the reader—Joyce's vocabulary is enormous and the work requires a great deal of attention to figure out what is going on—and is primarily encountered in college literature courses (I'm not telling you not to read it, just to be ready!). In contrast, J.K. Rowling's *Harry Potter and the Sorcerer's Stone* (released in the UK as *Harry Potter and the Philosopher's Stone*), which came out in 1998, spent a year, more or less, at the top of the *New York Times* list of best-selling fiction, and has sold millions of copies, is often absent from such lists (see, for example, the Modern Library's "100 Best Novels" list). Why? Just what are the criteria one should use to evaluate the "quality" of a literary (or cinematic, or musical, or artistic, etc.) work and to what extent should *popularity* be considered a marker of quality?

> **YOUR TURN:** Pick a category of the arts such as literature, film, music, painting, or sculpture, and develop a list of criteria you would use to assess quality. Depending on the category you choose, you may wish to be more specific. For example, rather than films in general, you may wish to consider action films in particular.

To be fair, critics and scholars often do articulate their criteria for evaluation. In considering Joyce's *Ulysses* as the best—or at least among the best—twentieth-century novels, critics and scholars often point to its progression of styles, its use of symbolism and **allusion**, its complexity, its linguistic inventiveness, its humor, its **themes**, and just its overall ambitiousness. For Ben Heineman Jr., a writer for *The Atlantic*, for example, *Ulysses* is a "deeply humanistic novel which is bursting with the enormous variety of life" (Heineman). These are all reasonable things to consider when evaluating a novel—but there is another side to the story here as well. Heineman also notes that *Ulysses*, "[l]ike many great works of literature, ... requires repeated reading and deep study fully to understand—and ultimately to enjoy—the many dimensions and layers" (Heineman). The question then becomes—and this is an important question: who has the time, energy, and preparation needed to learn to appreciate a complicated and confusing novel full of allusions, parodies, and riddles by reading it multiple times? The answer is most likely people who have received a robust humanities-based education and have available leisure time. It is probably not someone exhausted from working several jobs who may prefer to spend any available free time with family, get caught up on housework, or just vegging out rather than trying to ferret out the nuances of a complicated Modernist novel.

All Work and No Play ...

What I am suggesting here is, to get back to the idea of culture as "the best which has been thought and said" and the associated charac-teristics of good taste and sophistication, that such pronouncements about quality often hinge on explicit or implicit criteria that have historically reinforced class distinctions. The best novel of the twen-tieth century, so say at least some of the critics, is one that requires a college education to attempt to read, immense concentration, and multiple readings to appreciate—not exactly the first thing that comes to mind when one thinks of "beach reading." This is not necessarily to allege malevolent intent—although, as we'll see below, early critics and theorists of popular culture certainly exhibit pronounced bias against working class culture (and, at least for some, popularity has implicitly been construed as antithetical to quality). I am not saying that scholars and critics and college professors such as myself privilege works as better or worse to the extent that they exclude those with less education or leisure time; I am, however, saying that this has been the practical effect for a long time.

Put differently, the classically educated, wealthy, and politically powerful elite have historically been the arbiters of taste, establishing criteria for quality in the arts that have often had the effect of reinforcing their own upper-class status. This is, in fact, the conclusion of sociologist Pierre Bourdieu who argues in an important work called *Distinction: A Social Critique of the Judgement of Good Taste* that "good taste" is—or at least has been historically—defined by those who possess power and social status, which then serves to reinforce their elevated social position. Those lower down the social class totem pole then are conditioned to aspire to possess the good taste and sophistication of the social elites by adopting their preferences (you may not be able to afford a Louis Vuitton original handbag, so look for a much less expensive knock-off); the upper class then responds, as sociologist Georg Simmel noted, by abandoning fashions once they are adopted by lower classes and turning to something new (see Simmel).

Definition by Opposition

All of this then brings us back to the conundrum of defining pop culture, which often has involved defining it by what it is not. Pop culture, for example, is not "**elite culture**" or "**high culture**," nor is it **folk culture**, the **avant-garde**, or general culture. The elite culture / pop culture divide, which we have already been talking about, differentiates practices and bodies of knowledge associated with the upper class from those associated with the middle and lower classes. As discussed above, upper-class practices and bodies of knowledge have historically been those that require money, leisure time, and, to a certain extent, education—so we can think of things like wine, opera, "art-house" film, classical literature, and so on. These practices and bodies of knowledge are then contrasted with their pop culture variations: beer, pop music, general release films, novels by the likes of Rowling and Stephen King, etc. This has sometimes, and usually dismissively, been referred to as **mass culture**—the culture of the masses, i.e., the lower classes. Mass culture, as we'll see, has in the past been criticized by cultural elites for a variety of reasons, but which all boil down to not meeting high culture standards for quality.

This kind of distinction between elite or high and pop culture, however, runs into two complications. First, it isn't just a binary opposition between two equal categories, but has historically been viewed as a hierarchy in which the elite side simply is better and more meaningful. Depth of knowledge of Shakespeare and classical mythology marks one as educated; depth of knowledge of *The Simpsons* means one has spent too much time watching cartoons. Giacomo Puccini's famous opera *La Bohème* is sublime; the latest pop song hit by (insert current pop star of your choice here) is formulaic fluff; and beer is for those who can neither afford nor appreciate fine wine. We're back to the ideas of "culture" as "the best which has been thought and said," and "good taste" as that which the upper class naturally possesses and everyone else should aspire to obtain. But again, we can and should question this: one can reasonably ask, for example, why an encyclopedic knowledge of Shakespeare is any more valuable or useful than being an expert on *The Simpsons*.

YOUR TURN: Having introduced the question, let's discuss it— why is a body of knowledge about Shakespeare or classical myth more valuable than a body of knowledge about *The Simpsons, Star Trek, Harry Potter*, or any other pop culture franchise?

Second, in the twenty-first century, to the extent that the lines between elite and pop culture ever really existed, they have become progressively fuzzier. A knowledge of wine is no longer the exclusive property of the monied classes, while craft brewing has elevated the status of beer. Outdoor opera performances draw enormous crowds (at least they did pre-COVID-19 and hopefully will again) while pop stars perform with philharmonic orchestras. The stark fact of cost still remains—only the super wealthy can afford giant yachts and private jets—but any automatic association between wealth and culture arguably exists today mainly as a form of nostalgia or a marketing strategy in which millionaires in limousines pass each other jars of mustard. Put differently: in the twenty-first century, culture in the sense of "being cultured" is no longer the exclusive property of the upper-class. Some have lamented this as the "waning of taste," in which, in the absence of an entrenched upper-class setting standards, "quality" has become a casualty and the world of art a kind of free-for-all. Further, some conservative standard-bearers decry the **commodification** of "great art" such that

one can decorate dorm rooms with prints of Van Gogh's *Starry Night* or dress up Michelangelo's *David* with refrigerator magnet outfits. This hand wringing, however, seems primarily to find its roots in upper-class resentment over the waning obeisance of the lower classes and their encroachment upon previously insulated environments.

Pop Culture vs. Folk Culture

Another form of negative definition—defining popular culture by what it is not—is the purported distinction between pop culture and

Mona Lisa *2.0*

folk culture, which depends on two concepts that will be very important in various ways to this investigation of popular culture: **authenticity** and commodification. Folk culture is connected to what are considered "traditional" customs and practices of a particular community in a specific place. Folk culture is generally rural, rather than urban, and is often considered as a kind of inheritance or heritage. Folk music is a familiar form of folk culture—music such as bluegrass or gospel spirituals associated with particular regions or ethnic groups. However, folk culture can extend to many other practices, such as dress, crafts, traditional foods, holidays and observances, and so on. Such practices can be construed as "authentic" in the sense of being historically grounded and sincere expressions of a way of life—or culture in its broadest sense—in a particular place. It is the culture of the "folk"—the "common" people. Such practices are also often associated with **artisanal** production; an artisan is a skilled craft worker who creates material objects partly or entirely by hand. As such, constraints are placed on how quickly such objects can be produced.

When defined against folk culture, pop culture is no one's traditional or "authentic" culture. Pop culture is instead from this perspective something invented for mass consumption—mass culture as mentioned

Folk Art

above—and may involve the commodification of folk culture. For example, woven Navajo rugs and blankets have a long history going back over a thousand years and may be considered an Indigenous artistic form expressive of Navajo folk culture. The mass commodification of Navajo rugs for non-Native consumers is the "inauthentic" pop culture version.

> **YOUR TURN**: Authentic Navajo rugs may sell for thousands of dollars. Copies sell for far less. If the original and the copy are identical, why is the original worth so much more?

In some cases, folk populations intentionally commodify their own culture as a source of income. Frankenmuth, Michigan, for example, markets itself as "Little Bavaria" and offers tourists German folk music, food, and German-inspired gifts. In other cases, those from outside a particular folk culture utilize elements of that culture, which has created a debate surrounding the ethics of **cultural appropriation**.

> **YOUR TURN**: Cultural appropriation can be considered as the adoption of the practices or customs of one group by members of another. Often, but not always, the appropriating group is part of the *dominant culture*. Under what circumstances, if any, do you consider cultural appropriation acceptable?

Popular culture as *not* folk culture need not entail questions of appropriation however. Sometimes the contrast is simply between something with an entrenched connection to a particular folk culture and a mass-produced **commodity** without a history associated with any particular group: the difference between a didgeridoo created by an Australian Aborigine and a kazoo.

As with the distinction between elite culture and pop culture, the contrast between folk culture and pop culture often is not just an opposition between two equal things but a hierarchy of value, with folk culture generally being considered more valuable due to assumptions about artistry as well as the contemporary Western fetishization of authenticity. The value of a commodity—that is, anything that can be bought and sold—is based on several factors, but central among these are the amount of labor involved in their creation and their scarcity. A table hand-carved by a skilled craftsman is considered more valuable than a similar mass-produced table from Ikea because the hand-carved one took much longer to produce and is one of a kind, and we have agreed to acknowledge these things as valuable qualities. Importantly, these values need to be recognized as **ideological** (see chapter 2) rather than natural—they reflect a set of values that have been shaped over time and reinforced to such an extent that they seem natural. As a thought experiment, one could imagine a group of future space aliens sifting through the rubble of extinct Earth civilization and being more impressed with the aesthetic and clever design of the Ikea table than with something made by hand.

Relatedly, contemporary Western culture places a great premium on authenticity. While I'll be discussing this more in chapter 4, the twenty-first-century tendency is to privilege "the real thing" over the "knock off"—the "real thing" being defined here as a sincere and appropriate expression of cultural affiliation and/or artistry. Folk culture wins over pop culture on both the artistry and authenticity counts—and this reflects a prevailing, but, again, contingent, structure of value in which handmade is privileged over mass produced. Although something mass produced may be indistinguishable from a hand-constructed original, and although mass-produced items may be aesthetically pleasing and well-constructed in their own right, contemporary Western society nevertheless historically equates value with scarcity and artisanal craftsmanship.

Pop Culture vs. the Avant-Garde

Another thing that pop culture is often defined against is the avant-garde (French for "fore-guard"—the vanguard or advance guard). The avant-garde is the "cutting edge" of a particular medium. Avant-garde works are experimental creations that often challenge conventional ways of thinking and run contrary to established tastes. Put differently,

Popified Cubism

avant-garde works often start off as hard to consume and enjoy; over time, society often becomes comfortable with the avant-garde, assimilating it as part of an artistic medium—today's avant-garde becomes tomorrow's mainstream. Cubism in art, bebop in jazz, and free verse in poetry are examples of forms that were once avant-garde but have now been assimilated into their categories and don't particularly vex or confuse contemporary consumers of art, jazz, and poetry respectively.

When evaluated in relation to the avant-garde, pop culture again always seems to come up short. The avant-garde is "edgy," "risky," "daring," sometimes "cerebral" or "provocative," and so on—and, for these reasons, it typically has selective appeal. There is in fact a kind of asymptotic connection between the avant-garde and elite culture as appreciating the avant-garde often depends on a process of education. Appreciating avant-garde art or music, for example, often requires knowledge of the history of the medium and an understanding of the artist and/or movement's intentions. Going back to my introduction, Cubism in painting was avant-garde art in the first two decades of the twentieth century. Those who initially hailed it as pioneering were artists, critics, and educated fans of art who understood the movement in relation to earlier forms of art and its intentions. Cubism has since become assimilated into popular culture and, while perhaps still seeming strange to some viewers, is certainly not unfamiliar.

Pop culture, in contrast, when considered in opposition to the avant-garde, is characterized as easily digestible. It plays to conventional ways of thinking and established tastes rather than challenging them. Where avant-garde art is subversive of or even hostile to established tastes, intentionally breaking with tradition and challenging its consumers to reconceive a genre, pop culture from this uncharitable perspective lacks awareness of its participation in an established artistic tradition and is, in essence, candy—empty calories—to be consumed by non-critical audiences. Popular culture is therefore popular precisely because it appeals to the "lowest common denominator."

> **YOUR TURN:** This contrast between the avant-garde and pop culture suggests that pop culture cannot be subversive of established tastes and cultural understandings. Do you agree?

Pop Culture vs. Culture

This last opposition takes the question of "the popular" in the other direction. Is there a point at which something is so commonplace, so ubiquitous, that it is no longer popular culture? Just what is the difference between "culture" in general and "popular culture" in specific? Many people in the US, for example, possess and drive cars. Does that mean that driving is popular culture? And what about religion? According to a 2014 survey done by the Pew Research Center, 70.6 per cent of Americans identify as Christian (see "America's Changing Religious Landscape"). That suggests Christianity is certainly popular. But is it pop culture? My sense is that many people of faith would quickly dismiss that idea as absurd, but why?

> **YOUR TURN:** To what extent would you include religion as part of popular culture?

This question about the difference between popular culture and culture in general gets at the heart of the confusion surrounding the idea of popular culture. If we think of **culture** as *the things that people make and do that convey meaning in a particular time and place*, then popular culture would be things made or done by vast numbers of people—and this is what some popular culture commentators have argued. Pioneering scholar of popular culture Ray Browne, for example, defines popular culture in his essay, "Folklore to Populore," as follows: "Popular culture consists of the aspects of attitudes, behaviors, beliefs, customs, and tastes that define the people of any society. Popular culture is, in the historic use of term, the *culture of the people*" (Browne 25). By "the people" here, Browne means the "common people"—the masses rather than the cultural elite. Similarly, Dustin Kidd defines popular culture as "the set of practices, beliefs, and objects that embody the most broadly shared meanings of a social system" (Kidd).

These definitions of popular culture, however, are weirdly at odds with the ways in which popular culture is discussed in the **popular press**—and discordant, I would propose, with the ideas about popular culture most non-scholars hold. Often, those who write about pop culture in the popular press seem to be operating with a kind of "**fuzzy set**" conception of pop culture—things at the center of the set are good examples; as one moves toward the periphery of the fuzzy set, examples shade toward something else: folk culture, the avant-garde, elite culture. So, recognizing that any attempt to define popular culture is going to elicit criticism, one might nevertheless start by working backward and considering the kinds of things routinely discussed as pop culture. Like pornography, pop culture is something people seem to know when they see it, and discussions of the topic often focus on things such as: comics, conventions, and **cosplay**; celebrity culture and fandom; video games; rock concerts and pop music—especially music marketed to teenagers and associated with urban environments such as hip-hop, rap, and techno; general release films; most genres of television (notably animation, sitcoms, melodramas, crime dramas); new technologies and new technological platforms such as podcasts and social media—again, especially those associated with teenagers and young adults; best-selling works of fiction (the *Harry Potter* books, the *Twilight* series, novels by Stephen King and Michael Crichton, fantasy and science fiction in general); sporting events popular with the working class (baseball, football, NASCAR); advertising; fast food; Ikea; and so on.

By looking at the things routinely described as being part of popular culture, we can extrapolate out a list of shared features that characterize events, practices, and objects discussed as pop culture. These features include the following:

- *Accessibility without significant training, education, or expense.* One need not have gone to college or to be a "trust fund baby" to participate in pop culture. Pop culture is "democratic" in this respect.
- ***Affective*** *engagement.* Events and media considered as pop culture often afford or evoke an emotional experience with a physical component—the exhilaration of a concert, the tension of a horror film, the arousal of pornography, the sobs elicited by a melodrama, the laughter of the sitcom.
- *Youth orientation.* Popular culture is often, although not always, associated with things "young people"—teenagers and those in their 20s in particular—make, do, and consume.
- *Trendiness.* Popular culture is often defined by a limited shelf-life. Fashion trends change quickly, media personalities fade rapidly, summer blockbusters and chart-topping albums quickly give way to new releases. While some celebrities and artists defy this, pop culture for the most part is defined by its protean nature and ephemerality.
- *Indifference to or antagonism toward established sources of authority and entrenched standards of taste, decorum, and "appropriateness."* Connected to its youth orientation, that which is considered pop culture often pays no heed to or displays an irreverence toward tradition, established standards for "quality," good taste, and those who seek to enforce these things.
- *Rejection of "age appropriateness."* A specific form of indifference to or antagonism toward established sources of authority and

entrenched standards of taste and decorum—and connected to pop culture's youth orientation—is pop culture's refusal to honor traditional expectations concerning "age appropriate" behavior. When "grown-ups" cosplay; play video games; read comics, fantasy, and science fiction; and so on, they are "acting like children"—that is, refusing to abide by long-standing expectations regarding maturation.

- *Frivolity.* The activities that constitute contemporary popular culture, particularly when they ignore or reject sedimented understandings of age appropriateness, are often construed (even by those who participate in them) as frivolous, in the sense of a being "unproductive." Pop culture activities are thus considered as "time wasters," leisure time activities, and sometimes forms of escapism. Pop culture is thus defined against the productive time of labor.

- *Individualistic.* As a form of escapism or leisure time activity defined against productive labor, popular culture events and activities are conceived of as *choices* reflective of an authentic identity. Pop culture privileges the notion of authenticity as a sincere reflection of an individual's talent, passion, creativity, or "uniqueness."

- *Depthlessness.* Pop culture is often characterized as lacking "deeper meaning." It is enjoyed primarily for its affective arousal—the stimulation, relaxation, or "fun" it affords the consumer. In some cases, attempts to derive deeper meaning are met with resistance or antagonism.

- *Community.* Participation in popular culture establishes a form of community among individuals with similar tastes. While the "popularity" of pop culture forms can be questioned, one never participates in pop culture alone.

The list above reflects characteristics of and attitudes toward popular culture that seem to pervade contemporary thinking and writing in the popular press and in social media—and these attributes suggest that, when we think about popular culture, we have something much more specific in mind than "the culture of the people." While we will take a closer look at some of these assertions as we move forward (notably the assumption that popular culture lacks depth or is frivolous), the list does allow us to propose a working definition for popular culture to govern our investigations:

> Popular culture can be defined as social practices and activities in which people can engage without significant training, education, or cost. Typically associated with youth culture and quick to morph or fade, pop culture practices and activities are often construed as forms of leisure that allow for personal expression, afford pleasure, and create community. Such practices and activities often ignore or display an irreverence toward tradition, established standards for "quality" and "good taste," age appropriateness, and those who seek to enforce these things. These practices and activities—and the objects and media that are their focus—are often presumed to lack interpretive depth or complexity despite their centrality to the lives of participants and consumers.

The Development of Popular Culture Studies

I want to focus on the last part of this definition—the assumption of a lack of depth and complexity—not just because it returns to a point I raised in the introduction to this book, but because it condenses the history of popular culture studies and captures the paradox of our lived experience of popular culture. In the introduction, I highlighted the irony of the "**pop culture paradox**"—the fact that activities and practices central to people's lives are at the same time devalued as trivial. We can spend hours each week gaming, binge-watching a Netflix series, reading popular fiction, going to movies, tailgating, and so on. We might describe these things as our passion, what we live for, and yet, there is nevertheless a tendency to say that these things are "just for fun" and don't really have deeper meaning. After all, what deeper meaning could there be to *Iron Man* or Ariana Grande or a Packers game?

Tailgating

In asking this question of what deeper meaning there could be to the things we enjoy, we're inevitably back again to questions of value and the criteria being used to establish it (get used to it—we're going to be talking about this a lot!). What's particularly fascinating about the pop culture paradox—pop culture as simultaneously incredibly important and totally meaningless—is the way that it is the product of and reflects a particular world view that has developed over time and been reinforced so consistently that it just seems natural—just the "way things are." There are the things we study in school that are important and meaningful (if often boring), there is the work we do that hopefully we enjoy but that we do even if it isn't to survive, and then there are the frivolous things that we do in our downtime that are crucial to our wellbeing, part of our "selfcare," and yet really not meaningful beyond that. But an important premise of this guide to popular culture is that the way things are is never "natural," but rather the product of historical forces and circumstances.

> *Any time you hear someone say, "that's just the way it is!" be on guard.*

As will be developed in the next chapter, this is how ideology functions: by presenting history as nature. Instead of just accepting the **status quo** as natural and inevitable, our goal here is to cultivate a mindset that asks why things are the way they are, how they came to be this way (this is often the starting point for excellent research projects), and how things might be different in the future. We will ask whose interests are served by the status quo, and then consider how they could be otherwise. Indeed, were I to boil this textbook down to a single objective, it would be precisely this: *learn to think critically about the world you inhabit and recognize that the way things are is always only one of many possible worlds.*

This is very much central to the pop culture paradox. There is absolutely nothing natural or inevitable about the devaluation of pop culture. Instead, it reflects a long history of social forces. Indeed, as suggested above, the first thinkers to give serious consideration to the development of what we are defining here as popular culture not only took a dim view of it, but considered it as an active threat to the entrenched interests of the upper class—pop culture was low culture, debased culture, *dangerous* culture. As John Storey notes, "[t]hose with political power have always thought it necessary to police the culture of those without political power, reading it symptomatically for signs of political unrest; reshaping it continually through patronage and direct intervention" (Storey 21). In the nineteenth century, spurred by forms of social change including industrialization and urbanization, the political dynamic between the haves and have-nots began to shift. The threat to the upper class posed by the lower classes is at the heart of Matthew Arnold's *Culture and Anarchy* (1869), the work that posits that culture is "the best which has been thought and said," that to be cultured is to be able to recognize the best, and that the pursuit of culture can "minster to the diseased spirit of our time" (Arnold 31). Arnold's recommendation to quell the threat of social unrest posed by an increasingly assertive working class is a mix of education and policing by the state.

Matthew Arnold certainly wasn't the first to pinch his nose at the "culture" of the "unwashed masses," but his *Culture and Anarchy* outlines in stark terms the divide between culture as what he refers to as "sweetness and light" and the trivial or debased popular culture of the underclasses, a distinction then elaborated upon more fully by later critics and commentators. Notable among these later commentators is

F.R. Leavis who, in a pamphlet published in 1930 titled *Mass Civilization and Minority Culture*, echoes Arnold directly:

> In any period it is upon a very small minority that the discerning appreciation of art and literature depends.... Upon this minority depends our power of profiting by the finest human experience of the past; they keep alive the subtlest and most perishable parts of tradition.... In their keeping ... is the language, the changing idiom, upon which fine living depends, and without which distinction of spirit is thwarted and incoherent. By "culture" I mean the use of such a language. (Leavis qtd. in Williams, *Culture & Society*, 253)

As Raymond Williams notes, Leavis, writing in 1930, was responding in particular to what he considered the debased culture of advertising, popular fiction, films, and radio broadcasting that were threatening to overwhelm "the ways that he and others valued" (Williams 257). "'Mass-civilization,' without discernable respect for quality and seriousness" (Williams 257) was threatening to swamp Western culture and erode upper-class privilege.

No doubt Arnold and Leavis and other standard-bearers of high culture believed strongly that their criteria for evaluation of art were universal and unquestionable, and that they possessed the necessary faculties of discernment to distinguish great art from trash. And there may well be significant value in cultivating the intellectual faculties necessary for engaging with classical works of art—the point here is not to devalue the classical tradition or to substitute a **canon** of popular culture works for classical works, but instead to raise questions about the criteria for establishing value that are being used in the first place. Nevertheless, from a twenty-first-century perspective, Arnold and Leavis and others like them may sound like pretentious snobs whose lamentations about the lower classes' lack of culture betray their own anxiety about retaining political and social status—and there is certainly much to that diagnosis. The irony however is that, while we might disdain or ridicule their elitism, it still retains a grip on our thinking about popular culture and is part of the pop culture paradox. Why is that?

YOUR TURN: To what extent do you think activities and practices associated with the wealthy and culturally elite still shape ideas of quality and value?

The Frankfurt School and the Mass Culture Industry

Part of the answer to that question of why we can thumb our nose at the snobbishness of cultural elites while still having our thinking shaped by their elitism can be found in the work of a group of intellectuals collectively referred to as the **Frankfurt School**. Associated initially with the Institute for Social Research at Goethe University in Frankfurt, Germany in the 1920s and 1930s (hence the name Frankfurt School) before relocating to the US due to the rise of Nazism in Germany, members of the group explored social conditions that facilitated and reinforced oppression, and theorized changes that might permit the emergence of a more egalitarian culture. As part of their investigation, they were especially critical of mass culture, which they theorized as an important means through which contemporary **capitalism** propped itself up. In a work titled *Dialectic of Enlightenment*, two thinkers associated with the Frankfurt School, Theodor Adorno and Max Horkheimer, developed a thesis that what they referred to as "the **culture industry**"— what we might refer to as popular culture—was essentially a factory pumping out standardized products such as movies, magazines, music, and so on, which had the effect of pacifying people and making them content with their situations despite difficult economic circumstances— pop culture as a tranquilizer for the masses.

People, according to Adorno and Horkheimer, have what may be referred to as **real needs**—psychological needs to be creative, independent, and autonomous. These needs, according to the Frankfurt School, cannot be met for most in a capitalist society because the majority of people have to work hard at boring jobs to eke out a living; what capitalism does is create and substitute **false needs** that can be satisfied through consumerism and suppress real needs. This is where the

culture industry comes in. The culture industry mass produces items for us to consume and gives us the appearance of freedom of choice and the ability to express ourselves, while taking over our imagination and asking us to choose from a variety of things that are basically the same. If we are hungry, we can choose from among ten different fast food restaurants offering more or less the same thing on the same main thoroughfare—and the advertising for them inevitably shows us happy people enjoying quality time with friends and family: we're not just buying a burger, but buying happiness. Similarly, if we want to go to the movies, we can choose among twelve different offerings at the local multiplex, all about the same length and with similar endings. If we need new shoes, we can select from 300 similar pairs available from a variety of online retailers. We buy, therefore we are, and, by being a consumer, we are told that we are expressing our individuality.

The especially pernicious part of this from the Frankfurt School's point of view is that, because our real needs are not actually being met,

Pop Music in the Smart Phone Age

culture industry products only offer a temporary sense of release and euphoria—just enough to relax or refresh us so we are ready to face the work week again. We enjoy our pop culture pursuits on the weekend so that we can return to being diligent workers during the week, earning profits for the businesses that employ us and make money off our labor. This is connected to the standardization of culture industry products: we aren't being asked to think. In a famous (and controversial) analysis of popular music of the 1930s—essentially big band standards—Adorno characterizes popular music as defined by repetition with minor variation—what he calls "**pseudo-individualization**" (see Adorno). His argument is that pop music essentially comes pre-digested; it doesn't require thought or attention. In contrast to classical music, which, according to Adorno, has an organic structure that requires active listening to appreciate, popular music is a distraction that can be absorbed in a state of inattention: it's there in the background. It's basically candy—tastes sweet, has no nutritional value, is ultimately bad for us.

> **YOUR TURN:** Thinking in terms of contemporary pop music or movies, do you find Adorno's critique of the mass culture industry persuasive? Why or why not?

Adorno and Horkheimer's positions on what we'll refer to as pop culture have the potential to elicit a knee-jerk rejection wherein we scrutinize our listening and viewing preferences, identify works that we consider original or complex, and use them to argue against the ideas of pop culture as dumbed-down standardized mass culture. Perhaps we're willing to grant that their description seems to fit genres that we don't know well or particularly enjoy, or even that it works for much of a genre that we do know well and enjoy, but then we point to a particular song or band or movie marked by what we consider its originality or mastery. Or maybe we take issue with the premise of pseudo-individualization entirely, using our knowledge of superhero movies or hip-hop or detective novels to argue that there is in fact immense variation within the genre. These kinds of responses conform to what we might call the "my mama" rule—I can make a joke about my mama, but you can't!—and they speak to our emotional attachment to pop culture practices as we defend the thing we enjoy against what seems an unfair attack by a biased critic. This, too, is part of the pop culture paradox: we will defend this thing we are passionate about against attack even as we dismiss it having "real value." The point here is that we have been conditioned to associate pop culture with "leisure" and then to devalue such practices as less important when compared with "work" or "school"—and the educational system has been deeply implicated in maintaining this hierarchy.

Popular Culture Studies

At this point, given such a history of deeply entrenched bias against popular culture, you may be starting to wonder how modern popular culture studies ever came into being. The birth of contemporary popular culture studies can be traced to a shift in thinking initiated in the field known as **cultural studies** in the 1960s—indeed, pop culture studies today can reasonably be thought of as a subdivision of cultural studies. Much of the approach to popular culture that informs this textbook derives from the tack adopted by the Centre for Contemporary Cultural Studies (CCCS) at the University of Birmingham starting in the 1960s. Sometimes referred to as the Birmingham School of Cultural Studies, the CCCS used and combined a variety of critical lenses, including **Marxism** and **feminism**, to explore the various ways we endow our world with meaning through the things we make and do. The important thing about the CCCS is that they took popular culture as a serious topic of investigation, analyzing what pop culture had to say and how it said it. This extended to things like punk rock, **subcultures**, media audiences, celebrities, film, and television. The academic study of popular culture in the US was officially inaugurated in 1972 when English professor Ray B. Browne founded the first academic department of popular culture at Bowling Green State University in Ohio, as well as the Popular Culture Association.

Fast forward to the twenty-first century: attitudes toward the study of popular culture have shifted ... somewhat. The canon of great books has been shaken up, but not displaced entirely. Universities offer courses on popular culture (often as electives rather than "core" courses) and primary and secondary schools increasingly incorporate things like popular music, TV, and comics into their curriculums. And yet, the tendency to think of these things as supplements to "traditional learning" or ways to get kids' attention rather than valuable and meaningful in their own right persists. To borrow from George Orwell's 1945 novel *Animal Farm*, all forms of culture are now equal, only some forms are more equal than others.

Our task here, again, is not to invert the high culture / pop culture opposition and to insist that *Family Guy* should replace Faulkner or that Metallica is better than Mozart. Nor is the intention to jettison criteria for evaluation entirely and abandon all attempts at assessing the quality of something. Instead, our goal is to take popular culture seriously and see in it complex and meaningful expressions of shared understandings and beliefs. As will be developed in the next chapter, we will consider popular culture as consisting of **signifying practices**—things that people make and do that convey meaning. And to the extent that we wish to evaluate the quality of something, we will work to articulate clear criteria that explain how we arrive at our conclusions—always bearing in mind the question of whose interests are served by such pronouncements. And maybe, just maybe, by thinking about popular culture from a new perspective, we can start to untangle the pop culture paradox and to reconsider pop culture as something other than mindless amusement.

Suggested Assignments

1. Look more deeply into the ideas of one of the thinkers introduced in this chapter, such as Matthew Arnold, F.R. Leavis, Raymond Williams, or Theodor Adorno. Alternatively, explore the ideas of either the Frankfurt School or the Birmingham School of Cultural Studies in greater depth.

2. Develop and apply your own criteria for evaluating the merit of a popular culture **text**. For example, devise a set of criteria for evaluating the quality of an amusement park attraction such as a haunted house, a diner, or a comic book and then apply those criteria to a particular example.
3. Explore changing ideas of the avant-garde in relation to a particular artistic genre.
4. Reflect on your personal tastes in relation to a particular aspect of popular culture such as television or popular music. How did your tastes develop and what influenced their development most?

Works Cited in the Chapter

"100 Best Novels." *Modern Library*, http://www.modernlibrary.com/top-100/100-best-novels/.

Adorno, Theodor W. "On Popular Music." 1941. *Soundscapes.info*, vol. 2, Jan. 2000, http://www.icce.rug.nl/~soundscapes/DATABASES/SWA/On_popular_music_1.shtml.

"America's Changing Religious Landscape." *Pew Research Center*, 12 May 2015, https://www.pewforum.org/2015/05/12/americas-changing-religious-landscape/.

Arnold, Matthew. *Culture and Anarchy: An Essay in Political and Social Criticism*. 1869. Oxford: Project Gutenberg.

Bourdieu, Pierre. *Distinction: A Social Critique of the Judgement of Taste*. Harvard UP, 1987.

Browne, Ray. "Folklore to Populore." *Popular Culture Studies Across the Curriculum*, edited by Ray B. Browne, McFarland & Company Inc. Publishers, 2005, pp. 24–27.

Heineman, Ben W., Jr. "Rereading 'Ulysses' by James Joyce: The Best Novel Since 1900." *The Atlantic*, 29 Nov. 2010, https://www.theatlantic.com/entertainment/archive/2010/11/rereading-ulysses-by-james-joyce-the-best-novel-since-1900/67092/.

Horkheimer, Max and Theodor W. Adorno. *Dialectic of Enlightenment: Philosophical Fragments.* Edited by Gunzelin Schmid Noerr, translated by Edmund Jephcott, Stanford UP, 2002.

Kidd, Dustin. "Popular Culture." *Oxford Bibliographies*, 28 Feb. 2017, https://www.oxfordbibliographies.com/view/document/obo-9780199756384/obo-9780199756384-0193.xml.

Simmel, Georg. "Fashion." *International Quarterly*, vol. 10, no. 1, Oct. 1904, pp. 130–55.

Storey, John. *An Introduction to Cultural Theory & Popular Culture.* 2nd ed., University of Georgia Press, 1998.

Williams, Raymond. *Culture & Society: 1780–1950.* 1958. Columbia UP, 1983.

Additional Reading Suggestions

Ashby, LeRoy. *With Amusement for All: A History of American Popular Culture since 1830.* UP of Kentucky, 2012.

Fiske, John. *Understanding Popular Culture.* 2nd ed., Routledge, 2010.

Gans, Herbert. *Popular Culture and High Culture: An Analysis and Evaluation of Taste.* 2nd ed., Basic Books, 1999.

McRobbie, Angela, editor. *Postmodernism and Popular Culture.* Routledge, 1994.

Ross, Andrew. *No Respect: Intellectuals & Popular Culture.* Routledge, 1989.

CHAPTER 2

THE SEMIOTIC APPROACH

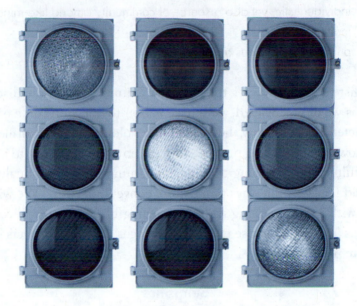

I Like Traffic Lights

In chapter 1, I offered a condensed overview of the development of popular culture studies, highlighting two curious facts: first, there has been a lot of debate over just what popular culture actually is and, second, until recently there was, in contrast, very little debate over the fact that, whatever popular culture was and is, it is inferior when compared to **elite culture**, **folk culture**, the **avant-garde**, and so on. Buried in the middle of chapter 1, I took the apparently daring step of offering a list of characteristics we can use to pinpoint what it is we are talking about when we discuss popular culture. To recap: as conventionally understood in the twenty-first-century **popular press**, popular culture is:

- accessible;
- affectively engaging;
- youth oriented;
- trendy;
- indifferent to or antagonistic toward sources of authority, taste, age appropriateness, and decorum;
- individualistic, yet also a source of community among like-minded individuals; and
- purportedly frivolous and depthless.

This list reflects the ways that popular culture is routinely discussed and, as we move forward, we'll have reason to question some of these characteristics—notably, the charges of frivolousness and depthlessness. For now though, having proposed a set of criteria we can use to identify pop culture, we are going to put aside assumptions about quality and instead focus on the ways pop culture conveys meaning. We will first start with *how* something is made meaningful, and then will consider various lenses we can use to bring into focus particular aspects of pop culture phenomena.

Semiotics

Our privileged approach to popular culture in this textbook will be through the lens of something called **semiotics**. Semiotics is the study of **signifying systems**—rule-governed systems of meaning production. Spoken and written languages are obvious examples of signifying systems, but then so are things like semaphore (a system of communicating using flags), fashion, and tattoos. The building blocks of any semiotic system are **signs**, which are little units of meaning. Signs themselves consists of two parts: the **signifier** and the **signified**. The signifier is the way in which a particular concept is expressed. The signified is the concept being expressed.

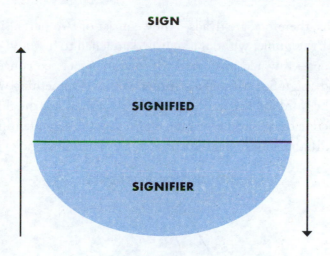

Fig. 2.1 The Sign

To see how this works, let's take the most famous example: the sign tree (see Figs. 2.1 and 2.2). The letters T–R–E–E and how we pronounce them is our signifier, and our mental impression corresponding to the word tree (what we think of when we see or hear the word) is the signified.

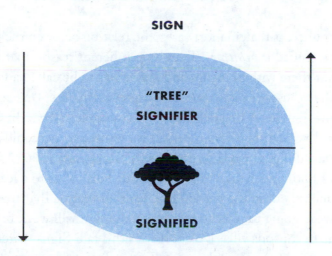

Fig. 2.2 Signifier / Signified

Signs, therefore, are dyads—they consist of two parts: signifier + signified. A signifier without a signified attached to it would make no sense to us—it would be a word without an associated concept, snerkle? And a signified without a signifier would be something we can't ... what's the word for it again? The sign, by the way, is not the thing itself. The concrete thing out there in the world that the sign identifies is the **referent**. This relationship is sometimes represented as a kind of pyramid:

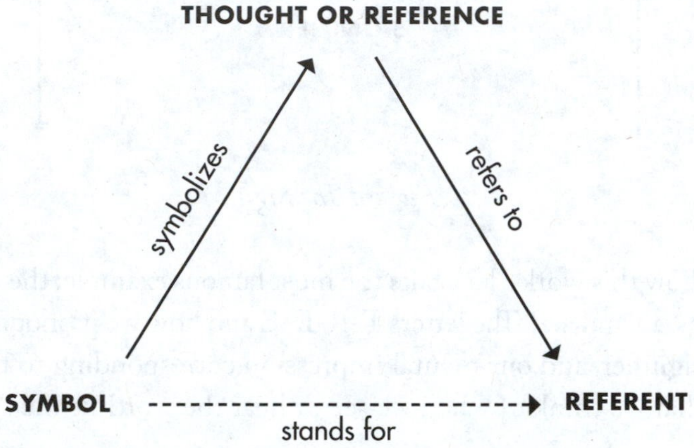

THOUGHT OR REFERENCE

SYMBOL ------------------------> REFERENT
stands for

Fig. 2.3 The Semiotic Triangle

Important here is that, in most cases, the relation between the signifier and the signified is *arbitrary*. There's no inherent reason that that tall thing over there with branches and leaves has to be called a tree—we know this because the same concept is expressed in other languages with a different signifier. A tree in Spanish, for example, is *arbol*. In German, it's *baum*. In Swedish, it's *träd*. And, if we wanted to, we could agree to substitute a different word for tree—say "trashpanda villa." As long as you and I both understand that trashpanda villa refers to a leafy thing with branches out in the world (and, for that matter, that trashpanda is how we're going to refer to raccoons), the sign will work fine for us. Don't the trashpanda villas look gorgeous this fall? Signs therefore rely on *convention*: learned and shared understandings of how signifiers and signifieds go together.

Now, let's take things the next step. The arbitrary nature of the **sign** on its own is interesting to contemplate. Even more fascinating though is the way in which most signs become meaningful to us: through their relationship with other signs. Here, we can talk about two different types of relationships among signs—and these will be important to us moving forward: **paradigmatic** relationships and **syntagmatic** relationships. The way to think of the paradigm is as a category of related signs. If we go with the paradigm "tree," then that includes oak, maple, larch, willow, banzai, yew, and so on. The paradigm "racket sports" includes tennis, ping pong, racquetball, badminton, etc. Each sign within a paradigm acquires meaning by virtue of not being others of the same type. An oak is not a maple, willow, or larch. Thinking about color can help make this clear: looking at your box of 64 Crayola crayons, how would you describe the color "blue"? Well, its darker than cornflower blue, but lighter than midnight blue. The meaning of "blue" therefore depends on its difference from other members of the same paradigm.

50 Shades of (Bluish) Grey

Syntagmatic relationships, in contrast, are relationships of position—where one sign is in relation to others. If we are talking about spoken or written language, then the meaning a sign acquires has to do with what precedes and follows it in a sentence. If I say, "Oh, no! The dog ...!" our understanding of "dog" here won't be fixed until the sentence is finished: "Oh, no! The dog ordered take-out again!" Here, the syntagm is a sequential arrangement—a kind of chain of meaning. It is only when we get to the end of the sentence that we can retroactively impose meaning on words in the chain—the dog is now busted for stealing your credit card. Where visual elements are concerned, syntagmatic relationships can also be spatial—the visual relationship between one sign and others. A picture of one person alone in the bleachers of a stadium means something very different to us than a picture of that same person surrounded by many other people (see Figs. 2.4 and 2.5). Meaning is constructed by the relationship of one sign to others that surround it.

Figs. 2.4 and 2.5 Go Team!

In thinking about the meaning conveyed by signs, it is also important to distinguish between **denotation** and **connotation**. The denotative meaning of a sign is what we might consider its dictionary definition:

its most basic or literal meaning. The denotative meaning of a rose is "a prickly bush or shrub that typically bears red, pink, yellow, or white fragrant flowers" and so on. However, we know that roses come saturated with connotations—associations attached to the sign that come from our culture and our personal experience. Roses, we have been taught, mean love, passion, Valentine's Day, and so on.

A useful example to help clarify these semiotic concepts is the category of tattoos. Tattoos are a type of language—a signifying system (see Figs. 2.6, 2.7, and 2.8). Individual tattoos are **signs**—the signifier is the design, the signified is what it conveys. But what does a tattoo tell us? First, we may

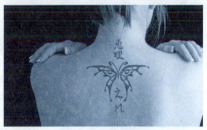

Figs. 2.6, 2.7, 2.8 Tattoos

consider the design itself: a "tribal" pattern, a detailed Japanese koi fish, rudimentary blue ink letters, or a rose will each signify—mean—differently to us based upon our understandings of and associations with these images. And then we consider the syntagmatic relationships: on whose body does the tattoo appear? Where is it placed? And what is its connection to other tattoos or forms of body adornment? A rose tattoo signifies differently depending if it is on a conventionally feminine woman or conventionally masculine man, if it is on the small of the back or on the face, and if it appears alone or is part of an elaborate cluster of tattoos.

YOUR TURN: Consider each of these images—in each case, what meaning is conveyed to you by the tattoo and why does it signify that way to you?

Another useful example of thinking about **signs** and signifying systems is fashion, which is also a rule-governed system of communication (see, for example, Figs. 2.9, 2.10, and 2.11). We can think of pieces of clothing as signs. Shoes and hats and everything in between are meaningful objects. Just what they mean, however, depends not only on the signs themselves, but their combination and their context. A slinky black dress may be appropriate for a formal evening event, but not for bowling. And that slinky black dress signifies quite differently if it is on a conventionally feminine woman or on a big burly dude. A blue blazer with a blue-and-red-striped tie on a man is regarded as conservative. However, what if the man wearing the blazer and tie is also wearing shorts and sandals?

YOUR TURN: What rules do you know that govern fashion— about how, when, and where articles of clothing are conventionally worn?

Figs. 2.9, 2.10, 2.11 Outfits

YOUR TURN: Consider each of these images above—in each case, what meaning is conveyed to you by the articles of clothing and why do they signify this way for you?

The kinds of **signs** we have been discussing in which the relationship between signifier and signified is arbitrary and must be learned are sometimes called **symbolic signs**. Before moving on from semiotics, it is important to note, however, that there are two types of exceptions to this rule. **Iconic signs** are words or images that resemble the thing they represent. A picture of pancakes on a Waffle House menu, for example, is an icon: it is a delicious visual approximation of the concept associated with it. The connection between a picture of a stack of pancakes and the concept of pancakes is not arbitrary; it is instead one of resemblance. The signifiers of **indexical signs**, in contrast, may not look or sound like their signifieds, but nevertheless are directly connected in some way. Smoke, for example, points (as with your index finger) to fire. A sign at the beach with a shark fin is a warning that there may be ... wait for it ... sharks in the water! These associations still need to be learned, but there is a kind of causal connection tethering them together.

Types of Signs

YOUR TURN: Would you categorize each of these signs above as symbolic, iconic, or indexical?

Myths and Ideology

Much of what we'll be doing in our considerations of popular culture is thinking about both what popular culture means and how it creates and conveys those meanings. Using the language introduced above, we'll be thinking about categories of popular culture as rule-governed systems of communication composed of **signs** that acquire meaning in light of their denotative and connotative meanings, as well as their paradigmatic and syntagmatic relationships with other signs. One sitcom or hip-hop artist or social media app becomes meaningful to us in particular ways through its relationships to others in the same paradigm, the context in which it is consumed or used, and all the associations we bring to bear upon it. As a starting point though, before we attempt to assign meaning or to interpret the significance of a pop culture object or practice, we need to ask a series of questions about just what the thing is in the first place. Signs as part of signifying systems are where we start our investigation. Only after we consider what something is and how and why it is performed or used can we then start to consider its larger significance within its historical context. Questions to ask at the start therefore include:

- What makes this thing or practice what it is?
- What qualities does it possess?
- How is it used or performed?
- How does it compare or contrast with other, similar things?
- Who uses it?
- In what contexts is it used?
- Why is it used?

The **sign** is our beginning point. Where we end up is with **myths**, **ideology**, and **codes**. The idea of myth within semiotics differs a good bit from the commonplace understandings of myths as either traditional stories, often set long ago and involving gods and monsters (such as those including Greek gods and goddesses), or widely held but false beliefs (such as that George Washington chopped down a cherry tree and then confessed when busted for it). Within semiotics, the idea of myth was developed by the twentieth-century French literary theorist and philosopher Roland Barthes in a seminal work called *Mythologies* in which he defines myth as the disguising of history as nature. As discussed above, signs are little units of meaning consisting of signifiers and signifieds that are initially connected arbitrarily but then cemented together by convention. English-language speakers have agreed (without ever really having been consulted or thinking about it) that "rose" is a sign that consists of the letters R-O-S-E attached to a mental image of a flower—likely red, having a stem with thorns, and so on. What myth does, according to Barthes, is to take that sign and overlay an additional meaning on it: passion. Because roses have been associated so consistently and for so long with romance—in poetry, literature, film, and television; in Valentine's Day marketing; in wedding ceremonies, and so on—the concept "passion" seems to be intrinsically associated with roses, as if the rose itself somehow naturally expresses the ideas of passion, love, and romance. This connection between roses and passion is convention. There is no reason at all that roses have to be the go-to gift

Passionate Roses

for Valentine's Day—it's just the way things have developed over time. However, we've heard and seen roses connected with love and romance so often that the connection now seems "the way it is."

This, for Barthes, is how myth functions: it takes an association that is the product of historical forces—repetition over time in the case of the rose—and presents it to us as natural, just the way things are. To put it into technical terms, Barthes refers to myth as a "second-order semiological system": "That which is a **sign** in the first system, becomes a mere signifier in the second." Here's how this looks schematically using the example of horseshoes in Fig. 2.12:

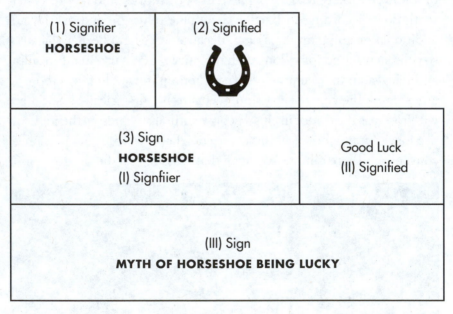

Fig. 2.12 Myth

At this point, you may be saying, "OK. What's the big deal?" What is important about myth for Barthes is that it illustrates how ideology functions. While there may be a tendency to think of ideology as something other people have, we are all subject to ideology because ideology refers to the ideas, beliefs, and principles that structure our world view. From the moment we are born, we are immersed in ideology—bombarded by messages from family and friends and institutions and **texts** that tell us what we should believe to be right, normal, and natural. In some cases, our ideological beliefs may be the result of conscious deliberation—we may march in the cause of Black Lives Matter (BLM), for example, or petition the government to be more active in addressing climate change because our beliefs and experiences lead us to conclude that engaging in these ways is an important expression of our values. Although it is difficult, we may also choose to depart from the views we were raised with or that we subscribed to at some point in our lives. In other cases, ideological beliefs may be unrecognized or unconscious. Many people for a long time simply assumed that men were better suited for professional careers and women for domestic and childcare duties. Some people questioned this, but many did not because, they assumed, "this is just the way things are." Today, some may simply assume, for example, that the "natural" trajectory for personal growth is school, work, marriage, perhaps children, home-ownership, and so on, because that is a narrative we have heard repeatedly. This is how ideology functions. A particular social configuration that has emerged over time and, importantly, benefits some members of society, is presented as the "right" and "natural" way things are done. In many cases, as we'll discuss in the next section of this chapter, people are even coerced into participating in their own disenfranchisement.

The thing about ideology is that our ideological beliefs, to us, seem obvious, right, and natural. Of course democracy is the best political system! Of course people should be free to say whatever they want! Of course **capitalism** is the best economic system! Other people are the crazy ones for not sharing our beliefs—and if they would only think on the matter carefully, no doubt they would realize they are wrong, we are correct, and then shift their views, right? It can be difficult to consider that, from someone else's perspective, our ideological views are equally suspect or pernicious, because we generally act in ways congruent with our "values"—what matters to us, what we have been told and/or come to believe is important. Indeed, we can become quite defensive when our ideological beliefs are questioned—wars have been fought over which religion or economic system is the best or truest.

YOUR TURN: A powerful example of ideology in action is the idea of the American Dream. The American Dream is the belief that, through hard work and honest dealings, all Americans, no matter how humble their origins, can achieve material success and rise to a place of prominence within American society. Where have you seen this idea before? Do you believe it is true? Whose interests does it serve and what would happen if lower-class Americans stopped believing in it?

For the purposes of our investigation of popular culture, we're going to save our conclusions about whether we agree with something or not until the end. We will, however, be very, very suspicious of anything presented to us as "natural," "the right way," "just the way things are," and so on. Rather than accepting these claims, we will consider instead:

- How did this particular way of doing things or thinking come about? That is, we may seek to recover its history.
- Whose interests does it serve?
- What other ways of thinking or doing things are there?

Congealed Ideology

Here is where things get even more interesting (I know—you're saying, "not possible!" Well, hang on to your hat). It is relatively easy to appreciate things like political movements, advocacy groups, religious sects, and so on as motived by ideology. But what about a desk?

Maybe you've had the misfortune of sitting at a desk such as the ones pictured in Fig. 2.13 below (maybe you are even "sitting" in one right now). The molded plastic seats are uncomfortable and the desktop is awkward and slippery. What does the desk—and the classroom in which it exists—tell us about the philosophy of education that governs the school or university in which it is placed? Lots, actually. It tells us for one thing that education is not supposed to be fun, relaxed, or comfortable, but serious business—this is emphasized as well by the absence of

Fig. 2.13 Desks as Congealed Ideology

carpet, the bare walls, and the florescent lighting. Students are supposed to sit upright and utilize the space afforded them for taking notes. The placement of desks in rows facing forward discourages collaboration and directs student attention across the great divide toward the teacher at the front of the room—the teacher, who is standing and free to move while students are awkwardly stuffed into seats in rows, is the authority. It is the teacher's job to unscrew the tops of their students' heads and pour in knowledge, which the students will then regurgitate to show they have been paying attention on exams and in papers. In short, the desk is what we can consider "**congealed ideology**"—the distillation of a conventional philosophy of education in the form of aluminum, plastic, and wood. The desk—a **sign**—in conjunction with the other signs that surround it tells us a lot about the understandings of what teaching and learning are that will prevail in that classroom.

If classrooms organized as in the image above—rows of singular desks facing the front of the room—are all you've ever seen, no doubt because of its familiarity, this would seem the natural and correct way to do it. But we can pause for a moment and ask our questions: what other kinds of desks—or seating arrangements—could be substituted? How else could the space of learning be organized? What other models of pedagogy could be substituted?

YOUR TURN: What ideas about teaching and learning are conveyed by the two images in Figs. 2.14 and 2.15 and how do they compare to the traditional classroom pictured above? Which educational space do you think would be most effective in facilitating student learning and why?

Figs. 2.14 and 2.15

What's true of desks in classrooms is true of all the things we encounter: they are—or become—congealed forms of ideology that reflect and naturalize particular ways of thinking about the world. Here's another example. Consider the object in Fig. 2.16:

Fig. 2.16 Baseball Mitt

We can start by asking our questions:

- What makes this thing or practice what it is?
- What qualities does it possess?
- How is it used or performed?
- How does it compare or contrast with other, similar things?
- Who uses it?
- In what contexts is it used?
- Why is it used?
- What associations are connected with it?

Many people will recognize the object as a baseball mitt—a tool used in a game of sport to protect the hand and facilitate catching a ball. In what ways could there be anything ideological about that? If we start by asking what this thing is and what qualities define it, we might notice that it is made of leather—an animal product. Right there, we can see one way in which the baseball glove is congealed ideology: it is one object among many (shoes, belts, jackets, sofas and chairs, and so on) that helps to naturalize the idea that animals are objects available for human use (and, I would add, at this point, we are bracketing off our feelings about the use of animals in this way. Our goal now is first to explore the ways that this material object reflects larger social patterns, beliefs, and understandings before then evaluating those positions).

Noticing that the glove is made of leather and, therefore, participates in the naturalization of animals as raw materials for human objects is a good starting point. But we can go further, because consideration of the mitt prompts us to think about what baseball is, who plays it, and the contexts in which it is played. Baseball is a rule-governed competitive sport in which teams square off with players having specialized positions (pitcher, catcher, outfielder, etc.) and, usually, a coach who directs the players—it is a game that combines collaboration with competition, and naturalizes the ideas that individuals or groups must compete with others to win and be "the best," and that individuals have particular roles to play within the collective of the team. Baseball reinforces the ideas that one must follow the rules of the game (there are penalties for breaking the rules) and that there will always be winners and losers—and that winning "within the rules" is the ultimate goal. Further, players are supposed to be "team players" and to collaborate by playing their parts— independent action is discouraged and creative thinking is minimized. In organized play (leagues and professional), the rules are policed by umpires and line judges, who have the final say.

Baseball, when described in this way, is weirdly like a corporation: workers play their prescribed roles within the "team" overseen by a boss with the goal of "winning"—beating their competitors and making the most profit possible for the company and its investors. Perhaps this is why baseball has often been described as "America's pastime"? However, one could reasonably push back here and say that other team sports are organized in the same way: football, hockey, soccer, and so on all are rule-governed sports in which players have positions, coaches make decisions, and winning is the objective. You would be exactly right to point this out (go you!)—and it leads to a significant realization: the forces telling us that "winning" means beating our opponents, that there will always be winners and losers, that we need to play our roles, play by the rules, and respect those in position of authority are *everywhere* and, as we'll talk about a bit in the next chapter, reflect how capitalism functions. The baseball mitt then—when used as intended at least—is emblematic of a complete worldview. This is how ideology functions: it presents one possible configuration—in this case, of sport—as just the way things are done. This now raises the question: how else could sports be played? Are there ways that sports can be wholly collaborative rather than competitive? Can sports have goals other than "winning"? Can sports allow participants to play various roles and exercise independent thinking?

We could go on here and talk about how sports in general and baseball in particular naturalize a division between work and leisure— similar to our discussion of the **Frankfurt School**'s opinion of popular music, going to a ball game on a summer afternoon allows us to return to "the grind" refreshed—a kind of escape valve to blow off steam and keep the system stable (serving the interests of those in positions of power and authority who benefit from the present status quo). We could also consider the history of baseball and the kinds of bodies it has conventionally privileged (what does it mean that the professional participants in "America's pastime" have been all male, all able-bodied, and primarily white?). We could talk about player salaries in the major leagues, how they compare to what teachers and civil servants make, and what that tells us about American culture and its priorities. But I think you get the point: we started with a baseball mitt and ended up with a consideration of the ideological beliefs that structure the game and baseball's role in naturalizing a particular worldview.

The idea here is that all the objects we encounter find a place in our ideological worldview. Certainly, human-made objects from baseball gloves to classroom desks to paper plates to giant inflatable holiday decorations are the products of human assumptions and intentions. But even elements of the natural world are made meaningful in light of our ideological beliefs and understandings. Going back to our initial **sign** "tree," the denotative mean-ing of tree is "a woody perennial plant, typically having a single stem or trunk growing to a con-siderable height and bearing lat-eral branches at some distance from the ground." However, the meaning of a particular tree—or group of trees—for us in the real world will have everything to do with not just our personal experi-ences and connotations with trees, but with also the larger systems of thinking that have shaped our understandings. Fig. 2.17 is a pic-ture of a larch.

Fig. 2.17 The Larch

What do you think this tree would mean to you if you were (a) a logger whose livelihood depended upon harvesting trees; (b) a developer seeking to build a housing development where it stands; (c) an environmental activist interested in preserving the habitat of the endangered Northern Spotted Owl who nests in these trees; (d) a climate change activist who recognizes deforestation as an important component in global warming; (e) an artist who paints landscapes. Human beings don't make trees in the same ways that we intentionally manipulate materials to create objects for use or enjoyment (although we can genetically manipulate trees and plant them); however, what they mean for us depends upon their place in our ideological worldview.

YOUR TURN: In what way can the objects pictured below (Figs. 2.18 and 2.19) be considered congealed ideology? What beliefs or assumptions about the world do they naturalize?

Figs. 2.18 and 2.19 A Hummer and a Cell Phone

Codes

In our discussion of baseball and trees above, we have already shifted from a consideration of the denotative and connotative meanings of signs to their participation in what we can refer to as codes. In this case, unlike with myth, the semiotic understanding of codes is relatively close to the common understanding. Codes in general are systems of communication. To **decode** a **message**—that is, to render it intelligible, to make sense of it—one needs a "key," a set of instructions that help translate elements of the code. Morse code, for example, famously uses dots and dashes in place of letters to form words. Three dots equal the letter "S" and three dashes equal the letter O. Originally established for maritime use, "SOS" is a distress call, sometimes translated as "save our ship." (Incidentally, SOS is a great example of the arbitrary nature of the sign. There is no reason at all that three dots should equal an "S" or three dashes an "O." It's just convention.) In order to translate dots and dashes into letters, one needs a key. After a while, once one has memorized the key, dots and dashes can be immediately translated into letters forming words.

In semiotics, codes function more or less in the same way: as interpretive frameworks for making sense of **signs**. Codes guide us in making sense of something—a statement, an action, an object, etc. For example, the idea of a "dog whistle" can be understood as a political message intended for a very specific group and which one can't "hear" unless one understands the code of which it is a part. The use of former US President Barack Obama's middle name, Hussein, was often construed as a "racist dog-whistle"—part of a xenophobic and Islamophobic code intended by the president's detractors to highlight his skin color and to stoke intolerance. The political message of the "dog whistle" can't be interpreted unless one is conversant with the code of which it is a part.

Codes in general, however, aren't always or even usually as pernicious as racist codes that permit one to make sense of political dog-whistles. Codes are, at bottom, shared understandings among users of **signs**—learned sets of conventions that allow us to make sense of signs. According to Carl W. Jones, codes function as "general maps of meaning, belief systems about oneself and others, which [imply] views and attitudes about how the world is and/or ought to be" (Jones 500). Codes, in short, are the point at which semiotics and ideology meet. Let's take our example of the Hummer in Fig. 2.18 above. To the person who buys one, it not only signifies wealth but is part of the code of "rugged masculinity"—derived from military HUMVEEs, the Hummer signals "toughness"; it takes up space and fuel efficiency is a minimal concern. (This is what we might call a displaced code as the Hummer stands in for the owner's rugged masculinity.) Interpreted using a different code, however, the same features of the Hummer can be understood as representative of "**toxic masculinity**"—traditional cultural norms of masculinity that are harmful to men, women, and society. The same object, therefore, can be interpreted in light of multiple codes.

YOUR TURN: Consider the following images in Figs. 2.20 and 2.21. What "key"—that is, what cultural understanding—is needed to decode their meaning?

Figs. 2.20 and 2.21

Encoding / Decoding

This brings us then to what is often referred to as the "**encoding** / decoding" model of communication developed by cultural studies scholar Stuart Hall in the early 1970s. While we'll be discussing this in greater depth in chapter 5 on film and television, this model of communication addresses how messages result in meaning. The first step is encoding in which the sender of a message uses signs to "package" a meaning they wish someone else to receive. These signs may be verbal or non-verbal. The decoding of the message is how the recipient of the message interprets it—and there are three possibilities here for a message that is understood in some way:

- The **dominant / hegemonic** position is one in which the message is interpreted in the way it was intended.
- The **negotiated** position is a mixture of acceptance and rejection. The message is understood, but not fully taken up.
- The **oppositional** position is one in which the recipient understands the message but rejects it.

Our Hummer can again serve as a good example here. If someone buys a Hummer intending to signal their rugged masculinity and someone else is impressed by their purchase for that reason, then the recipient of the message occupies the dominant / hegemonic position. If someone responds to the Hummer by envying the rugged masculinity aspect but being bothered by the fuel inefficiency and ostentatious display of wealth, the recipient of the message occupies the negotiated position. And if someone responds to the Hummer by viewing it as emblematic of toxic masculinity—disdain for the environment, taking up excessive space, fetishizing military violence, and so on, this would clearly be an oppositional position. All three positions understand the code of "rugged masculinity" being deployed through the Hummer; the way in which the they interpret the message, however, reflects the recipients' own ideological beliefs.

YOUR TURN: What message is conveyed by the following image in Fig. 2.22 and what form would a dominant / hegemonic response, a negotiated response, and an opposition response take?

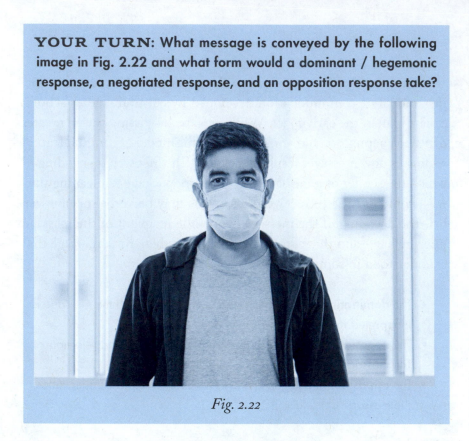

Fig. 2.22

Code Switching

Much of what I've said about codes above as shared understandings by users of signs can be illustrated by attending briefly to the phenomenon of "**code switching**." Code switching refers to the practice of alternating between two or more languages or language variants in conversation. This can refer to something obvious, such as a bilingual speaker switching from English to Spanish. It can also, however, refer to consciously adopting or disguising an accent to facilitate a particular agenda. For example, a National Public Radio story from 2013 noted that US restaurant servers who adopt a convincing Southern accent "get better tips and more sympathetic customers" ("Five Reasons"). In the hilarious 2018 cinematic send up of American racism and stereotypes,

Sorry to Bother You (Boots Riley), telemarketer Cassius Green (Lakeith Stanfield) is instructed by his co-worker (played by Danny Glover) to use his "white voice" when trying to sell encyclopedias. Disguising his usual intonation with a pinched, nasal parody of whiteness results in increased sales and preferential treatment.

Lakeith Stanfield as Cassius Green in Sorry to Bother You

In the cases of restaurant servers adopting Southern accents and Cassius Green in *Sorry to Bother You*, code switching is a conscious strategy—a way to encode messages such that they will be decoded by recipients in a dominant / hegemonic way. However, we all do this to varying extents in our daily lives—you probably don't speak the same when hanging out with friends as you do when addressing your boss at work. That's code switching, too, and it reveals a sophisticated understanding of the relation of code to context.

YOUR TURN: What other examples of code switching can you think of?

Much of what has been introduced in this chapter will be returned to and developed more fully in the chapters to come. The main idea to take away here, however, is that everything in some sense is ideological as we are all constantly engaged in a process of making our world meaningful in light of our current understandings, values, beliefs, and the codes we speak. What we will continue to investigate is how signs are produced, interpreted, and circulated.

Suggested Assignments

1. Focusing on a particular sign (such as a tattoo or outfit, as discussed above), explore the syntagmatic and paradigmatic relationships that govern how it **signifies**.
2. Looking deeper into Roland Barthes's idea of mythologies, analyze a myth you see as important and explain how history is disguised as nature.
3. Explore how a common object can be considered congealed ideology.

Works Cited in This Chapter

Barthes, Roland. *Mythologies*. Translated by Annette Lavers, Farrar, Straus and Giroux, 1972.

Hall, Stuart. "Encoding and Decoding in the Television Discourse." Discussion Paper. *CCCS Stencilled Occasional Papers*, University of Birmingham, 1973, http://epapers.bham.ac.uk/2962/.

Jones, Carl W. "Personal Branding: 'Encoding a Personal Brand Through Semiotics: A Case Study.'" *Semiotics and Visual Communication III: Cultures of Branding*, edited by Evripides Zantides, Cambridge Scholars Press, 2019, pp. 492–511.

Thompson, Matt. "Five Reasons Why People Code Switch." *National Public Radio*, 13 Apr. 2013, https://www.npr.org/sections/codeswitch/2013/04/13/177126294/five-reasons-why-people-code-switch.

Additional Reading Suggestions

Berger, Arthur Asa. *Signs in Contemporary Life: An Introduction to Semiotics*. 2nd ed., Sheffield Publishing Company, 1999.

Blonsky, Marshall. *American Mythologies*. Oxford UP, 1992.

Chandler, Daniel. *Semiotics: The Basics*. 3rd ed., Routledge, 2017.

Danesi, Marcel. *Of Cigarettes, High Heels, and Other Interesting Things: An Introduction to Semiotics*. St. Martin's Press, 1999.

Eco, Umberto. *A Theory of Semiotics*. Indiana UP, 1976.

Sebeok, Thomas Albert. *Signs: An Introduction to Semiotics*. University of Toronto Press, 2001.

CHAPTER 3

THE CRITICAL THEORY TOOLBOX

The Right Tool for the Job

In chapter 2, I introduced the **semiotic** approach, which we will utilize throughout this textbook to understand how popular culture is made meaningful. The starting point for us in our considerations of various forms of popular culture will always be to consider the **signs** before us in terms of their **denotative** and **connotative** meanings, as well as their **paradigmatic** and **syntagmatic** relationships. We will think about how **messages** are **encoded**, transmitted, and **decoded**. And then we will consider how signs function **ideologically**—how they seek to persuade us to think in particular ways, and how they naturalize certain understandings of the world, while challenging other ways of thinking.

This chapter pertains to that final step: decoding popular culture as **congealed ideology**. To do this, we will quickly survey various forms of **critical theory**, which we can think of as reflective approaches to cultural practices and artifacts that seek to unmask ideology that naturalizes oppression. Developed in the first part of the twentieth century by the **Frankfurt School** (see chapter 1) specifically in relation to class-based oppression, the approaches and insights of critical theory have been adapted to address issues of **gender**, sexuality, race, and their intersections. When applied as **criticism**, the various forms of critical theory can be considered as special types of lenses that bring particular aspects of culture into focus, allowing them to be scrutinized carefully and their implications considered. The end goal, ideally, is always to understand ourselves and our world more fully, with an eye toward living better and more justly.

Marxist Theory and Criticism

Marxist theory and criticism, unsurprisingly, started with the nineteenth-century writings of German philosopher Karl Marx and his collaborations with fellow German thinker Friedrich Engels, so a bit of background here is needed. While Marx is best known for his 1848 pamphlet *The Communist Manifesto* and his foundational work of economic theory, the three-volume *Das Kapital* (1867–83), translated into English as *Capital: A Critique of Political Economy*, it is important to distinguish Marxism from **communism**. Marxism can be understood as a philosophy of history—by this, I mean that Marxist thought presents a theory about the forces that shape how cultures develop and where they are headed. Communism, in contrast, is a specific form or mode of cultural organization in which the **means of production**—the raw materials, machines, and factories needed to produce goods and services—are collectively owned by everyone, no one gets rich off of the labor of others, and private property doesn't exist.

At the core of Marxism and Marxist critical theory is the idea of **historical materialism**, which asserts that the economic organization of a society (what is referred to as the **base**) influences everything else in that society and shapes the way people think (everything that rests on the base is called the **superstructure**). For Marx, a society's economic **mode of production** (**capitalist**, **socialist**, communist, etc.) fundamentally determines the way that society is organized, how it functions, and how it develops—the way the society is organized in terms of economics influences everything else in that society. This is obviously the case in relation to social class. Capitalist societies are split into two primary groups: the **bourgeoisie** who own the means of production and purchase the labor power of others, and the workers, called the **proletariat**, who do not own the means of production and are forced to sell their labor power (that is, they are mostly forced to work for someone else to survive). Those who own the means of production accumulate wealth by profiting off of the labor of their workers—they sell a good or service for more than they pay for labor and raw materials (the profit is called **surplus value**). So, if it costs $10 to produce a chair—$8 to pay the worker and $2 for the raw material—the factory owner then sells it for $30 and pockets the $20 as profit. At its most distorted, we end up with a company such as Walmart, which made a 2019 profit of $514 billion while paying many workers minimum wage ("Fortune Global 500").

Marxist critical theory sees history as propelled by economics and **class struggle**: those who own the means of production and profit off the labor of others seek to maintain that structure because it works to their advantage—those making big bucks want to keep making big bucks; the workers who struggle to make ends meet, in contrast, feel **alienated**—disconnected—from their labor because they are just cogs in a machine, and resent what they perceive as their exploitation by the bourgeoisie who profit off their labor, so they may push to change things. Workers may mount protests or go on strike and, Marx proposed, if they get fed up enough and things seem entirely hopeless, they may burn things to the ground: revolution. Marx in fact assumed the inevitability of working-class revolution within capitalist society due to growing discontent. Marxism as a philosophy of history maps out a trajectory in which capitalism is ultimately a stage toward communism in which human beings reject the class system, refuse to let people exploit the labor of others for their own profit, and hold all things in common. Capitalism has, however, proven remarkably resilient, if not always especially adroit, when it comes to defusing working-class resentment.

Here is where Marxist critical theory comes in. What a Marxist approach to popular culture focuses on are ideological messages about class encoded in objects and practices—and, it is worth noting, that examining what a **text** has to say and how it says it are not the same as agreeing with it. Adopting a Marxist approach does not automatically make you a Marxist. As mentioned above, those in positions of wealth and power—the "ruling" or "dominant" class—inevitably seek to preserve that privilege and have at their disposal various means to compel or solicit the consent of the governed. As explained by French philosopher Louis Althusser, the dominant class can compel the consent of the working class directly through what Althusser refers to as **repressive state apparatuses (RSAs)**—the police, the national guard, the military, the courts, the government—which work to maintain the existing social order. However, there are also more diffuse means of coercing consent from the working class, which Althusser refers to as **ideological state apparatuses (ISAs)**. ISAs include schools, religious institutions, the media, social clubs and organizations, and so on that influence how we think by naturalizing particular economic and social formations (the process through which individuals internalize a particular set of values is referred to by Althusser as **interpellation**). ISAs reinforce positions that favor the dominant class and the existing order—and their role, to put things cynically, is not only to influence people to accept the existing social order as "the way the things are" but to convince them to act against their own best interests (see Althusser). How do you get people without health care, for example, to reject political candidates and policies that would give them health care? And how do you get people making minimum wage at two or three different jobs to think it is OK for corporate CEOs to make $14.5 million a year? ("Highest-Paid CEOs"). For a start, by repeatedly demonizing socialism—an economic mode that primarily disadvantages the ruling class by putting the means of production into the hands of the community as a whole and in which class difference is diminished.

The flip side to that equation then is to persuade people that they can change their situations. As quoted in *A Short History of Progress* (2004) by Ronald Wright, the author John Steinbeck once quipped that "socialism never took root in America because the poor see themselves not as an exploited proletariat but as temporarily embarrassed millionaires" (124). The problem from this perspective is not that CEOs make too much; it is, rather, that working-class people make too little—and here is where the idea of the American Dream does its most powerful ideological work. The notion of the American Dream is that anyone, no matter how humble their origins, can, through hard work and acting with integrity in one's dealing with others, rise to a position of wealth and prominence in American culture. Belief in the American Dream quells the specter of class struggle by persuading working-class people that they, too, can achieve money and fame, and that they are responsible for their own advancement. And it is certainly true that "average people" do hit it big now and again—we know this because we hear about their stories all the time. What the **myth** of the American Dream obscures is that inheritance is the quickest way to wealth and that there are millions and millions of honest hard-working people who will never overcome the conditions of their birth no matter how hard they try and how honest they are. Indeed, for the overwhelming number of working-class people, the class into which they are born is their destiny—for them, the American Dream will remain forever that: a dream. What would happen if all these people concluded that they were in fact trapped with no way out of their situation?

YOUR TURN: Do you think the American Dream as described above still exists? Why or why not?

ISAs (here including stories about average people becoming million-aires) play a central role in helping the ruling class achieve **hegemony** over the working class. Associated in particular with Italian philosopher Antonio Gramsci, hegemony refers to the way a dominant group secures the consent of subordinate groups by making the ruling class's values and beliefs the norm for that society. Whoever is in charge works hard to promote and normalize their own views, which helps to secure their privilege.

> **YOUR TURN:** In the last chapter, we discussed ideology. Thinking back to that discussion, in what ways do you see particular ideological beliefs that serve the interests of those in positions of power and prominence normalized?

What Gramsci's work helps us understand is capitalism's resiliency. Despite the best efforts of the dominant class, subordinate groups can develop a sense of class consciousness that causes them to chafe against their positions and engage in acts of resistance. The dominant group then seeks to put out the fire through an act of incorporation that coopts the resistance for its own purposes, arriving at what Gramsci refers to as a **compromise equilibrium**. For example, as I'm working on this textbook in early 2021, BLM has achieved unprecedented visibility. How corporations have responded to BLM reflects the politics of their CEOs and boards of trustees. However, many big ones, including Facebook, Google, Walmart, and Amazon, have publicly attached themselves to—or, in Gramsci's term **articulated** themselves with—BLM. Why? While the decision to support BLM may well be the result of sincerely held principles, it is also a calculated business decision with the goal of profiting. BLM resistance has been incorporated by capitalism and a compromise equilibrium reached. BLM achieves greater visibility, but its resistance has been coopted as a strategy to maximize profit by big companies—businesses implicated in creating and perpetuating existing class divisions, which are very much skewed by race. These companies then package and sell the resistance right back to the protesters. Another example: in the 1970s, punk rockers gave the middle finger to corporate capitalism by wearing used, worn, beat-up clothing. Companies very quickly sought to incorporate this resistance by selling ripped jeans in boutiques and department stores. Punk became trendy, undercutting the antiestablishment ethos that galvanized it to begin with.

I'm a punk rocker, yes I am

YOUR TURN: Can you identify other ways that dominant groups coopt and seek to profit off of resistance movements?

For our purposes here, Marxist critical theory becomes a lens through which we can consider popular culture practices and artifacts as distillations of ideology in relation to class and class relations. This involves asking questions about how issues of class and class relations are represented, as well as whether the object or practice participates in naturalizing or challenging class division. It is important to acknowledge that sometimes the answer is not clear cut. And it is important to acknowledge as well that what a text says may be wholly at odds with its creator's intentions for it—Hollywood studios can make billions off of films critical of corporations making billions, and Ticketmaster can charge $300 a ticket to see Rage Against the Machine.

YOUR TURN: Consider the underlying messages related to class conveyed by the following examples. What values are being promoted? And who benefits?

1. American "Black Friday" sales that start on Thanksgiving Thursday
2. A TV commercial featuring a happy family enjoying fast food in a restaurant chain
3. A narrative franchise with which you are familiar such as *Harry Potter*, *Star Wars*, or *Star Trek*

Feminist Theory and Criticism

In the same way that Marxist theory and criticism focuses its lens on class and class inequality, **feminist theory and criticism** seeks to understand the nature of gender inequality through a focus on the social roles played by women in relation to men, how they have developed, and the forces that maintain them. And, in the same way that Marxist theory works to demystify ideology that supports a **status quo** in which many are disenfranchised, exploited, and repressed, feminist theory similarly attempts to identify and critique the mechanisms through which women have been discriminated against and controlled in **patriarchal culture**—cultures in which men have historically held positions of power and authority.

Two key dichotomies that have been central to the development of feminist theory and its deployment as criticism are the distinction between **sex** and gender on the one hand, and between **essentialism** and **constructivism** on the other. The sex / gender distinction has to do with the difference between the physical body and the social expectations that we overlay onto physical bodies. We can understand sex to refer to anatomy and biology including genitalia and genetics. Western culture has for a long time been accustomed to thinking of human biological sex as a binary opposition between two categories: male and female; in this binary opposition, men have a Y chromosome, penis, and testicles, while women have two X chromosomes, a vagina, and a female reproductive system. In reality, the situation is much more complicated. To begin with, medical studies suggest that 1 out of every 1500 to 2000 people is born intersexed—that is, having biological sex characteristics that are not all male or female (see Blackless). In some cases, intersex traits are visible at birth: some children are born with incompletely developed or ambiguous genitalia or born with two sets. What has typically happened in the past is that such infants were surgically and/or hormonally assigned a sex in conformity with Western culture's insistence that one identify either as male or female with corresponding anatomy. In other cases, intersex traits may not appear until puberty or, in the case of some chromosomal variations, become apparent at all—estimates, in fact, are that 1 out of every 100 people has some form of disorder of sexual development (DSD) in which an individual's anatomical sex is at odds with their chromosomal or gonadal sex (see Ainsworth). In reality, biological sex can be thought of as a spectrum rather than a binary opposition—there are in fact many different sexes rather than just two.

YOUR TURN: What do you think is at stake in maintaining the belief that there are only two human sexes?

Gender can then be thought of as a kind of **code** specifying the social expectations that are overlaid onto the sexed body—the way that a given culture expects biological males and females to act, think, look, talk, walk, and so on. For example, those with male bodies are supposed to act masculine, which historically has included being tough and avoiding outward displays of emotion: "act like a man!" Being feminine then maps onto female bodies, and permits displays of emotion and affection. Gender is thus the point at which culture and biological sex meet—which offers an excellent example of the semiotic proposition concerning the arbitrary nature of the sign. Below in Figs. 3.1 and 3.2 are two familiar signs: "businessman" and "housewife."

Figs. 3.1 and 3.2 Sexual Stereotypes

Why have modern men traditionally cut their hair short and worn suits while women have styled their hair longer and worn dresses? The answer is purely cultural convention. There is no inherent reason at all for particular hair styles or fashion trends. We know this because fashion differs from place to place and time to time. Scottish men wear kilts while in some parts of the world men wear thawbs or kandoras—a traditional male robe. Men who practice Sikhism don't cut their hair.

YOUR TURN: What are some other gender expectations that differ from place to place or that have changed over time?

In the twenty-first century, Western women can wear dresses or pants, and may choose to cut their hair short; it remains unusual, however, to see a conventionally masculine man in a gown—but, strange as it may sound, that could change if men began wearing dresses consistently. Dress expectations are part of a cultural code; they are arbitrary and naturalized over time via repetition—that men wear suits and women wear sundresses only seems natural to us due to its familiarity. The arbitrariness of fashion, however, doesn't mean that all trends are innocent. Many fashion trends for women, from bustles and corsets to high heels, for example, have had the effect of constraining movement—and a component of what has been called First-Wave Feminism of the nine-teenth and early twentieth centuries was dress reform: a movement to permit women more practical and comfortable clothing. In fact, until the twentieth century, women's clothing lacked pockets because pockets on dresses interrupted the aesthetic or "look" of the outfit—which makes sense if one considers the primary role for women to be objects to be looked at. Part of the dress reform movement, which advocated more functional clothing for women, was in fact the push for pockets—in 1910, something called the "Suffragette suit" came equipped with six of them!

.In any event, at least until relatively recently in the twenty-first century, gender expectations were tightly coupled with the biological sex binary opposition: male and female bodies were supposed to act in what the culture considered masculine and feminine ways. Here (see Figs. 3.3 and 3.4) we can think of gender expectations as semiotic codes:

Fig. 3.3 Male / Female Icons and Fig. 3.4 Traditional Gender Stereotypes

Traditional Gender Stereotypes

Male	Female
Aggressive	Passive
Independent	Dependent
Dominant	Submissive
Not nurturing	Nurturing
Insensitive	Sensitive
Logical	Emotional
Strong	Weak
Silent	Talkative

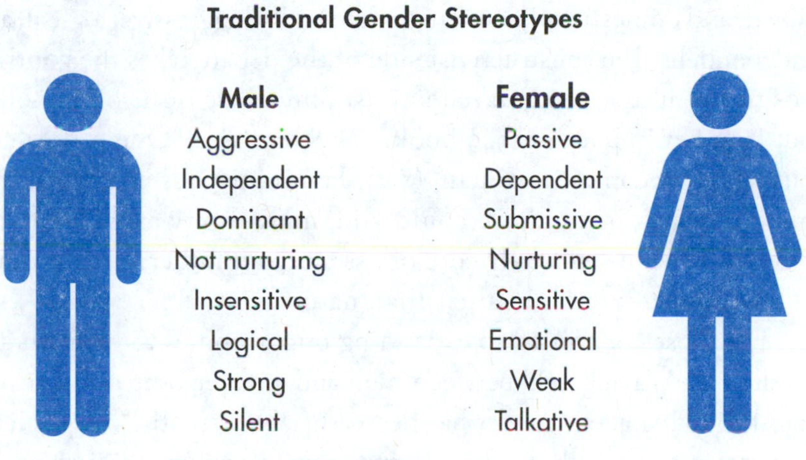

One of the more interesting twenty-first-century developments has been the extent to which conventionally rigid gender expectations have increasingly been challenged. Although discussions of gender often conflate biological sex, gender, and sexual orientation, social media plat-forms and other venues soliciting personal information now in many cases permit a variety of options for self-identification ranging from "cisgender" or just "cis," meaning that one's gender identity matches their sex assigned at birth, to "transgender," meaning that one's gender identity or expression differs from the biological sex assigned at birth, to "androgynous" and "gender-fluid." The fact that such options exist demonstrates a growing social awareness that there is no inherent connection between anatomical sex and gender. This suggests that Western culture is moving away from gender essentialism.

Closely tied to the sex / gender distinction has been the essentialism / constructivism debate, which raises questions as to whether or not there is some male or female "essence." Gender essentialism is the belief that men and women naturally think and act in particular ways and are better or worse suited to particular avocations and activities because of their biological sex. Such thinking attributes an "essence" to men and women—something universal that defines what it means to be a man or woman—and this has been the basis for stereotypes such as that women are "naturally" nurturing, emotional, and domestic, while men are "naturally" aggressive, logical, and independent. The constructivist side of the debate takes the contrary position that, as second-wave feminist Simone de Beauvoir famously put it in her important 1949 book, *The Second Sex*, "One is not born, but rather becomes, a woman" (152). Femininity for constructivists like de Beauvoir—and, we could add, masculinity as well—is not directed by some womanly core or essence, but rather is the product of environment: nurture rather than nature.

For those committed to expanding opportunities for women and leveling the playing field between men and women, overcoming essentialist thinking about gender has been crucial as essentialist arguments have often been the basis for denying women opportunities extended to men. The idea that women are "naturally" better suited to childcare and domestic duties, for example, has been used to prevent women from moving into the workplace. The idea that women are "naturally" more emotional and less rational than men has been used as an argument to prevent women from holding positions of authority—the word "hysteria" in fact derives from the Greek word for uterus, *hystera*, and remains more closely tied to women than men. Indeed, essentialist thinking about gender has been especially pernicious in that it naturalized discrimination against women in the name of protecting women: when men deprived women of opportunities for adventure, personal growth, and self-expression, it was often couched in the language of being for their own good.

This does not mean that biology does not influence at all the way we think and feel. It does mean, however, that there is immense variation from person to person. Some women are more aggressive than some men, while some men are more nurturing and sensitive than some women. Further, biology is so inextricably intertwined with culture that it is incredibly difficult to separate the two. If gender codes associate being "womanly" with being emotional and "manly" with being stoic—and conforming to those codes is considered important—then it is not at all surprising that women will be more emotional than men. As a thought experiment, one could image a society in which masculinity was associated with being emotional, and femininity with keeping emotions in check. In such a society, it would be "natural" for men to cry and unseemly for women to do so, and, no doubt, men would cry more and women less. Anatomy is only destiny if we believe and insist that it is—and, as was noted in the last chapter concerning ideology, this approach to popular culture would have you cultivate an attitude of suspicion toward any claim that something is "naturally" one way or another, because disguising history as nature is exactly how ideology functions—and ideology inevitably serves the interests of particular groups.

This then brings us to feminist theory and criticism. A feminist approach to popular culture considers popular culture representations, practices, and artifacts in light of the messages they convey and assumptions they make about women, with an eye in particular toward how those messages, assumptions, and representations participate in supporting cultural inequities between men and women. Among the questions such an investigation may include are:

- Are women present in or presumed by the text at all? (The absence of women can send as powerful a message in many cases as their presence.)
- If women are present, how are they described, depicted, or presumed to be?
- What roles do women play? Are women central or ancillary?
- Are women active or passive in their roles? Do they think and act, or are they simply there to be looked at?
- Do women conform to or defy stereotypes? To what extent is the object, practice, or representation coded in terms of traditional feminine associations?
- Are there essentialist assumptions conveyed about women's "nature"?
- How do the representations of women compare to that of men within the same text?
- What messages, finally, are conveyed about the nature and abilities of women?

In seeking answers to these questions, it is important to bear in mind that texts may not be entirely consistent and that there may be disagreement over whether a representation or message is empowering or inhibiting.

YOUR TURN: Use a feminist lens to consider the following popular culture images. What messages about women do you decode and how do you arrive at your conclusions?

Figs. 3.5, 3.6, and 3.7 Images of Women

Feminist theory and criticism arguably can be accommodated under the broader umbrella of **gender studies**—a rubric that, ironically, feminist theory helped to create. What gender studies does is to take de Beauvoir's proposition that "one is not born, but rather becomes, a woman" and extend it to gender identity in general. Thus, one can talk, on the one hand, in terms of women's studies, an interdisciplinary enterprise sometimes referred as the "academic arm of the women's movement" (Howe) that draws on feminist theory to explore, among other things, how ideas of femininity have developed and shifted, how gender impacts the lived experience of women, and the contributions women have made to society. On the other hand, one can also now talk about masculinity studies, which examines how understandings of masculinity are constructed and maintained. We, therefore, can ask the same questions concerning masculinity and popular culture representation that one asks of femininity: how are men represented? Is some essence of masculinity assumed? What messages are conveyed about what it means to "be a man"? How do the representations of men compare to those of women? Whose interests are served by such representations? A recent development in masculinity studies is the concept of **toxic masculinity**—the idea that certain cultural norms associated with being masculine such as the need to dominate others, the refusal to compromise, and the resolution of conflict through violence, have been harmful to women, children, society, and, indeed, men themselves.

> **YOUR TURN**: In what ways can codes of masculinity be considered as harmful to men?

Closely tied to gender studies is sexuality studies, which, like gender studies, is an interdisciplinary enterprise focused on how sexual identity, sexual orientation, and sexual desire are produced, maintained, and policed. As with sex and gender, sexuality has often been thought of as a binary opposition between heterosexuality (sexual attraction to someone of the opposite sex), naturalized as normative, and homosexuality (sexual attraction to someone of the same sex), often construed as aberrant.

And as with gender identification, sexual identity has been shown to be much more complicated than a simple hetero/homo opposition. Other recognized forms of sexuality include bisexuality, asexuality, and pansexuality (attraction toward people regardless of sex or gender identity), and some have suggested that sexuality exists along a continuum from exclusive attraction to the opposite sex to exclusive attraction to the same sex. While homosexuality was declassified as a mental disorder by the American Psychiatric Association in 1973 and has achieved significant levels of visibility and acceptance in Western culture in the twenty-first century, stigmatization of homosexuality nevertheless doggedly persists within particular populations. In the complete absence of such stigmatization it is interesting to conjecture what percentage of the population would actually identify as bisexual or pansexual. Adopting a sexuality studies approach to popular culture, one can ask a series of questions concerning how a given text or practice encodes messages about sexuality. The beginning point is with these two:

- Does the text or practice naturalize heterosexuality as the only option? Are other sexualities represented or implied in any way at all?
- If other sexualities are represented or implied, are they depicted or characterized as viable and equal possibilities? Or are they depicted as deviant, exotic, and/or comic?

The most straightforward way to naturalize heterosexuality as "normal" and "right" is to render other sexualities invisible, which was in large part the mainstream media practice for much of the twentieth century. If all one ever sees is conventionally masculine men pursuing conventionally attractive women, all other possibilities are marginalized and implicitly construed as deviant. Where characters coded as non-hetero did appear in twentieth-century media, they tended to be villainized or comic—e.g., the murderous man-hating lesbian or the female protagonist's gay friend. The twenty-first century has seen a proliferation of non-hetero characters in literature and media presented in ways that seek to avoid and undercut sexual stigmas.

In raising questions about the naturalness of gender and sexuality, gender and sexuality studies often engage in a strategy of **queering**. When used as a verb, to queer something is to look at it in such a way that it becomes strange, and this often involves questioning the foundations on which a belief or idea rests or reading a text or practice "against the grain." Connected to **queer theory**, a branch of gender and sexuality studies that emphasizes the social construction and maintenance of ideas of normalcy and deviancy, the practice of queering can be applied to a range of practices and texts to highlight how they seek to naturalize certain ideas especially as related to gender and sexuality. For example, a queer approach to activities or practices generally considered as hypermasculine, such as aggressive sports, could consider them as means through which men are permitted to touch in a culture that stigmatizes physical displays of affection between men.

Ethnic Studies, Postcolonialism, and Critical Race Theory

In the same way that women and members of the LGBTQIA+ community fighting for recognition and equality have developed strategies to critique and contest the politics of oppression and exclusion, members of other historically disenfranchised groups have similarly sought to highlight the richness of their histories and traditions while challenging forms of discrimination. The shape that these approaches have often taken within the world of academia is, as we have already seen, often in the form of "studies"—programs or departments with a particular racial or ethnic focus. Thus, one can speak of Black studies, Africana studies, or Africology programs; Latino, Chicano, and Raza studies programs; African American, Asian American, and Native American studies programs; Jewish and Arab studies programs; and so on. Outgrowths in the US of the Civil Rights movement of the 1960s and early 1970s, these programs can generally be accommodated under the umbrella of what is termed **ethnic studies** and, implicitly or explicitly, share the goal of challenging the Eurocentric bias of traditional approaches to education, as well as of Western culture more broadly. As explained by Alvaro

Huerta, "As an interdisciplinary scholarly field, ethnic studies is about self-respect and self-determination. It's about racialized groups—workers, students, scholars, organizers, and others—refusing to be viewed or gazed upon from a Eurocentric paradigm as inferior or less than. It's about rejecting the scholarly practice of being objects of studies. Instead, we demand to be the subjects in this equation" (Huerta).

And, in the same way that women's studies programs find their basis in feminist theory, contemporary ethnic studies programs draw to varying degrees upon the approaches and insights of what is known as **postcolonial theory and criticism**. As summarized by J. Daniel Elam, postcolonial theory, which developed in the second half of the twentieth century, concerns itself with "the political, aesthetic, economic, historical, and social impact of European colonial rule around the world in the 18th through the 20th century." "Postcolonial theory," continues Elam, "takes many different shapes and interventions, but all share a fundamental claim: that the world we inhabit is impossible to understand except in relationship to the history of imperialism and colonial rule" (Elam). Intimately intertwined with issues of race and ethnicity, postcolonial theory and criticism has sought to explain and explore the cultural dynamics and legacy created by one group subordinating another. In a seminal work of postcolonial theory, the French West Indian psychiatrist and political philosopher Frantz Fanon explored in *Black Skin, White Masks* (1952) the psychology of the colonized and how they are persuaded to accept their own inferior status. In *Orientalism* (1978), another foundational postcolonialist study, cultural critic Edward Said considers how Western ways of imagining "the Orient" as exotic and irrational facilitated imperialist politics. Fanon, Said, and other postcolonialist theorists and critics have therefore explored how dominant groups seek to perpetuate their hegemony through securing the consent and compliance of subordinate groups. Ethnic studies programs, in turn, have drawn on these insights as approaches to "decolonizing" the thinking of program participants by recovering overlooked histories, celebrating the richness of culturally specific practices and traditions, and highlighting how ideology circulates and hegemony functions to preserve the status quo.

In the twenty-first century, the insights of postcolonial theory and criticism also inform **critical race theory** (CRT), an approach to culture that focuses on systemic racism—the ways in which racism is deeply entrenched in contemporary social structures. Emerging out of legal studies, CRT began by critiquing the notion that the US legal system is colorblind, asserting instead that the American legal system (and, by extension, the legal systems of other predominantly white countries) has been and continues to be skewed by attitudes about race—facts put into stark relief by the 2020 death of George Floyd at the hands of the police in Minneapolis, which added new urgency to the BLM movement. CRT scholars have explored the ways in which US laws and policies are biased against people of color and the ways that legal institutions reinforce that bias. According to the UCLA School of Public Affairs, "CRT recognizes that racism is engrained in the fabric and system of the American society ... [and] that institutional racism is pervasive in the dominant culture.... CRT identifies that these power structures are based on white privilege and white supremacy, which perpetuates the marginalization of people of color" ("What Is Critical Race Theory?"). Now having extended well beyond legal studies, CRT has been utilized to investigate the racial structures of everyday life. "Opposing racism," assert Omi and Winant in their study of US racial history, "requires that we notice race" (Omi and Winant 159).

CRT scholars, it should be pointed out, as well as women's and ethnic studies scholars, also emphasize **intersectionality**—the idea that forms of social stratification such as race, class, sexual orientation, age, disability, and gender do not exist separately but are interwoven together. People are not just one thing—white or black, male or female. Instead, people are complex combinations of features and affiliations subject to various forms of privilege and exclusion. One, therefore, must be careful to avoid sweeping generalizations about "women," "men," "people of color," and so on because the experiences of those thus categorized will be radically different depending on other factors—an upper-class white woman and a poor woman of color are both women, but their experiences navigating American culture are likely to be dramatically different.

Disability Studies

In keeping with the other forms of critical theory introduced in this chapter, **disability studies** is an interdisciplinary scholarly discipline that focuses its attention on the ways in which disability has been defined, how disability has been represented in various media, and its consequences for individuals characterized as or who identify as disabled. According to the Society for Disability Studies, the goals of the discipline include "challenging the view of disability as an individual deficit or defect," studying definitions of and responses to disability from a cross-cultural perspective, and encouraging participation in academia by disabled students and faculty ("What Is Disability Studies"). Adopting an intersectional model, disability studies emphasizes the ways that other factors such as race, class, and sexuality can influence the experience of disability.

> **YOUR TURN**: What popular culture representations of persons with mental and/or physical disabilities can you think of? Focusing on one or two representations, in what ways do you see them as either reinforcing or challenging stereotypes?

Conclusions

This chapter has offered a condensed overview of different forms of critical theory and criticism that can be used to help us understand what popular culture is and what it does. A reasonable question you may be left with, however, is which approach to utilize in a given situation. The not especially helpful answer is: it depends. It may be that you have a particular interest, such as popular culture and gender, that you wish to explore in a variety of different contexts. If so, that's fine—you can certainly explore the gender politics of just about any aspect of popular culture, from the marketing of toys to children to Halloween costumes to song lyrics. In other cases, it is often useful to allow the text you are analyzing to direct you toward the approach—a film such as Jordan Peele's *Get Out* (2017) seems to lend itself to a critical race theory approach, for example, while a Marxist approach to punk music and **subculture** might be a fruitful direction to take. In some cases, with an eye toward intersectionality, critical approaches can be combined, although in shorter essays the danger may be attempting to cover too much. If you become interested in a particular approach—and my overviews here have been quite "bare bones"—suggestions for additional reading are provided below.

The overarching goal of this section—and, indeed, of this approach to popular culture as a whole—is to provide tools that can assist with honing critical thinking skills that allow us to appreciate popular culture texts as inevitably encoding messages about our world. In some cases, these messages reinforce conventional understandings and participate in shoring up the status quo—the way things are. In other cases, these messages may be subversive, asking us to rethink or reject aspects of our reality we may previously have taken for granted. In still other cases, we may receive mixed messages—a text may be "progressive" on race while being conservative in relation to gender. The first step, however, in becoming someone who acts deliberately rather than someone who is acted on and directed by cultural forces is to begin to see the ways in which ideological messages about how we should think and act bombard us constantly. It's a revelation that can be exhausting. But it is a necessary preliminary step toward actualizing a better reality.

Suggested Assignments

1. Compose a reflective essay that uses one of the critical approaches outlined in this chapter as a lens through which to consider your own life experience. How has a component of your identity such as race, class, or gender identification shaped your experiences? Here, you may also wish to think in terms of intersectionality.

2. This chapter has outlined critical approaches to popular culture in broad strokes. Research one particular approach that appeals to

you in greater depth. You may wish to consider who the primary figures in the field are, how the field has developed, and debates within the field. (The "suggested additional reading" section below may serve as a starting point.)

3. Use one of the approaches outlined in this chapter as a lens through which to explore a popular culture object or practice with which you are familiar as congealed ideology. What assumptions about class, gender, physical ability and so on are encoded in and naturalized by the object or practice?

Works Cited in the Chapter

Ainsworth, Claire. "Sex Redefined: The Idea of 2 Sexes Is Overly Simplistic." *Scientific American*, 22 Oct. 2018, https://www.scientificamerican.com/article/sex-redefined-the-idea-of-2-sexes-is-overly-simplistic1/.

Althusser, Louis. "Ideology and Ideological State Apparatuses." *Lenin and Philosophy and Other Essays*, translated by Ben Brewster, Monthly Review Press, 2001, pp. 121–76.

Beauvoir, Simone de. *The Second Sex*. 1949. Translated by Constance Borde, Vintage, 2011.

Blackless, Melanie, et al. "How Sexually Dimorphic Are We? Review and Synthesis." *American Journal of Human Biology*, vol. 12, no. 2, Mar. 2000, pp. 151–66.

Elam, J. Daniel. "Postcolonial Theory." *Oxford Bibliographies*, 15 Jan. 2019, https://www.oxfordbibliographies.com/view/document/obo-9780190221911/obo-9780190221911-0069.xml.

Fanon, Frantz. *Black Skin, White Masks*. 1952. Translated by Richard Philcox, Grove Press, 2008.

"Fortune Global 500." *Fortune*, https://fortune.com/global500/2019/.

Gramsci, Antonio. *The Antonio Gramsci Reader: Selected Writings 1916–1935*. Edited by David Forgacs, New York UP, 2000.

"Highest-Paid CEOS." *AFL-CIO: America's Unions*, https://aflcio.org/paywatch/highest-paid-ceos.

Howe, Florence. Editorial in *Women's Studies Quarterly*, vol. 7, Summer 1979, p. 2.

Huerta, Alvaro. "The Right to Ethnic Studies in Higher Education." *Inside Higher Ed*, 15 May 2020, https://www.insidehighered.com/advice/2020/05/15/why-students-should-be-required-take-ethnic-studies-opinion.

Omi, Michael and Howard Winant. *Racial Formation in the United States*. 2nd ed., Routledge, 1994.

Said, Edward. *Orientalism*. 1978. Vintage Books, 1979.

"What Is Critical Race Theory?" *UCLA School of Public Affairs*, https://spacrs.wordpress.com/what-is-critical-race-theory/.

"What Is Disability Studies?" *Society for Disability Studies*, https://disstudies.org/index.php/about-sds/what-is-disability-studies/.

Wright, Ronald. *A Short History of Progress*. Carroll & Graf, 2005.

Suggested Additional Reading by Topic

Marxist Theory and Criticism

Eagleton, Terry. *An Introduction to Ideology*. Verso, 2007.

——— . *Marxism and Literary Criticism*. University of California Press, 1976.

Nelson, Cary and Lawrence Grossberg, editors. *Marxism and the Interpretation of Culture*. Macmillan, 1988.

Simon, Roger. *Gramsci's Political Thought: An Introduction*. Lawrence & Wishart, 1982.

Williams, Raymond. *Marxism and Literature*. Oxford UP, 1977.

Feminist Theory, Gender and Sexuality Studies

Adams, Rachel and David Savran, editors. *The Masculinity Studies Reader*. Blackwell, 2002.

Butler, Judith. *Gender Trouble: Feminism and the Subversion of Identity*. Routledge, 2006.

Connell, Raewyn. *Gender: In World Perspective*. 3rd ed., Polity, 2014.

Cranny-Francis, Anne et al. *Gender Studies: Terms and Debates*. Palgrave Macmillan, 2003.

Franklin, Sarah, Celia Lury, and Jackie Stacey, editors. *Off Centre: Feminism and Cultural Studies*. Routledge, 2017.

Gottzén, Lucas, Ulf Mellström, and Tamara Shefer, editors. *Routledge International Handbook of Masculinity Studies*. Routledge, 2019.

Lips, Hilary. *Gender: The Basics*. 2nd ed., Routledge, 2018.

McCann, Carole and Seung-kyung Kim, editors. *Feminist Theory Reader: Local and Global Perspectives*. 4th ed., Routledge, 2016.

Naples, Nancy A. *Companion to Sexuality Studies*. Wiley-Blackwell, 2020.

Richardson, Diana and Vitoria Robinson, editors. *Introducing Gender and Women's Studies*. 5th ed., Red Globe Press, 2020.

Saraswati, L. Ayu and Barbara L. Shaw. *Feminist and Queer Theory: An Intersectional and Transnational Reader*. Oxford UP, 2020.

Saraswati, L. Ayu, Barbara L. Shaw, and Heather Rellihan. *Introduction to Women's Gender and Sexuality Studies: Interdisciplinary and Intersectional Approaches*. 2nd ed., Oxford UP, 2020.

Wade, Lisa and Myra Marx Ferree. *Gender: Ideas, Interactions, Institutions*. 2nd ed., W.W. Norton & Company, 2018.

Ethnic Studies, Postcolonial Studies, and Critical Race Theory

Ashcroft, Bill, Gareth Griffiths, and Helen Tiffin. *Postcolonial Studies: The Key Concepts*. 3rd ed., Routledge, 2013.

Ashcroft, Bill, Gareth Griffiths, and Helen Tiffin, editors. *The Post-Colonial Studies Reader*. 2nd ed., Routledge, 2006.

Baker, Brian, et al. *Introduction to Ethnic Studies*. 3rd ed., Kendall Hunt Publishing, 2011.

Crenshaw, Kimberle, et al. *Critical Race Theory: The Key Writings That Formed the Movement*. The New Press, 1996.

Critical Ethnic Studies Editorial Collective. *Critical Ethnic Studies: A Reader*. Duke UP, 2016.

Delgado, Richard and Jean Stefancic. *Critical Race Theory: An Introduction*. 3rd ed., New York UP, 2017.

Huggan, Graham, editor. *The Oxford Handbook of Postcolonial Studies*. Oxford UP, 2016.

Yoo, David, Pamela Grieman, and Charlene Villasenor Black, editors. *Knowledge for Justice: An Ethnic Studies Reader*. University of California Los Angeles American Indian Studies Center, 2020.

Disability Studies

Berger, Ronald J. *Introduction Disability Studies*. Lynne Rienner Publishers Inc., 2013.

Connor, David J., et al. *DisCrit—Disability Studies and Critical Race Theory in Education*. Teachers College Press, 2015.

Davis, Lennard J., editor. *The Disability Studies Reader*. 5th ed., Routledge, 2016.

Goodley, Dan. *Disability Studies: An Interdisciplinary Introduction*. 2nd ed., Sage, 2016.

McRuer, Robert. *Crip Theory: Cultural Signs of Queerness and Disability*. New York UP, 2006.

CHAPTER 4

POPULAR CULTURE PIVOT POINTS

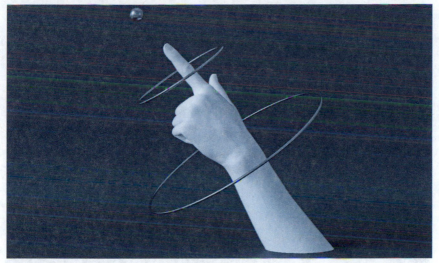

Putting Your Finger on It

The preceding two chapters have outlined different approaches to popular culture. While **semiotics** will be our starting point—thinking about popular culture as **encoding messages** to be **decoded** by consumers of popular culture—**Marxist theory, feminist theory, queer theory, critical race theory,** and so on, can then be used as lenses bringing into focus particular messages embedded in popular culture. This chapter will be a bit different. My goal here is to introduce five pop culture "pivot points": **authenticity, convergence culture, intertextuality, structure of feeling,** and **subculture.** These five ideas are important concepts in popular culture studies that can further help us refine our approaches as we develop an increasingly large shared vocabulary.

Authenticity

To start thinking about the importance of authenticity to contemporary popular culture, let me ask you a few questions (you'll notice this is becoming a trend):

- What would you think if you learned that Bruce Springsteen didn't actually write his own songs?
- What would you think if you learned that rappers Ice Cube and Lil Wayne actually came from privileged backgrounds?
- What would you think if you learned that your favorite independent coffee shop was actually owned by a large chain?

It's possible—likely, even—that you would feel let down or betrayed in each case, but why? Springsteen, Ice Cube, and Lil Wayne's songs would still be as good and the coffee would taste the same, right? You'd be let down because contemporary Western culture privileges authenticity, which we can consider as a kind of semiotic code translating to honesty or sincerity of expression when it comes to identity, artistry, and even, bizarrely, to marketing.

The Real Thing?

Where personal expression is concerned, how many times have you been told that what's most important is to "be yourself" or to "be true to yourself" or to "follow your dream" or something along those lines? This presumably means to act in accordance with your personal beliefs, passions, and preferences—to express your "core" identity, often including **gender** and sexuality, without regard for what other people expect or will think. This imperative to "be yourself" is very much a part of our twenty-first-century Western *zeitgeist*—the spirt of the moment in which the imperative to "be yourself" is paramount. This kind of oxymoronic "individualistic culture" prioritizing self-expression and personal goals over moderation of expression, adherence to **social codes** and authority, and collective action is one particular cultural formation resulting from and reinforced by various social forces—notably **capitalism**, which creates competition among individuals for material and social advancement. Other cultures in different times and places have emphasized cooperative action and conformity to authority and expectation more fully—even the US has moved back and forth between periods of loosening and tightening of individualistic emphasis, although the overall trend has arguably been toward increased individualism.

Although it doesn't prevail universally, even within Western culture (e.g., certain orthodox religious sects), in the twenty-first century, individualism is arguably the dominant ethos—an important part of the contemporary structure of feeling—and authenticity is its privileged framework. To be an authentic person, to be "true to yourself" rather than fake, is to act in conformity with one's personal beliefs and desires, even if, as memorably put by American poet and philosopher Ralph Waldo Emerson in his famous essay "Self-Reliance," the world will whip you with its displeasure for your nonconformity.

This cultural imperative to "be yourself"—to express your authentic personality—is not without its complications and ironies. On the one hand, the insistence that we be ourselves comes at the precise moment that **essentialisms** of all forms are being questioned. We can reasonably ask: do we have one core self or many? Is our weekend self our "true self" and our work-a-day self fake? Or are these equally valid and true forms of our self? On the other hand, capitalism has been remarkably adept at coopting the imperative to self-expression by selling us our non-conformity (as a kind of **compromise equilibrium**). You can customize everything from your truck to your burger to your laptop skin, but you are still buying them from corporations. And then there's the overarching oxymoron of individualistic culture: if everyone is a non-conformist, is anyone really nonconforming?

> **YOUR TURN:** What makes a person authentic in your eyes? To what extent and why do you value this?

An emphasis on authenticity has been particularly important to evaluating contemporary popular music—the perception of the "real-ness" of a music artist or band is inevitably central to their appeal to audiences, although what that realness consists of varies depending on **genre**. As P. David Marshall discusses in *Celebrity and Power*, ideas of authenticity in relation to musical performance and performers have shifted across time—notably in the twentieth century in response to new technologies—but have focused on the performer with an increasing emphasis on the sincere expression of emotion (155).

Like gender **codes** discussed in the previous chapter, authenticity can be considered as a kind of semiotic code: a "language" spoken by artists and bands and understood by audiences. Authenticity in post-1960s rock and roll has arguably pivoted around two tightly coupled elements: sincerity of expression on the one hand, and rule-breaking on the other. To avoid being inauthentic—or "fake"—and to be regarded as "serious" artists, rock and roll artists and bands in the twenty-first century need to write their own songs, play their own instruments, and "follow their vision"—that is, to create music without regard for the anticipated response from critics and audiences (which leads to an artist or band being construed as a "sell-out"). The assumption is that the music, created by the artist or band, is a reflection of their genius, and that the song lyrics offer a sincere snapshot of the artist or band's history and/or "feelings"—the lyrics "make a statement" about "who the artist is" or what they stand for. Marshall speaks of this in terms of "commitment," which can mean either emotional sincerity or a form of solidarity with an audience, or both (164). This is why fans feel duped if it turns out that the music or lyrics weren't written by the band or if the performer's beliefs or background are at odds with lyrical content. And, while it is often crucial that rock and roll artists or bands write their own songs and lyrics, and play their own instruments, sincerity of expression is more important than technical precision or virtuosity. What punk rock of the 1970s proved is that three chords and an attitude, rather than a trained voice and years of practice on an instrument, are all that's required for rock and roll stardom. Indeed, lack of polish is itself a marker—part of the code—of authenticity in rock and roll. Anything too polished or overproduced has the potential to come across as fake.

Closely connected to sincerity of expression in the code of rock and roll authenticity is rule breaking—which I consider related to what Marshall refers to as "difference" (163–64). Ironically, we expect rock and roll celebrities to flout conventional rules of decorum: the whole "sex, drugs, and rock and roll" mantra. This can be in terms of outrageous personal behavior and onstage antics. We not only license but expect rock and roll bands and performers to violate the social rules and expectations that typically govern the rest of us—this is part of the reason rock and roll stardom is particularly appealing, even within an ostensibly individualistic culture. Rule breaking, however, also applies to musical composition. Authentic bands and artists differentiate themselves from other similar bands and artists (and here we can think about the **paradigm** rock and roll bands) through innovative approaches to their genre. (Interestingly, there is a kind of formula at play here in which a band's first two albums develop a particular sound or approach, the third album is then a departure, and the fourth a return to form.)

> **YOUR TURN:** The discussion above has focused on the code of authenticity specifically as related to rock and roll. How is authenticity performed in other music genres with which you are familiar such as country or hip-hop?

An important issue in relation to innovation and codes of authenticity worth mentioning here is **cultural appropriation**. Cultural appropriation—sometimes discussed as cultural misappropriation—can be said to take place when elements of one culture are adopted or utilized by another. This tends to become controversial when members of the **dominant culture** appropriate from a disadvantaged minority culture. In cases where appropriation reaffirms derogatory stereotypes, it is clearly offensive; however, the line distinguishing between appreciation and misappropriation can often be quite murky—and all of rock and roll, which originated in the 1940s and 1950s, finds its roots in other styles including blues, jazz, gospel, and country. As part of asserting their authenticity, musicians will often explore other musical traditions—as when, to use older examples, rock stars Peter Gabriel and David Byrne (the latter of the band Talking Heads) incorporated African and Brazilian elements respectively into their work. More recently, rap has been utilized by a variety of white artists from Taylor Swift to Iggy Azalea.

> **YOUR TURN:** Under what circumstances is cultural appropriation acceptable? When is it objectionable?

I've focused on codes of authenticity here primarily in relation to personal identity and music, but the concept is ubiquitous in individualistic Western cultures of the twenty-first century. The catch phrases "be yourself," "keeping it real," "follow your dream," and so on all reinforce the idea that what matters most is the performance of an authentic identity.

> **YOUR TURN:** How is authenticity performed in other areas of popular culture? What marks an authentic fan of a sports team or film franchise? When is a business or restaurant authentic? And is the authentic thing always best?

Convergence Culture

Coined by central media studies scholar Henry Jenkins, convergence culture refers to the way twenty-first-century technologies combine tasks and activities that previously were distributed among discrete systems, as well as to the ways consumers of media content interact with that content and each other. In his 2006 book, *Convergence Culture: Where Old and New Media Collide*, Jenkins defines "convergence" as "the flow of content across multiple platforms, the cooperation between multiple media industries, and the migratory behavior of media audiences who will go almost anywhere in search of the kinds of entertainment experiences they want" (2). "Every important story gets told," continues Jenkins, "every brand gets sold, and every consumer gets courted across multiple media platforms" (*Convergence Culture* 3).

Convergence culture, on the one hand, can refer to **transmedial** adaptation. Meaning "across different media," transmedial **adaptation** describes the process of adapting content presented in one medium into others. For example, Dracula was originally introduced as a character in the novel of the same name by Bram Stoker in 1897. Stoker's narrative, however, has subsequently been adapted for stage, film, radio, television, comics, video, video games, and so on, and the character Dracula has been marketed in an endless variety of consumer products ranging from mugs to masks to cereal. *Harry Potter*, similarly, began life in a series of books by J.K. Rowling and has subsequently been adapted across media into films, consumer products, and even a theme park.

Jenkins connects this idea of transmediality to what he calls **participatory culture**. Instead of an older model of media consumption in which media producers and consumers occupied separate spheres, in participatory culture, the process is much more interactive with private individuals creating and publishing their own media content and then circulating it via various means, most notably social media platforms. As will be discussed in chapter 10 of this book, **fandom** is an important example of participatory culture, and is something Jenkins associates with **collective intelligence**—the ways in which consumers of media interact with one another discussing the media they've consumed and collectively arriving at shared understandings. "Collective intelligence," writes Jenkins, "refers to [the] ability of virtual communities to leverage the combined expertise of their members" (*Convergence Culture* 27) to shape understandings of a media property.

Convergence culture, on the other hand, is also used by Jenkins to refer to technological shifts that have allowed different technological systems to share the same tasks. Phones used to be solely for the purpose of making telephone calls. Now, however, your phone can be used to text, play games, watch movies, surf the web, and so on. Amazon.com used to be a site for buying books; now, not only can you purchase just about anything, but you can also stream media content. Computers used to be for data processing; now, they can do everything your phone can. "Convergence," explains Jenkins, "involves both a change in the way media is produced and a change in the way media is consumed" (*Convergence Culture* 16).

Converging Platforms

YOUR TURN: In what ways have you been a producer of media content? And in what ways have you experienced or benefited from the "collective intelligence" of participatory culture?

Intertextuality

The animated television show *Family Guy* is notable for its "cutaway gags"—moments when the program shifts away from the story being told to a short, usually unrelated scene, and then back again. For example, in the fourth episode of the first season, main character Peter Griffin's explanation to his wife about why he can't help with housework involves a short cutaway to him having disappeared into the land of Narnia through the dryer (such as the episode shown below, from the fifteenth season, in which Stewie and Brian play Sherlock Holmes and Watson) *Family Guy* has literally hundreds of such sequences that briefly refer to celebrities, politicians, other television programs, movies, and so on, all of which are examples of intertextuality—moments when one **text** (in this case, *Family Guy*, see Fig 4.1) makes a connection with another.

Fig. 4.1 Family Guy

At its most basic, intertextuality refers to the ways in which the meaning of one text is shaped by its connections with another: "inter" as in "between" texts. Of course, as discussed in chapter 2, this is how meaning is produced in general. The meaning of a given **sign** depends on its paradigmatic and **syntagmatic** relationships to other signs, as well as the **connotations** overlaid on the sign by individual users. Put differently, when we think of a sign as a kind of text, its meaning will be shaped by its differences from other similar signs that could be substituted, its position in relation to other signs, and the associations we bring to bear on the sign, some of which may be widely shared, others of which may be idiosyncratic. A Rottweiler is a black and tan dog breed that is not a Doberman or a dachshund. A Rottweiler will signify differently playing happily in a dog park or barking on the end of a chain guarding an impound lot. And a Rottweiler will certainly be regarded differently by someone who grew up with them as pets and by someone who was once bit by one while jogging!

All meaning production therefore depends on an element of intertextuality, as the meaning of one sign is shaped by its interrelations to others. However, the idea of intertextuality tends more commonly to focus on the ways more sophisticated assemblages of signs—art, music, literature, and media of all kinds—refer to others, as when *Family Guy* mentions the land of Narnia from C.S. Lewis's fantasy series or the familiar Cat in the Hat cartoon character from the works of Dr. Seuss. Intertextuality comes in several forms, including quotation, allusion, **pastiche**, and parody. Quotation and allusion are similar: to quote something is to repeat a sentence or phrase someone else has said or written. In chapter 3, I quoted a phrase attributed to author John Steinbeck: "socialism never took root in America because the poor see themselves not as an exploited proletariat but as temporarily embarrassed millionaires." Quotation isn't limited to spoken or written language however; pieces of any other semiotic system can be repeated in new contexts by someone else, including sections of music, dance, and visual art. Digital sampling in music, for example, is a form of quotation and can include anything from samples of speeches or film dialogue to drum beats, horn blasts, and sections of bass lines.

Allusion is a bit less direct than quotation. To allude to something is to reference it or call it to mind without mentioning it explicitly. If you refer to something that makes you weak or that you can't resist as your "kryptonite," you are making an allusion to Superman. A greeting consisting of a raised hand with palm forward, thumb extended, and fingers parted between the middle and ring fingers to form a "V" shape is an allusion to the *Star Trek* franchise. In some cases, quotations themselves can also be allusions. If I wave my hand and say, "these are not the droids you're looking for," I'm both quoting directly from and also alluding to *Star Wars: A New Hope*. If I sing the two-note dah DAH dah DAH theme from *Jaws* as I creep up on my kids, I'm both quoting a musical passage and alluding to the film from which it originates.

Quotations and allusions are both forms of intertextuality that enrich texts by connecting them to others, thereby inflecting their meaning. Direct quotation with attribution—by which I mean quotation that acknowledges its source—is often used to lend authority to a statement, as well as to establish one's knowledge in a particular area. This is standard practice in academic research—if I'm writing about convergence culture, for example, I can acknowledge my debt to Henry Jenkins and show that I've done my homework by judiciously quoting Jenkins directly. Quotation to establish authority, however, may be as simple as telling your older brother, "Dad says you have to give me a turn!"

Because an allusion is an indirect reference, decoding it requires knowledge on the part of the recipient of a message and, as a result, rewards the recipient for their understanding. The listener to Public Enemy's iconic "Fight the Power" who recognizes that the song samples, among others, James Brown and Sly & the Family Stone, has their knowledge of funk and soul music validated. This, in turn, creates a kind of bond between the encoder and the decoder of the message as having a shared appreciation for these genres. Something similar takes place with media references. If I quote a line from *The Rocky Horror Picture Show* and you respond in kind, we then acknowledge each other as members of a community with a shared love for the famously campy film.

YOUR TURN: What examples of quotation and allusion can you find in the pop culture texts with which you are familiar?

Two ideas associated with intertextuality important to popular culture studies are textual poaching and **textual nomadism**. As developed in Henry Jenkins's foundational study of television fandom, *Textual Poachers: Television Fans & Participatory Culture* (1992), textual poaching is the process of appropriating aspects of a published work and redeploying them in new creative contexts. As will be discussed in chapter 10, fans of a particular source text—a published book, television program, film, and so on—may "poach" characters and elements of the fictional world in which the characters exist and use them in creative ways. This may involve creating new stories involving them, creating works of art featuring them, editing together clips to create fan videos, and so on. Such works are inherently intertextual as they require some knowledge of the source text on the part of the audience to be understood as intended by their creator. Textual nomadism refers to the ways in which we make sense of the media we consume. The meanings we derive from a text are shaped by all the associations we make as we read, view, or listen—this may involve connecting **themes** in a work to similar themes in other works with which we are familiar (e.g., paradigmatically), looking at a work within the context of other works by the same creator, interpreting a work in relation to one's own subcultural affiliation, and so on. The notion of "nomadism" here is that, as we seek to make sense of a text, we range widely across our own experiences, which inevitably shape and inflect our understandings of texts.

Quotation and allusion can often be put to more sustained use in the development of pastiche and parody. A pastiche is an imitation of another work or a particular style. For example, Banksy is a contemporary visual artist whose work combines graffiti with stenciling techniques. Someone else trying to emulate that style can be said to be pastiching Banksy. Similarly, a sonata written by a contemporary composer in the style of Beethoven can be considered a pastiche. Importantly though, recognizing a pastiche as a pastiche requires knowledge of what is being pastiched—pastiche is therefore inherently intertextual. To decode the work as intended by its creator, one needs to be aware of the work or style being imitated.

In contrast to pastiche, which tends to be respectful, although some-times playful, a parody is a work that imitates another, often exaggerating certain notable features, for the purpose of making fun or commenting on the source text. While a parody may be funny or interesting in its own right, as with pastiche, a full appreciation of the work's intentions requires one to recognize what is being parodied. Singer Weird Al Yankovic, for example, has made a career out of parodying pop songs by everyone from Nirvana to Billy Ray Cyrus in a light-hearted way. His songs can be enjoyed on their own, but to fully grasp the intended humor, one must be conversant with the songs—and sometimes the videos as well—that are being parodied. Similarly, the film *Young Frankenstein* (Mel Brooks, 1974) is most immediately a parody of the classic film version of Mary Shelley's 1818 novel, the 1931 *Frankenstein* directed by James Whale, while the *Scary Movie* franchise parodies the horror genre writ large. *Saturday Night Live* has across its history parodied celebrities and politicians—with Alec Baldwin's portrayal of President Donald Trump as a famous case in point. Parodies are by definition intertextual because they require knowledge of the text being parodied to achieve their intended effect.

A clever example of intertextual parody took place in 2013 at the annual correspondents' dinner for the journalists who cover the White House. A short video was presented in which Hollywood director Steven Spielberg announced that, following on the success of his 2012 biopic *Lincoln*, his next project would similarly be a biopic, but this time about the life of then-President Barack Obama—and playing Obama would be the star of *Lincoln*, white actor Daniel Day-Lewis. The rest of the sketch featured President Obama pretending to be Daniel Day-Lewis discuss-ing the challenges of playing President Obama (see "Barack Obama").

The video was very well received, but appreciating it as funny requires some background knowledge: one must know who Barack Obama is, of course, and the kinds of challenges he confronted as President (at one point, Obama playing Day-Lewis questions why Obama never gets mad, noting, "If I were him, I'd be mad all the time! But I'm not him. I'm Daniel Day-Lewis"). It's also useful to be familiar with Steven Spielberg as among Hollywood's most successful directors. But what the humor of the piece really hinges on is a two-part recognition on the part of the viewer: (1) Daniel Day-Lewis (who retired from acting in 2017) has been hailed as among the greatest actors in cinematic history and has played a remarkable range of roles, and (2) it would nevertheless still be absurd to have him play Obama because Day-Lewis is white and Obama is black. Indeed, were Lewis to actually appear in the video as Obama rather than Obama himself, in all likelihood the video would end up absurd if not actively offensive rather than funny. But because it is Obama himself pretending to be Lewis playing Obama, viewers can recognize the sketch as a parody of biopics like *Lincoln*, as well as of the kind of media coverage films receive in which famous actors discuss the challenges of their roles.

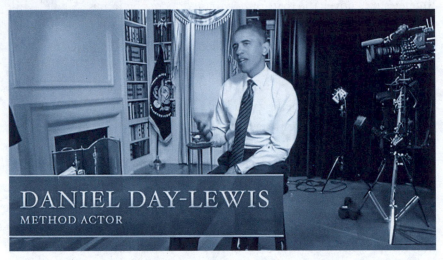

Obama Playing Day-Lewis Playing Obama

The "Barack Obama as Daniel Day-Lewis with Steven Spielberg" video is thus an intertextual work that, for full effect, requires viewers to know something about actor Daniel Day-Lewis and the roles he has played, Steven Spielberg and the films he has directed, President Barack Obama, biopics in general, and interviews with celebrities in which they discuss preparing to play difficult parts. Parody is in this way inevitably intertextual—and often, one might add, metatextual. The adjective "meta" has come to signify a work or concept that refers back to itself or the conventions of its genre (this is called *self-referentiality*). A film about filmmaking for example, or a country song that lists all the common clichés of country songs can be described as "meta" or "metatextual." A parody that calls attention to itself as a parody—as, by for example, having President Barack Obama say that he isn't Barack Obama but Daniel Day-Lewis—is thus an example of **metatextuality**.

Intertextuality is a defining characteristic of contemporary popular culture. Intertextuality is central, for example, to the process of adaptation, which typically involves shifting the medium through which a text is expressed, but may also involve altering a text within the same medium. We are often used to thinking about adaptation primarily from written form to visual, as, for example, the film versions of the *Harry Potter* books; however, adaptation can work in a variety of directions: the 2006 horror film, *Silent Hill* (Christophe Gans), for example, is an adaptation of the 1999 video game of the same name (and really is better than it has any right to be!). Bram Stoker's novel *Dracula* (1897) has been adapted for ballet. Disney's film *The Lion King* and the band Green Day's album *American Idiot* were both adapted for theater, and so on.

Adaptations do not necessarily have to translate a text from one medium to another. **Mash-ups** are contemporary adaptations that combine texts, sometimes across media, sometimes not, to create something new. The graphic novels (later adapted to film) *The League of Extraordinary Gentlemen* and the Showtime / Sky series *Penny Dreadful* bring together characters from various Victorian novels for example; Theodora Goss's *The Strange Case of the Alchemist's Daughter* (2017) does the same thing in literary form. Grahame-Smith's 2009 novel, *Pride and Prejudice and Zombies* is a mash-up that fuses Jane Austen's 1813 novel of manners, *Pride and Prejudice*, with the zombie genre. **Remakes** are, as the name implies, new versions of an older text. Sometimes, the remake is faithful to the original (which may itself be an adaptation). The American vampire film *Let Me In* (2010) is, for example, a generally faithful remake of the Swedish horror film *Let the Right One In* (2008), itself adapted from the book by John Ajvide Lindqvist. More often, however, remakes diverge in significant ways from the source text being remade, often leading to debates among fans over the virtues and flaws of each version. The 2016 remake of the 1984 film *Ghostbusters*, for example, diverges markedly from its source text, notably in having women play all the lead roles performed by men in the original. Remakes that alter the plot of the source text significantly are sometimes referred to as **reimaginings**. Remixes are alternate versions of the same story—Valerie Martin's novel *Mary Reilly*, for example, retells Robert Louis Stevenson's famous novel, *The Strange Case of Dr. Jekyll and Mr. Hyde*, from the perspective of Jekyll's housemaid. And then there are reboots, which present a new version of an established fictional universe. In 2005, for example, NBC rebooted the older series *Battlestar Galactica*, which originally aired from 1978 to 1979, to some acclaim.

While adaptations can often be consumed (and even sometimes enjoyed!) without knowledge of the source text being adapted or updated, all these forms of adaptation are by definition intertextual inasmuch as they find their basis in a previously existing work, and their ubiquity raises the fundamental question of why—why is our moment in the twenty-first century marked by such a profusion of remakes, reboots, reimaginings, mash-ups, and remixes? Is this a symptom of the exhaustion of our imagination? Are we just seeking comfort in something familiar? Or is it something else?

> **YOUR TURN**: What other forms of intertextuality do you see at play in contemporary popular culture?

Structures of Feeling

This popular culture studies pivot point is in some ways the most elusive. The concept of structure of feeling derives from the foundational cultural studies work of British Marxist critic Raymond Williams, and refers to the ways in which shared generational experiences and common values shape subjective experience. In Williams's *The Long Revolution* (1961), he describes the structure of feeling as the "felt sense of the quality of life at a particular place and time: a sense of the ways in which the particular activities [combine] into a way of thinking and living" (63). We can think of the structure of feeling as a kind of spirit of the moment, something shared to various extents by all the people living in a particular time and place, although significantly inflected generationally, as well as by other social factors such as class, race, and **sex**. In Williams's later *Marxism and Literature* (1971), he uses the idea to refer to what O'Connor refers to as a "pre-emergent cultural phenomena: a trend that is developing but is not yet clearly emergent. We may have a sense of something new developing but as yet not fully formed" (O'Connor 84). These traces of a structure of feeling are often there, according to Williams, in works of art and literature. They are found there, as Williams puts it, as "social experiences in *solution*," dissolved in the work rather than precipitated out (*Marxism and Literature* 133–34).

Williams's idea of **structures of feeling** has interesting applications when thinking about popular culture because Williams developed the notion in relation to the study of culture in general. For Williams, the analysis of culture has to grapple with the funnel-like structure of culture itself. At the top of the funnel is the complete culture of a time and place itself, which is where structures of feeling are located. This is the lived, felt experience of a time and place, embodied in practices, beliefs, objects, and understandings of that culture. There is then what Williams calls the "recorded culture," consisting of the surviving texts or practices of a certain culture. Finally, there is what he refers to as the culture of the "selective tradition," which refers to recorded culture materials that actually get studied or are privileged in a certain way. This is easiest to think about in relation to an earlier time period. How should we go about studying nineteenth-century America? None of us was alive then, so we have to instead look to recorded culture—all the materials that can give us insight into the period: books and magazines and newspapers, works of art and music, clothing and furniture and houses, tools and games, and so on. There are two problems here though: first, lots of materials produced in the nineteenth century no longer survive. What we have are durable materials that managed to last a century or longer, as well as materials that, either by accident or design, were preserved. Our picture of the nineteenth century, therefore, will inevitably be incomplete and is very much influenced by the selective tradition: nineteenth-century objects that someone felt were worthwhile. The further back we go in time, by the way, the more of a problem this becomes for the analysis of culture—because, as we go back in time, fewer and fewer material objects remain available. The other problem for cultural historians, at least of the nineteenth century, is the opposite: while the selective tradition has winnowed the percentage of available materials, there still remains an overwhelming amount—even a dedicated professional historian can only survey a relatively small amount of everything that was printed in the nineteenth century.

The result is that, when studying past cultures or present ones, we are drawing conclusions based on a small number of texts—and, where past cultures are concerned, without benefit of access to the overall structure of feeling that prevailed in a particular time and place. We end up a bit like paleontologists attempting to reconstruct a prehistoric animal on the basis of a tooth. This, however, doesn't mean that we shouldn't try to understand earlier cultures or our own. With an ideal goal of trying to get as close as possible to the structure of feeling that existed or exists in a given location at a given time, Williams asks us to focus on *patterns*: "it is with the discovery of patterns of a characteristic kind that any useful cultural analysis begins, and it is with the relationships between these patterns ... that general cultural analysis is concerned" (*The Long Revolution* 63). Thus, the goal is to work backward by making connections among **primary texts** and attempting to reconstruct an overall structure of feeling—always bearing in mind that our perspective on what matters is shaped by our own experiences and values. The past always becomes meaningful in light of present values and concerns.

The way that this will work in practice for us as investigators of popular culture is to start by considering individual primary texts—films, musical compositions, works of art, buildings, fan practices, what have you in terms of how they convey meaning and what they tell us. This, on its own, can be revealing about those primary texts and our relationships to them. However, we need to be wary of drawing broad generalizations on the basis of a limited number of primary texts. So, we then start looking for patterns: do other texts that are part of the same paradigm send similar messages? If so, we may be on to something culturally significant—perhaps something reflective of an emerging structure of feeling.

As an example, let's say you are interested in the role of race in contemporary horror films, and this leads you to a consideration of Jordan Peele's film *Get Out* from 2017. After careful analysis, you conclude the film's message to be that, far from being post-racial or color-blind, America remains haunted by its legacy of racist exclusion. This is a supportable interpretation of the film—but does it tell us anything more broadly about race and American culture? Well, maybe. The next step would be to look for a pattern: other primary texts—probably films and television shows, but possibly literature, art, even BLM marches—that work together with the message of *Get Out* to suggest a broader emerging structure of feeling. One must be careful of "**cherry-picking**" though—that is, one must avoid carefully selecting primary texts that support your conclusions while ignoring everything that doesn't.

One additional warning about using the idea of a structure of feeling. It's a very useful concept but, in the same way one needs to be wary of making broad generalizations on the basis of limited data—one or even a handful of carefully picked primary texts doesn't necessarily tell us anything definitive about "culture"—one also needs to be careful about making big assumptions about a particular culture. The tricky part about structures of feeling is that they are clearly inflected not only by way of age, but race, class, gender, and other social determinants. The challenge then becomes to try to determine just how far a particular attitude or sensibility or "feeling" extends within a given time and place.

> **YOUR TURN:** This is a difficult question, but what do you think characterizes or defines the structure of feeling that prevails in your community? What emerging sense, sensibility, or understanding seems to connect you to others of your generation?

Subculture

One final pivot point related to popular culture studies to be introduced here is the idea of a **subculture**. A subculture is a group that differentiates itself within the broader culture by having a set of beliefs and/or practices that are to some extent at variance with prevailing norms or beliefs. Examples of subcultures include bikers, skaters, punks, goths, hippies, and metalheads. In an important 1979 study called *Subculture: The Meaning of Style*, sociologist Dick Hebdige argued that subcultures are "subversive" in the sense of refusing to abide by a given culture's expectations concerning deportment and behavior. Hebdige focused on what he referred to as "spectacular subcultures"—that is, groups that use style as a form of confrontation such as bikers with tattoos, punks with mohawks, or goths in whiteface.

Bikers

For Hebdige, these styles are a way to express "a refusal" (3)—that is, style is used as a form of "intentional communication" (100) to convey resistance to **hegemonic** expectations. This takes us back to our chapter on semiotics. Every culture has dress codes—understandings of what combinations of clothing and stylings of the body are acceptable for different bodies in different situations. This codes are both learned and widely shared within a culture—so the members of a given culture will mostly share a general sense of what is appropriate for little girls to wear and what is appropriate for grown women to wear, how one should look for a job interview and how one can look going to the gym, and so on. When someone doesn't know the codes, we may think of them as being naïve—someone may not understand, for example, that it is conventional to look formal for a job interview. Spectacular subcultures, in contrast, intentionally ignore cultural codes governing how one should look and comport themselves. Of course, cultures are fluid things—acts of resistance are quickly coopted and what is subversive at one moment quickly becomes assimilated as part of a compromise equilibrium. Tattoos and piercings (apart from pierced ears on Western women), for example, used to be aggressive forms of resistance. Now, they are quite commonplace (except for yours—those are really cool!).

Subcultures, by definition, differentiate themselves from the culture at large, so will in some sense be "deviant." Not all subcultures, however, particularly in the Internet age, must be "spectacular" in the sense of visible displays of refusal—and deviance is a matter of degree. It is more accurate to think of subcultures as asymptotic to mainstream culture with some coming very close and others diverging more markedly. As will be discussed in chapter 10, contemporary fandoms can be considered as participatory subcultures in which individuals share a more intense affection for a particular focus—book, band, film, television series, podcast, etc.—than the general public and engage in various practices in relation to the object of their shared affection. Deadheads, Potterheads, Parrotheads (fans of Jimmy Buffett), metalheads, Trekkies, and so on can also be considered participatory culture members, but fandoms of this sort have become increasingly commonplace in the twenty-first century, so can be conceived of as less of a refusal and more of an expression of personal taste.

Fandom

A useful concept related to the idea of subculture is the notion of **subcultural capital**. Capital in general refers to wealth—the money or other assets someone or something possesses. Proposed by Sarah Thornton in her 1995 study, *Club Cultures: Music, Media, and Subcultural Capital*, subcultural capital refers to the resources a member of a subculture possesses that afford that person status within the subculture: this can include longevity within the subculture, perceived commitment to it through style or action, knowledge of the subculture or its focus, and personal possessions. For example, a *Dungeons & Dragons* (*D&D*) gamer who helped create the game in the 1970s will have far more subcultural capital within the *D&D* gaming subculture than a newbie who was inspired to start playing after watching *Stranger Things*. Subcultural capital has a positive correlation with authenticity. The more subcultural capital the member of a subculture possesses, the more authentic that person is perceived to be.

YOUR TURN: What subcultures are you familiar with? Do you participate in one yourself? If so, what forms does cultural capital take within the subculture?

Suggested Assignments

1. Explore how authenticity is constructed within a particular subculture. How do members of the subculture demonstrate their commitment?
2. Trace the transmedial adaptation of a particular media property. How has a source text been adapted for different media platforms? What kinds of changes were made to accommodate the new medium?
3. Create your own parody of a pop culture property, such as a song or film. Explain clearly what aspects of the source text you intend to parody.

Works Cited within the Chapter

"Barack Obama as Daniel Day Lewis with Stephen Spielberg." *YouTube*, 29 Apr. 2013, https://www.youtube.com/watch?v=Pq9QxnY0miE.

Emerson, Ralph Waldo. "Self-Reliance." *The Essential Writings of Ralph Waldo Emerson*, edited by Brooks Atkinson, Modern Library, 2000, pp. 132–53.

Hebdige, Dick. *Subculture: The Meaning of Style*. 1979. Methuen, 1988.

Jenkins, Henry. *Convergence Culture: Where Old and New Media Collide*. New York UP, 2006.

——. *Textual Poachers: Television Fans & Participatory Culture*. Routledge, 1992.

Marshall, P. David. *Celebrity and Power: Fame in Contemporary Culture*. 2nd ed., University of Minnesota Press, 2014.

O'Connor, Alan. *Raymond Williams: Writing, Culture, Politics*. Blackwell, 1989.

Thornton, Sarah. *Club Cultures: Music, Media, and Subcultural Capital*. Wesleyan UP, 1996.

Williams, Raymond. *The Long Revolution*. 1961. Broadview Press, 2001.

——. *Marxism and Literature*. Oxford UP, 1978.

Additional Suggested Reading

Barker, Hugh and Yuval Taylor. *Faking It: The Quest for Authenticity in Popular Music*. W.W. Norton & Company, 2007.

Firestone, Amanda and Leisa A. Clark, editors. *Harry Potter and Convergence Culture: Essays on Fandom and the Expanding Potterverse*. McFarland & Company, 2018.

Gelder, Ken. *Subcultures: Cultural Histories and Social Practice*. Routledge, 2007.

Gelder, Ken, editor. *The Subcultures Reader*. 2nd ed., Routledge, 2005.

Haenfler, Ross. *Goths, Gamers, & Grrrls: Deviance and Youth Subcultures*. 3rd ed., Oxford UP, 2015.

—— . *Subcultures: The Basics*. Routledge, 2013.

Scott, Suzanne. *Fake Geek Girls: Fandom, Gender, and the Convergence Culture Industry*. New York UP, 2019.

POP CULTURE UNITS

CHAPTER 5

TELEVISION AND FILM

Lights, Camera, Action!

Since this textbook on approaching popular culture is all about asking questions, let's once again start this chapter with a bunch of them:

- What's your favorite TV show?
- What's your favorite movie?
- Have you ever "binge-watched" a series?
- Do you stream programs on Netflix, Amazon Prime, Hulu, Disney+, HBO, Showtime, or any other of the constantly expanding number of content providers?
- Did you have a favorite TV show growing up?
- Did you ever dress up as a TV or movie character for Halloween?
- What role do TV shows and movies play in your life now?

As your answers to these questions likely indicate, audio-visual sources of information and forms of narrative—television, film, videos, and so on—are so intimately intertwined with our day-to-day existence that it's hard to imagine our lives without them. According to the US Bureau of Labor Statistics, in 2018 nearly 80 per cent of the US population watched TV on any given day, while a 2019 study concluded that the "average U.S. adult" (18 years or older) "now watches almost six hours of television and video per day" (Roberts). No doubt numbers grew even higher in 2020 and 2021 during the COVID-19 pandemic.

So, most of us watch. A lot. What we don't tend to consciously consider, however, is that when we watch TV, movies, videos, and so on, we are engaged in a complicated process of making meaning out of images and sound. Because of our familiarity with how visual narrative forms work, **decoding messages** beamed at us becomes second nature. We've learned the **signs** and **codes**: when things get fuzzy and we hear dreamy harp music playing, this signals a flashback; a rapid-fire montage of different shots of an athlete training signals the passing of time as a character prepares for a competition—and we know the music playing underneath the montage is for us, not the character (this is called **non-diegetic** music; we hear it but the characters don't); we know if something is a comedy that the seemingly incompatible lovers will end up together; if we are shown a character and hear that character's voice without seeing their lips move (called a voice-over), we know this is what they are thinking in their head; we know that when we have a shot of a character looking out a window, then a shot of the street out the window, that we are seeing through the character's eyes; we know when ominous music starts playing in a horror film (again, non-diegetic music) to be on our guard and get ready for a jump-scare—we also know, because this isn't our first rodeo, that the horror movie monster is never really defeated the first time; we know red-shirted characters in *Star Trek* aren't coming back; we know that an unsteady camcorder aesthetic or "found footage" is meant to convey "realism"; and we absolutely know that when a sitcom mom makes a huge breakfast, the family members will only grab a piece of toast and dash out the door. I'm mixing up different kinds of codes here, as I'll explain below, but the point is that all of this knowledge is *learned*—what we know about TV and film and other audio-visual media, from how to identify a shot through the eyes of one of the characters to the fact that sitcom characters never, ever sit down for breakfast, is the result of repetition over time. We've seen it all before, so understanding these conventions just feels natural; like learning to ride a bike or drive a car, after we've mastered it, we don't think about it (unless and until something goes wrong).

YOUR TURN: Can you supplement the list of conventions of televisual and cinematic media above with others—the things we learn to expect and understand as consumers of visual narrative media?

Although making sense out of audio-visual media is second nature to us, pop culture munchers that we are, there is in fact a lot going on when we watch TV or a movie—and to unpack this a bit, we are going to have recourse to two important frameworks developed to explain how we make sense out of visual narrative media, the first developed by cultural studies scholar Stuart Hall in 1973 and the second by communications scholar John Fiske as explained in 1987.

The Encoding / Decoding Model of Television Spectatorship

The **encoding /** decoding model of communication was developed by cultural studies scholar Stuart Hall in 1973 in a creatively titled essay called "Encoding and Decoding in the Television Discourse" and offers a useful approach for thinking about how meaning is conveyed, not just through TV, but film, videos, and other forms of technologically mediated communication. While the article itself is dense, its essence is relatively straightforward and works along these lines: those creating a television show or movie have something that they want to communicate to viewers on the other end—this may be a story (fictional or not) or it may be information on some topic. Not only that, the creators of what

Hall refers to as a message (a TV show in his discussion, but equally applicable to film and video) also want their audience to respond in particular ways to their message: if I'm creating a comedy, I want people viewing it to find it funny and laugh; if I'm creating a horror movie, I want people to be on the edge of their seats; if I'm creating a documentary on the history of vaccines, I likely want people to understand not only how vaccines developed but why they are important; if I'm a meteorologist on the news, I want people to understand what the weather is likely to be for the next few days. The question any content creator then faces is this: *bearing in mind the nature of the medium transmitting the message*, how do I "package" information so that it is likely to be received the way I intend on the other end? The encoding end of the process takes place when a content creator packages a message to be transmitted for consumption—and a lot goes into this. For a movie or TV show, this includes the script, the acting, the filming, the editing, and so on. The message is then transmitted to an audience via a particular form of technological mediation—it may be screened in a theater, aired on TV, streamed to your phone or computer, etc. What happens on the other end then is a process of decoding—of attempting to make sense of the encoded message.

The role of the medium here is central. When we watch TV or a film, even if what we are watching is "live," the message is still being packaged in particular ways for our consumption. We aren't experiencing the event itself, but a kind of staging of it that takes into consideration the **affordances** and limitations of the medium. A radio broadcast of a baseball game, for example, has to narrate information very differently than a television broadcast of the same game due to the nature of the medium. Famously for communications theorist Marshall McLuhan, "the medium is the message" (7 and *passim*)—the nature of the means of communication inherently shapes and limits that message.

So, the encoding of a message always has to bear in mind the medium of communication that will be used to convey it to the recipient of the message. The especially tricky part about encoding messages is that there are always possibilities for misfires that result in their being decoded in unintended ways: "decodings," explains Hall, "do not follow inevitably from encodings" (136). Hall discusses three possible decoding positions—three reactions to a received message. The first is the **dominant / hegemonic** position, which decodes the message the way that it was intended and accepts it. If, for example, I make a documentary celebrating the life of Thomas Jefferson and you come away from the program deeply impressed with Thomas Jefferson, you've occupied the dominant / hegemonic position, having accepted what I've proposed. If you come away from the program conflicted, thinking "yes, he did important things, but he was also a slaveholder who fathered six children with Sally Hemings who were not emancipated on his death," you occupy a **negotiated** position: you are acknowledging the dominant message, Jefferson did important things, but are not accepting it entirely. And then there is the **oppositional** position; if you view my documentary on Jefferson, understand its intention to celebrate his achievements, and come away wholly disgusted with what you perceive to be Jefferson's hypocrisy, you've decoded the message differently than I intended entirely.

> **YOUR TURN:** The three positions outlined above, dominant / hegemonic, negotiated, and oppositional are possible responses to any decoded message. What would each mean in relation to a political advertisement or comedy sketch?

Importantly, these three positions all presume that decoders of a message grasp the intended message—I get it and I agree, I get it but have mixed feelings, I get it but reject it. There is always the additional possibility, however, of encoding misfires resulting in message recipients not appreciating the sender's intentions or failing to make any sense of it at all—that is, of just not getting it. These misfires can occur for many different reasons. Sometimes misfires have to do with a lack of proficiency with televisual and cinematic codes on the part of the message creator—if I'm trying to create a scary film but don't get the lighting right, or the soundtrack is too frisky, or the acting is poor, you'll probably appreciate what I'm trying to do, but it just won't work. Sometimes, misfires have to do with the lack of a shared context for understanding a message. If I make a **parody** of a Steven Spielberg "prestige" biopic, and you aren't familiar with these, you aren't likely to decode the parody as a parody and may end up just confused.

Visual Narrative Codes

Hall's approach to how consumers of television derive meaning from what they watch has an elegant simplicity to it: we start with ideas someone wishes to communicate; these are encoded into messages designed for transmission in a particular medium; the messages are then decoded on the other end by someone who can agree, partially agree, disagree entirely, or just not get it. What Hall makes clear is, *whether we are aware of it or not, we're always engaged in a process of decoding*—of interpretation, of making sense of messages beamed at us (which is true of not just television and film, but life in general). We can now add more precision to the idea of encoding and decoding in visual narrative media by turning to the work of scholar John Fiske, who discusses the types of codes that come into play when visual narrative messages are encoded and decoded.

A code, according to Fiske, as we discussed in chapter 2, is "a rule-governed system of signs, whose rules and conventions are shared amongst members of a culture, and which is used to generate and circulate meanings in and for that culture" (Fiske 4). Television—and by extension other visual narrative media—can be addressed, according to Fiske, in relation to four types of codes organized into three "levels" (see Fig. 5.1).

Fiske begins his discussion of televisual codes by outlining what he calls **social codes**. These are not specific to television or film but instead circulate in a particular **culture**—this is the level of "real life" or "reality." For example, as we discussed in chapter 3, all cultures have **gender** codes that dictate how those who are biologically male and female should look, act, dress, and so on. A burly guy with a deep voice and a beard

An event to be televised is already encoded by **social codes** such as those of:

Level one:
"REALITY"

appearance, dress, makeup, environment, behavior, speech, gesture, expression, sound, etc.

these are encoded electronically by **technical codes** such as those of:

Level two:
REPRESENTATIVE

camera, lighting, editing, music, sound

which transmit the **conventional representational codes**, which shape the representations of, for example: narrative, conflict, character, action, dialogue, setting, casting, etc.

Level three:
IDEOLOGY

which are organized into coherence and social acceptability by the **ideological codes**, such as those of: individualism, patriarchy, race, class, materialism, capitalism, etc.

Fig. 5.1 Fiske's Codes

is "manly"; a petite woman with long hair in a dress and make-up is "feminine." As Fiske puts it, "People's appearance in 'real life' is already encoded" (Fiske 4). Codes in our daily life are everywhere and govern the way we make sense of our reality—we can think in terms of codes of politeness, codes of location (rural life vs. a small town vs. a big city), ethnic and racial codes, and so on. "The point is that 'reality' is already encoded," writes Fiske. "[T]he only way we can perceive and make sense of reality is by codes of our culture" (4).

Social codes are the starting point for visual narrative media. Let's say we want to tell a story about someone who worked hard and achieved the "American Dream." Our program will likely start with a setting signaling poverty. The show might not state this outright, but will give the viewer all the signs we need to interpret it as such: a rural setting, modest house, characters in worn clothes, etc. The setting will be staged for us of course, but the point is that making sense of the staging will depend upon pre-existing codes that allow us to interpret the setting in the desired way: *humble origins*. Next, we need physical bodies on screen to perform the roles. Given our story about the American Dream, we're likely going to start with a child—in generations past, a white boy with sandy hair and blue eyes. Today, a greater range of possibilities. The child for our story will, of course, be an actor, picked for their appearance and ability to deliver lines; however, the body of the child actor picked will come to us pre-defined by certain cultural codes and expectations—before the child delivers any lines or does anything at all, the viewer has already interpreted the child's body as a complicated sign: young, rural, poor.

Our Young Protagonist

Once the creators of our program on the American Dream start casting bodies based on how they look and talk, and building sets to reflect social realities, we've moved from the level of "reality" to what Fiske calls "representation." This is the nuts-and-bolts level of content creation, consisting of **technical codes** and **conventional representational codes**. Technical codes refer to how our narrative is staged and recorded, and include camera shots and angles, lighting, editing, music, and sound. Technical codes, according to Fiske, transmit conventional representational codes that shape the representation of things such as character, narrative, dialogue, action, setting, and so on. To get a sense of how these codes go together, let's go back to our program on the American Dream. How can we represent our protagonist's family as *poor but hard working*? Perhaps a montage of family members doing various tasks: scrubbing laundry, chopping wood, harvesting crops—all brightly lit, all outside, with a spritely major key classical music piece beneath it all. Editing together these different scenes into a rapid sequence will encode the message that they are *poor but virtuous*. We might then contrast these scenes with one of the program's villains—perhaps the greedy banker who owns the deed to the house our protagonist and his family live in and is demanding the rent knowing that the family, despite working hard, can't pay it. How can we show that he is a villain? He's likely old, well-dressed in contrast to our hard-working family, shot in a dimly lit interior space perhaps with a kind of blue filter to make it look cold and lifeless. The music beneath the scene will shift to something slower and in a minor key. In each case, the technical codes—filming, editing, lighting, music—combine to transmit conventional representational codes: youth and the vigorous warmth of rural life contrasted against the solitary greed of the bitter old man in his sterile house full of lifeless objects.

The Villain

Social codes are where we start—our pre-existing understandings of reality, of the "real world." Creators of visual narrative forms use those social codes as starting points and building blocks toward encoding a particular message. In order to package it in a way that the recipient hopefully will decode as intended, technical codes are employed—scenes are filmed, lit, edited, scored, and so on—to shape conventional representational codes, which themselves are furthered by dialogue, action, setting, and character. Our sympathetic protagonist will appear outdoors in bright light helping someone and light-heartedly joking; our villain will utter ominous lines while filmed alone inside in dim light. These representational codes will then all conspire to create Fiske's third level of televisual codes: **ideological** codes.

Ideological codes refer to the beliefs or values encoded in the **text** that the viewer is finally supposed to accept. The inspiring story of our protagonist's achievement of the American Dream reinforces the idea that with pluck, honesty, grit, and determination, anyone can rise to a position of privilege in American culture. It naturalizes the idea that some people are rich and some are poor—that's OK, says our show, because people, if they are honest and hard-working, can overcome their humble beginnings—indeed, it is their reward for adhering to these virtues; and when they are rich, they will remember their roots and be charitable rather than miserly. Along his journey, our protagonist probably met a woman and fell in love but, goes the story, he was too poor to marry her when they first met, so he left to seek his fortune, returning just in time to save her from the clutches of someone less deserving. Marriage was always the destiny for both of them, although she had to wait for him. Close scrutiny reveals that our familiar story comes freighted with ideological codes we are asked on some level to decode and accept: **capitalism**, family, heterosexual monogamy, gender distinctions permitting men more free-dom of action, and so on. And we may come away impressed and inspired to work hard ourselves (the dominant / hegemonic position), we may come away conflicted (the negotiated position), or the whole thing may leave us cold because the program clearly supports a system of values to which we do not subscribe (the oppositional position).

The ideological codes that we identify in a given work may then direct the kind of inquiry we undertake and the critical lens we utilize for our analysis. For example, noting the way that our story of the American Dream works to make a capitalist system in which there will be winners and losers feel natural and right, we may decide to

The Dream Achieved

adopt a **Marxist** critical lens and explore how the work conveys this ideological message. Or, alternatively, we may wish to adopt a **gender studies** approach and focus our attention on how the narrative participates in normalizing particular conventional gender dichotomies that have permitted men a greater range of freedoms and opportunities than women. Interpretation of pop culture texts is in this way a bit like cutting a gem: our goal is to bring out the qualities already present in a particular text—and then to consider their significance for our understanding of the work and for our understanding of the world.

YOUR TURN: Explore the technical, conventional representational, and ideological codes present in a scene from a television program, film, or video of your choice.

Approaching Visual Narrative

The purpose of this discussion of encoding, decoding, and televisual codes has been to foreground the idea that making sense out of visual narrative forms is in fact a complicated process and to provide us with a **semiotic** framework and shared vocabulary we can use as we begin to think critically about television, film, and video. So, with this in mind, what then does it mean to approach television, film, video, and other visual narrative forms from a pop culture studies perspective? Here John Fiske is again instructive. He proposes in *Television Culture* that, in thinking about television, there are three aspects we need to attend to: "the formal qualities of television programs and their flow; the intertextual relations of television within itself, with other media, and with conversation; and the study of socially situated readers and the process of reading" (16). What this means is that we need to consider individual texts and their qualities, the relationships of televisual texts to other texts and contexts, and the ways in which different viewers make sense of the television programs they consume. Put differently, we can ask: what are we watching? How does it relate to its context? And how do different viewers make sense of it?

The question of what it is that we are in fact watching asks us to consider the televisual codes outlined above—that is, we can ask both *what* messages are conveyed by the program, film, video, etc., and *how* these messages are conveyed. Let's use a real-world example this time: Jordan Peele's 2017 film *Get Out*. In this Academy Award-winning film, a young black man, Chris (Daniel Kaluuya), goes with his white girlfriend, Rose (Allison Williams), to visit her family in rural upstate New York. There he discovers (sorry, spoilers!) that she and her family serially kidnap black men and women whose bodies are then taken over by rich people who want to avoid death. The film ends up as an allegory of American race relations, condensing into two hours—and caustically critiquing—a history of wealthy white people appropriating and controlling black people. But how does the film guide us to this conclusion?

There is a lot to consider in answering this question: obviously, this involves considering the elements of the narrative itself: the characters, the plot, the action, the setting, and the dialogue—the conventional representational codes that shape what happens in the film, where it happens, to whom it happens, and how the characters respond. And we also need to consider how these things are packaged for us: the editing of scenes, their lighting, the camera shots and angles, music and sound, the role of special effects, and so on—the technical codes that shape the way the narrative is represented for us. Because films and TV shows more than a few minutes long give us lots to work with, an analysis such as this typically involves close attention to moments or scenes that stand out as being particularly important, striking, or illustrative (although one must be careful to avoid **cherry-picking**). Using *Get Out* as our example, let's focus on two scenes: the Sunken Place and the silent auction.

In the first scene, the protagonist, Chris, has been hypnotized by his girlfriend's mother, Missy (Catherine Keener). Compelled to recall the events surrounding the death of his own mother when he was a child and his related guilt, he is then forced by Missy to sink into a kind of internal psychological void called the Sunken Place. Two of the most striking aspects of this scene are Chris's paralysis as he is controlled by Missy—the iconic shot of Chris with tears running down his face

Fig. 5.2 Chris in the Sunken Place

used for the film's publicity comes from this scene—and the surreal image of him then sinking into darkness as though he is deep in the sea or floating in space (see Fig. 5.2). The shot of Chris crying is done as a close-up, which creates intimacy with him. The shot of him sinking is perhaps the most intrusive way special effects are used to create a particular image. Both shots and the scene as a whole are about loss of control as Missy takes over control both of Chris's body and mind. He is dispossessed of his autonomy and becomes a kind of puppet whenever Missy taps a spoon against a china teacup, symbolic of her own social status and ethnic heritage.

The scene of the auction is notable not for special effects, but for editing and sound. The first thing to point out is that the scene is actually not one scene but two as the action has been edited to move back and forth between a distraught Chris talking with his seemingly sympathetic girlfriend Rose about his suspicions and an auction taking place in which what is being auctioned off is Chris himself; this creates a kind of ironic juxtaposition revealing Chris's concerns as entirely warranted. Both scenes are tied together by an ominous musical score beneath the action that tells us the events are taking place simultaneously. And what stands out about the auction itself is that it is a silent one—the auctioneer (Rose's father, played by Bradley Whitford) and the participants communicate solely by gestures (see Fig. 5.3). Like Chris's descent into the Sunken Place, the meaning here is conveyed

Figs. 5.3 and 5.4
The Auction and the Flag

by image and music rather than dialogue. And, as a subtle nod to the larger significance of the action, Chris and Rose are together dressed like the American flag: Chris in blue, Rose in red and white stripes (see Fig. 5.4).

In attending to these scenes as part of building a larger argument concerning the **themes** and meanings of the film, I am considering both what happens in the scenes and how it relates to the overall plot of the film, as well as to the technical aspects that shape the viewer's response: music, editing, special effects, costuming. All of these individual elements participate in the encoding of the film's larger ideological messages about race and the persistence of racism in American culture. The primary theme of the film is arguably that racism still in fact persists twenty-first-century America—and the film takes a dim view of it, using the conventions of the science fiction and horror **genres** to make its point.

This last observation concerning genre introduces another important point: films, television shows, and videos are by their nature **polysemic**, which means that they have multiple meanings and support different interpretations. Race is a clear thematic focus of *Get Out*, so, for the purpose of this illustration, it makes sense to focus on race—indeed, the film is ready-made for a kind of **critical race theory** approach, given that it actively plays on the difficult relationship between people of color and law enforcement in American culture. However, one could certainly attend to other elements of the film. For example, one could consider how the film plays with genre, using elements of science fiction and horror to advance political critique; one could focus entirely on the soundtrack to the film and how it shapes the viewer's response; one could adopt a Marxist approach to the film by attending to the curious class positions of the film's characters; one could focus on how recurring **motifs** and **tropes** such as deer and photography help tie the film together; one could use a **feminist** lens to consider how women are represented; one could then consider the **intertextual** elements of the film—how it **alludes** to and compares with other related texts; and this just scratches the surface of possible approaches.

Looking for Patterns

The first step in the analysis of popular culture is thus often a process of close reading—attentive analysis of the program, practice, or object that considers the qualities of the thing in question and how it creates meaning. Our starting point always needs to be to ask: what is this thing? How is it put together? What makes it tick? From there, we can expand outward with a consideration of how the object under scrutiny—in this case, a film or television show—connects, as Fiske puts it, "with other media, and with conversation" (16). A full appreciation of the thematic message of *Get Out*, for example, requires some knowledge of American history as the film's meaning is shaped by its context, both present and historical. The auction scene with Chris is a straightforward reference to antebellum American slave auctions, Chris's getting hassled by a police officer on the way to Rose's family connects to the BLM movement, and the film even references US President Barack Obama—before giving us a picture of an America that is far from being "post-racial."

In addition to thinking about how both present and past history inform a work and the context that is needed to interpret the work as intended, one can also ask questions, as Fiske suggests, about how the work relates to media—and here we can either proceed **diachronically** or **synchronically**. "Diachronic" means across time, so a diachronic study looks at how something has developed (or not) over a period of time. For example, one could do a diachronic study of how black bodies have been represented in horror films from the early twentieth century up to and including *Get Out* in the twenty-first. It would ask when, where, and how people of color are represented in the genre, and look for trends—general directions in which things changed. Such a study might then consider what social factors influenced these trends, asking why things changed in the way that they did.

In contrast, a synchronic approach considers related works produced at more or less the same moment in time. In relation to horror films, one could then ask: how are people of color represented in horror films released in the past five years and how does this reflect prevailing understandings of race and racism? Bearing in mind that Stuart Hall privileges patterns as particularly meaningful when trying to capture the **structure of feeling** of a particular moment, if a pattern of representation emerged, this could provide sociological evidence of shifting ideological understandings of race. Here again, one would need to be wary of cherry-picking one's examples or making broad generalizations on the basis of a limited number of **primary texts**. One film or two films or even a handful that have received special attention don't really provide a firm footing for making big assumptions about "culture," although they may allow one to present a kind of hypothesis for further investigation.

And then there is the question of who watches what and in what circumstances—as Fiske puts it, "the study of socially situated readers and the process of reading" (16). In thinking about the significance and meaning of a particular work, we can also explore patterns of consumption: with whom was *Get Out*, for example, popular? How was the film watched—theater? Streaming service? DVD? And what meanings did different viewing groups decode from the film? Patterns that emerge from gathering sociological data based on questions such as these can also be very important in helping us to understand the cultural significance of a given popular culture text—in this case, a film or television show.

Asking Questions

The beginning point of an analysis of pop culture audio-visual media begins—as with any pop culture form—with the asking of questions. Lots and lots of questions. These questions may include the following:

Qualities

- **MEDIUM**. What is the medium of the message? (TV, film, video?) And how / where is the message consumed? (On a hand-held device? On a computer? On a conventional television? In a theater?)

- **CHARACTERISTICS**. What qualities define the message? For example, how long is it? Is it animated or live action? Is it self-contained or part of a series? Is it 2D or 3D? Color or black and white? Is it in English? If not, is it dubbed or are there subtitles?

Codes

- **GENRE**. What genre does the message belong to? (E.g., comedy, tragedy, horror, science fiction, biography, documentary, etc.). What generic markers make this clear?
- **CONVENTIONAL REPRESENTATIONAL CODES**. What types of settings and characters are present? What do you notice about costuming and make-up? How would you summarize the plot? What role does dialogue play?
- **TECHNICAL CODES**. What stands out about camera work, music and sound, editing, lighting, and special effects?
- **IDEOLOGICAL CODES**. What are the larger themes of the work? What picture of the world does the work naturalize? What should the ideal viewer of the work think and feel having completed watching it? How does the work either reinforce or contradict social codes of its moment?
- **METATEXTUALITY**. Does the text play with the conventions of genre or adhere to them uncritically? Does it foreground its own status as a text in any way, calling attention, for example, to itself as a show or film?

Intertextuality

- **CONTEXT**. What kinds of knowledge does decoding the text as intended require? For example, is the text based on a comic book? Is it part of a series? Does it require knowledge of a particular history, social group, or lifestyle? How is the text a reflection of its particular historical moment? If the text being considered is an older one, how does its decoding today compare with that of its moment? That is, is it received differently today due to shifting social codes or has its meaning remained stable?

- **ALLUSION**. Does the text reference or allude to other works either in the same medium or other media?
- **SYNCHRONIC COMPARISON**. How does the text's style, themes, and ideological messages compare to other works of its genre produced at around the same moment?
- **DIACHRONIC COMPARISON**. How does the text compare or contrast with similar works from earlier periods, demonstrating trends or a lack of development?

Audience

- Is the text intended for a particular audience? If so, how does the text signal this and what marks the intended audience? How was the work marketed?
- How have different groups—e.g., men / women, old / young, people of color / white, cisgender / LGBTQIA+, wealthy / not wealthy, religious / non-religious, and so on—responded to the text and what aspects of the text have shaped their responses?

Sample Essay

The following sample essay by Kathleen Hudson is an excerpt from a longer work titled "'Something from Your Life, Something that Angers You ...': Female Rage and Redemption in Netflix's *Stranger Things* (2016–2017)." The essay, which was originally published in an online scholarly journal titled *Refractory: A Journal of Entertainment Media*, adopts a gender studies approach to the Netflix series *Stranger Things*.

"'Something from Your Life, Something that Angers You …': Female Rage and Redemption in Netflix's *Stranger Things* (2016–2017)"

Kathleen Hudson

The political events that defined 2016—the year in which the Netflix series *Stranger Things* was released—sparked a wave of female rage in the United States of America. In November of that year the first female major party presidential candidate, Hillary Clinton, narrowly lost the election to Donald Trump, a man who had openly bragged in the past about sexually assaulting women. Discourses on women's health, sexual commodification, gender identity, and "family values" dominated political and social life and exposed profound, seemingly irreconcilable divisions in the national ideology. Moreover, the language applied to Clinton, in particular, illuminated a pervasive assumption that women in public spaces must repress their emotional responses as part of a culturally informed behavioral standard. Gendered norms problematized any actions or words made by women that might be construed as aggressive, rendering those who allegedly violated this standard alternately "unfeminine" or monstrously hyper-feminine. "Censorious anger" was widely identified as a "liability" for women, to the point where one critic noted that many "are so sure that our resentments—especially any resentments toward men—are corrosive, and make us appear pathetic and vengeful, that we ask for divine help to simply stop feeling them" (Traister).

The concept that angry or frustrated women threaten both socio-political stability and gender identity itself is hardly a new one. Midcentury psychology and sociology, such as that organized in Orville G. Brim Jr.'s "Table of Traits Assigned to Male and Female" (1958), based off Talcott Parsons and Robert Bales's materials in *Family, Socialization and Interaction Process* (1955), suggests that "Quarrelsomeness," "Revengefulness," and "Insistence on rights" are not only traits that are primarily female but are also "incongruent" or contradictory characteristics of the proper "performance" of that gender (Brim 203). While based on a faulty understanding of biology, it hardly matters whether such assumptions are scientifically accurate or not. As Kate Millet argues in her examination of this study in *Sexual Politics*, in many social discourses that define gender roles "the vices of the oppressed and all their serviceable virtues are acknowledged, with the usual implication that the under class ... is expected to bear its ignoble status with a better fortitude and a more accommodating mien than it does" (Millet 232). Female anger and frustration, regardless of how justified such emotions might be, are frequently characterized as irredeemably and almost monstrously paradoxical parts of female identity, and thus subject to strict social and personal policing.

The Duffer Brother's Netflix series *Stranger Things* openly marketed itself as a homage to the 1980s. Featuring 90s "It Girl" Winona Ryder and a collection of stock characters and familiar tropes plucked from a number of beloved films and books, the show incorporated a patchwork of popular culture which signaled a return to a politically and socially complex decade and suggested that we view this period, at least initially, through the lens of sentimental nostalgia. However, deviations from recognizable cultural

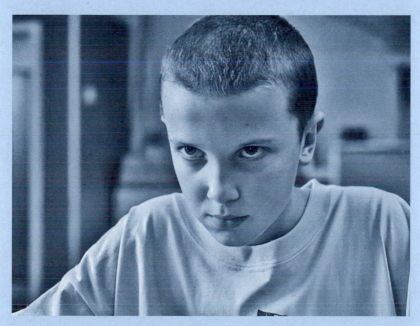

Fig. 5.5 Eleven from Stranger Things

references provide audiences with new negotiations of gender politics. For example, in the show's second season Eleven [see Fig. 5.5] is tasked by Kali to use her telekinetic abilities to move a disused train compartment from one end of a field to another, and by tapping into an inner source of power she manages to do so. This moment is taken directly from the 1980 film *The Empire Strikes Back*, the second installment of the original *Star Wars* trilogy. In this film protagonist Luke Skywalker is taught to use the "Force" to move objects without physically touching them. However, the homage in *Stranger Things* differs from its source material in two very important ways. Firstly, both trainee and mentor in the show are female. Secondly, instead of freeing oneself from aggression, as Yoda instructs Luke to do in *Empire*, in *Stranger Things* Kali tells Eleven to "find something from your life … something that angers you" and use the emotions those memories inspire to accomplish her goal (2.07). Unlike Luke, who is told that fear, anger, and hate lead only to suffering, Eleven interrogates and embraces feelings of resentment and channels those emotions into a constructive manifestation of rage.

Though initially coded as recognizable female archetypes drawn from the horror and science fiction films of the 1970s and 80s, *Stranger Things* characters Eleven and Joyce Byers speak to a contemporary moment. At the beginning of 2017 many disaffected voters, despite the prevalence of rhetoric that identified female fury as monstrous, began more actively embracing the image of a righteously angry "nasty woman" whose emotional response is a natural reaction to social injustice.[1] Protesters turned out in force for the Women's March in January 2017, just a few days after the presidential inauguration, and women soon began running for political office in record numbers. The #YesAllWomen and #MeToo movements emerged as a parallel, related attempt to promote female-centered narratives and thus expose the full extent of sexual harassment and gender-based violence in a variety of professional and social situations. These Twitter hashtags offered platforms through which women and men could share stories of suffering, abuse, and alienation, providing a plethora of real-world examples of the widespread impact of rape culture. They eventually became just a few of the more well-known movements gaining ground after 2016 that utilized female anger and the female narrative as a means of enacting social change. The instant popular appreciation for Eleven and Joyce as well as the full-throated calls by the show's fans for "Justice for Barb," referencing a character who is on one of the lowest levels of a high school hierarchy and who is killed in Season One, underscores the *Stranger Things* viewing audience's willingness to not only accept complex women characters but to also utilize politicized anger in defense of those who are unfairly marginalized or abused. Rejecting self-censorship and recharacterizing their own emotional narratives, women have increasingly accepted that, as Laurie Penny's *Teen Vogue* article suggests, "Most Women You Know Are Angry—and That's All Right" (Penny).

Both conforming to and deviating from the generic tropes that inform their characterizations, Eleven and Joyce's attitudes and attributes in *Stranger Things* problematize the allure of uninterrogated nostalgia and recontextualize negotiations of female anger in both the show's setting and in contemporary discourse. Living on the border between monstrosity and victimhood, Eleven and Joyce suggest that anger against a regressive regime is justified and constructive when undermining oppressive systems and developing personal identity. Both women are positioned in opposition to the monstrosity and/or incompetence of the "father," and their weaponized anger is most often depicted as an affirmation of the self. Perhaps most critically, Eleven and Joyce's depictions suggest that anger does not diminish one's gender identity—it may complicate reading of gender from a socio-cultural perspective, but ultimately female anger does not detract from either Joyce's role as a mother or Eleven's "coming of age" story. Boyish "Final Girls," androgynous "others," and the bald-shaved almost-mother Ellen Ripley from the *Alien* film franchise haunt the text, invoking popular and critical discourses while complicating easy assumptions regarding gender and emotional self-expression. Though heavily reliant on 80s novels and films as source materials and hampered by an overarching reluctance to compromise "heroic" male characters, *Stranger Things* pushes the boundaries of its own "nostalgia" by inviting re-imaginings of female anger in both new socio-political contexts and classic cultural works.

Note

[1] This phrase was used by then-candidate Donald Trump when referring to opponent Hillary Clinton during the third presidential debate on October 19, 2016. The phrase has since been widely adopted by various outlets.

Works Cited in the Sample Essay

Brim, Orville G. "Family Structure and Sex Role Learning by Children: A Further Analysis of Helen Kock's Data." *Selected Studies in Marriage and the Family*, 2nd ed., edited by Robert Winch, Robert McGinnis and Herbert Barringer, Holt, Rinehart and Winston, 1962, pp. 619–26.

Millet, Kate. *Sexual Politics*. New York: Columbia UP, 2016.

Parsons, Talcott and Robert Bales. *Family, Socialization and Interaction Process*, Routledge, 1955.

Penny, Laurie. "Most Women You Know Are Angry—and That's Alright." *Teen Vogue*, 2 August 2017, https://www.teenvogue.com/story/women-angry-anger-laurie-penny.

Traister, Rebecca. "Hillary Clinton Is Finally Expressing Some Righteous Anger. Why Does that Make Everyone Else So Mad?" *New York Magazine*, 15 September 2017, https://www.thecut.com/2017/09/hillary-clinton-what-happened.html.

Suggested Assignments

1. With attention to particular scenes, analyze the social, technical, conventional representational, and ideological codes present in a film, video, or episode of a television program.
2. Adopt one of the critical approaches introduced in chapter 3 and use it as a lens through which to consider a film, video, or episode of a television program.

3. Research the history of a particular film or television show and consider it within the context of its historical moment. How does the **text** reflect a particular **structure of feeling**?

4. Create a short script for a television program—either an existing one or one of your own invention. Explain the ideological messages encoded in your script and how you would seek to make sure viewers decoded those messages in keeping with your intentions.

Works Cited in the Chapter

Fiske, John. *Television Culture*. 2nd ed., Routledge, 2010.

Hall, Stuart. "Encoding and Decoding in the Television Discourse." 1973. *Culture, Media, Language: Working Papers in Cultural Studies, 1972–79*, edited by Centre for Contemporary Cultural Studies, Hutchinson, 1980, pp. 128–38.

Hudson, Kathleen. "'Something from Your Life, Something that Angers You': Female Rage and Redemption in Stranger Things (2016–2017)." *Refractory: A Journal of Entertainment Media*, vol. 31, 26 Feb. 2019, https://refractory-journal.com/vol-31-2019/.

McLuhan, Marshall. *Understanding Media: The Extensions of Man*. 1964. The MIT Press, 1994.

Roberts, Nicole F. "Psychological Research Explains Why TV Viewing Is Higher than Ever." *Forbes*, 4 Dec. 2019, https://www.forbes.com/sites/nicolefisher/2019/12/04/psychological-research-explains-why-tv-viewing-is-higher-than-ever/#63828c403b0b.

Additional Suggested Reading

Benshoff, Harry. *Film and Television Analysis: An Introduction to Methods, Theories, and Approaches*. Routledge, 2015.

Bignell, Jonathan. *An Introduction to Television Studies*. 3rd ed., Routledge, 2012.

Calvert, Ben, et al. *Television Studies: The Key Concepts*. 2nd ed., Routledge, 2007.

Hayward, Susan. *Cinema Studies: The Key Concepts*. 5th ed., Routledge, 2017.

Mittell, Jason. *Television and American Culture*. Oxford UP, 2009.

Nichols, Bill. *Engaging Cinema: An Introduction to Film Studies*. W.W. Norton & Co., 2010.

CHAPTER 6

MUSIC

This chapter was prepared in consultation with
Nicholas Laudadio of the
University of North Carolina Wilmington

Put the Needle to the Record

This book's approach to popular culture is all about asking questions, because asking questions is the beginning point for investigation, which leads to hypotheses, often more questions, tweaking of hypotheses, and, hopefully, at the end, illuminating conclusions. So, to get us going thinking about popular music (like a broken record), let me again ask you a bunch of questions:

- What types of music do you listen to?
- What is your favorite band or musical artist?
- Who was your favorite when you were fifteen?
- What are your favorite albums? Favorite songs?

- When do you listen to music?
- What was the last concert you went to?
- Which band or artist would you like to see most?
- What role does music play in your life?
- Who or what do you think has shaped your musical tastes most?

In the same way that most of us would find it difficult to imagine our lives without television and movies, it is similarly hard to conceive of contemporary life without popular music—which we can think of as being forms of music with wide appeal (with all the ambiguities that "wide" entails, as discussed in chapter 1), including rock, reggae, soul, funk, rap, hip-hop, forms of electronic dance music, country, and so on. After all, we're surrounded by popular music, more so than even television. Sometimes, it's in the foreground, as when we go to a concert, sing along to music while driving, or go dancing; it is a central part of social events like weddings and parties, and gets played loudly to pump us up at sporting events (when, typically, we can either choose to get on board the crazy train or contemplate who let the dogs out). Sometimes, it's in the background, as when we dine out, shop for groceries, or ride in elevators (while trying not to make eye contact with other people). It's part of the movies and television shows we enjoy—often rising to the level of our consciousness during the opening and closing credits—and is central to many videogames. In addition to employing older formats, such as CDs, vinyl, and terrestrial radio, we can now curate a streaming service playlist or seed an algorithm with songs we like to discover new bands. Perhaps we've even personalized our ring tone with a favorite song. Popular music is the music bed for our lives—we may wake up to it in the morning and fall asleep to it at night. We make lists of our desert island picks, follow our favorite bands and artists on social media, and delight in our favorite songs, which may serve as powerful triggers for reflection, reminding us of important moments in our lives. We love our music. And yet, as with other forms of popular culture, we may not ever really think too much about how we make sense of popular music, translating sound into meaningful experience, or how the music we enjoy fits into broader cultural patterns or a contemporary **structure of feeling**.

An unreflective attitude toward popular music is understandable for a number of reasons. In the first case, as with other **semiotic** systems, once we develop interpretive strategies and learn the **codes**, they become second nature to us, and we cease to be aware of ourselves as engaged in a process of **decoding** and making sense of music as **messages**. We only become aware of ourselves as engaged in a process of interpretation when we encounter something organized differently that confuses us. Second, the **pop culture paradox** comes into play: our music is incredibly meaningful to us—so much so that it is hard to imagine our lives without our favorite bands and songs—and yet, at the same time we may not attribute much overall importance to it. Indeed, that may be part of the appeal, at least in some cases: we love it because we perceive it as being an escape from the important, meaningful things that weigh us down: work, school, family obligations, and so on. (As we discussed in chapter 1, this was part of the **Frankfurt School's criticism** of popular music—they perceived it as a form of escapism or what we today might call "downtime," requiring little actual attention and serving to soothe the working class, allowing them to return to their labors refreshed so as to keep making money for those who own the **means of production**.) Third, music is often there in the background as we perform other activities, so it isn't something we're consciously thinking about; and fourth, music, frankly, can be difficult to talk about because being precise about music and its qualities requires a specialized vocabulary that non-musicologists and non-musicians often do not possess. Because music tends to move us just as much on an **affective** level—on the level of the body and our feelings—as it does on an intellectual level (or even more so), it's often hard to discuss. Thus, particularly in the absence of a background in music theory (including an understanding of things like pitch, scales, modes, rhythms, timbres, tempos), we may fall back on the familiar process of interpreting song lyrics—which, granted, are an important way that music can become meaningful for us—and then rely on general characterizations of music and how it makes us feel: fast, slow, happy, sad, soothing, aggressive, and so on.

One chapter on popular music in a textbook on understanding popular culture won't transform us into musicologists. Nevertheless, our approach to interpreting popular music will attempt to lend some precision to such discussions by adapting John Fiske's tri-pronged approach to television studies (as outlined in the previous chapter) as we focus on the formal qualities of music; the **intertextual** relations of music with itself, other artistic forms, and its broader context; and the ways different audiences respond to and make forms of music meaningful. The place to start then, as always, is by appreciating the formal qualities of the thing being analyzed: what makes a song what it is?

Mic Drop

What Is This Thing?!

In the same way we can't talk about the significance of crime dramas or television sitcoms or fantasy films without having some examples in mind to attend to in some detail in order to illustrate our claims and build our argument, we can't discuss musical **genres** such as hip-hop or country or electronic dance music in the abstract. The place to start our investigation then is with a general topic of investigation and with particular songs that interest us for some reason in relation to that topic. Our topic will, to a certain extent, govern our approach and what aspects of a song we focus on. Possible pop culture studies approaches to music (excluding for the moment video and performance codes) include, but certainly are not limited to, the following:

- What and how a particular song performed by a particular artist means. Here, we would consider how lyrical content, if present, works together with qualities of the song to **encode** meanings to be decoded by listeners.
- The **diachronic** study of the "life" and success of a particular song. Such a project might compare different versions of the same song in terms of their qualities, their reception, or both.
- A **synchronic** study that relates a song by a particular artist to other songs produced at the same time, either by the same band or artist or others, and within the same genre or across genres. Such a study could consider **ideological** messages as reflective of a particular structure of feeling, shared or contrasting musical qualities, or both.
- A diachronic study of the output of a particular artist or band, comparing songs from different periods to show different stages of artistic development.
- A diachronic study of the development of a particular style, sound, or genre, focusing on important songs from different periods to show shifts.

No matter what topic is pursued, some attention will need to be paid to individual compositions and their characteristics. We can't talk about what something means until we've carefully considered just what it is. For any musical composition, therefore, we can start with some general observations:

- When was the composition written and recorded, by whom, and in what context?
- Does it have vocals or is it instrumental?
- Was it recorded live or in a studio? And was an audience present or not?
- What stands out about the song?
- What does it make us think?
- How does the song make us feel?

Particularly in relation to the last three questions above, we can then examine the characteristics of the song itself, attending to qualities including the following:

- *Duration.* Duration refers to time and asks us to consider how long a song is, as well as how long its sections and individual elements last. We can include *tempo* (how fast or slow a song is, sometimes measured in beats pers per minute) and *rhythm* (the distribution of accented and unaccented notes) under duration.
- *Dynamics.* Dynamics refers to volume, either in relation to the song as a whole or its different notes and sections. Does the song get louder in particular parts or does it remain consistent all the way through? If there is a singer, does the singer's voice increase and decrease in intensity? Do the drums take over in places? Is it bombastic or very quiet overall?
- *Melody.* Melody refers to the "horizontal" or linear organization of the music. In popular music, it is usually the most identifiable part—the tune one sings or hums. Melodies are usually constructed out of smaller recurring pieces called phrases or **motifs**, which are themselves composed of individual notes. Melodies can be described as being in *major* or *minor keys* depending on the difference in pitch between two notes (called an interval). We typically perceive major keys as being brighter or happier and minor keys as being darker and sadder, although there is some

debate over why this is. Even without musical training or a background in musicology, we can ask of a song's melody whether it sounds happy or sad, bright or dark, melancholic or frisky.

- *Harmony*. Harmony refers to the "vertical" arrangement of a musical piece as other notes are overlaid on top of the melody. The combination of notes can also be major or minor and can create varying degrees of "tension" in listeners who then wait for a kind of resolution. Harmonies can be *consonant* (pleasing or sweet sounding) or *dissonant* (harsh and unpleasant) to the ear depending on how the notes work together.

- *Structure*. Structure refers to the arrangement of a composition. Different musical genres have characteristic structures for songs. For example, rock songs often feature repeating sections called verses and a chorus and heavy metal songs will typically include a guitar solo, often after the middle chorus.

- *Timbre*. Timbre (also called tone color) refers to the perceived quality of a musical note or sound—it is the frequencies of individual sounds that make two instruments playing or two people singing the same note sound different. Timbe can be flat, shrill, soft, rich, clean, distorted, bright, thick, thin, reedy, warm, deep, light, harsh, smooth, brassy, and so on. The timbre of Bob Dylan and Mylie Cyrus's voices, for example, is often described as nasal. The timbre of a cello can be described as deep and resonant.

- *Texture*. Texture refers to the overall "density" or "thickness" of a song, which has to do with the number of instruments or voices present and/or the number of tracks (individual recordings) overlaid on one another. Texture can be influenced by the use of effects, such as reverb and delay. While there are technical terms for musical texture, such as monophonic (a single melodic line with no accompaniment) and homophonic (melody with harmonic accompaniment), we can also describe texture more colloquially as thin, thick, rough, deep, light, and so on.

With reference to the list of qualities above, we can then generate a large list of questions to allow us to address individual musical compositions with a greater degree of specificity. This list includes the following:

- How long is the song? Is its length or brevity notable for some reason? (I.e., because it contrasts markedly with other songs in the same genre, conveyed in the same format, by the same artist, etc.)
- How would you describe the tempo? Is it very fast, moderate, or slow? Is the tempo notable for some reason?
- How would you describe the song's rhythm? Is there a consistent pattern of stressed and unstressed beats? Does the stress shift to a beat where one might not expect it (called *syncopation*)? Does the rhythm change at different points in the song? And, importantly, could one dance to it?
- How would you describe the song's dynamics? Does the composition "build" or does it stay consistent in terms of volume? Does the song feel quiet and intimate or big and loud? Do the dynamics change at different points in the song?
- While determining a song's key can sometimes require musical training, does the song sound happy or sad to you and why?
- Do the elements of the song blend in a pleasing way (consonance) or are there elements that don't mix well and sound harsh together (dissonance)?
- Does the song's structure follow a discernable pattern? Can you hear parts of the song repeated? Do digital samples play a role? These may be pieces of other songs, lines from films or television, real-world sounds, etc. If so, are samples *looped* (repeated) to form part of the song?
- How would you characterize the timbre of the different elements of the song? If there is a singer, how would you describe their voice? Are the instruments electronic in nature, acoustic, or a mix?
- How would you characterize the texture of the song? Does it sound stripped down and sparse? Or heavily produced and "thick"? Have effects been added to make it sound distorted or "dirty" or like the song is being performed in a big, echoey room (reverb)?

All of the questions above refer to how a composition *sounds* to us, which is vital to the meaning we decode from it and the affective response it evokes—that is, what it makes us think and feel.

> **YOUR TURN:** Pick a song that interests you for some reason and, using the questions above, consider the musical qualities of the song. How do these qualities work together to evoke a particular feeling from you?

Having considered these musical qualities, we can then perform what is likely for many the more familiar operation, which is analysis of lyrical content. Here, we treat the lyrics as a message—a chain of **signs** encoded for us to decode. We first have to interpret the lyrics as we would any other written or spoken **text** and thus attempt to understand the content of the message. Our reception of lyrical content, however, is substantially inflected in light of what we believe the singer's attitude is toward the subject matter—tone of voice and vocal dynamics, together with other musical qualities of the song, may lead us to believe, for example, that a singer is angry about a particular state of affairs, happy that something has changed, mournful over a perceived loss, and so on.

Once we have reached some conclusions about what the lyrics of a song mean and what the singer's attitude is in relation to the subject matter, we can then apply one of our **critical theory** lenses in an act of criticism to address the ideological content present. We may conclude, for example, that, in contrast to a long history of deeply engrained sexism, a recent song by a heavy metal group avoids objectifying women as sex objects and instead celebrates their autonomy; we might in contrast arrive at the conclusion that a song by a notable contemporary female artist reaffirms **gender** stereotypes that have historically disadvantaged women; a **Marxist** critique of a country-western song might conclude that it protests systemic patterns of inequality that trap particular populations in poverty and dangerous conditions; attentive analysis of a bubble-gum pop song, in contrast, might conclude that it reaffirms the familiar message for young listeners that their future is wide-open and they can be anything they want to be, thus reaffirming the **status quo**, and ignoring deep-seated forms of disenfranchisement.

Importantly, when interpreting how and what a song means, lyrical content cannot be abstracted from performance. How a singer delivers the lyrics—and how they are delivered in relation to the other components of the song of which they are a part—shapes the meaning we receive and our response to that meaning. This includes not only whether the lyrics are shouted or whispered, but whether they are intelligible at all. In some popular music genres, the timbre of the voice ends up as being more important than the meaning of the words in shaping our response.

One other consideration regarding lyrics is the extent to which they are congruent with the affect elicited by the music. What I mean by this is that the musical qualities of a song, including the timbre and dynamics of the singer's voice, evoke feelings from us. A minor key, slow tempo, and somber delivery of lyrics may make us feel sad or mournful. A major key, brisk tempo, bright electronics, and upbeat delivery of lyrics may make us feel happy and want to hit the dance floor. Shouted vocals, crashing cymbals, and distorted guitar may make us want to dive into the mosh pit (or get out the way!). In general, we expect the subject matter of the lyrics to correspond to the overall emotional tenor or feeling of the music, but this isn't always the case. In some instances, there may be an ironic dissonance created by lyrical content that seems at odds with the overall feel of the song. This is another reason why consideration of lyrical content must be done in relation to the overall song. Cynical lyrics overtop a happy major key pop song structure will mean differently to us than if they were sung together with an angry punk-rock music base.

> **YOUR TURN:** Consider the lyrical content of a song that interests you. How does the delivery of the lyrics by the singer shape your understanding of their meaning? To what extent does the mood of the lyrics correspond to the mood of the song? And what ideological messages are conveyed by the lyrics?

Intertextuality: From Song to History

If we are thinking and writing about the meaning of popular music, the starting point almost inevitably has to be the music itself—the songs and their qualities. In order to determine what and how something means, we need to think about what it is—how it is put together and what its qualities are. In the same way we can't talk about a movie or novel without discussing things like plot, **theme**, and character, we can't discuss music without thinking in terms of not only lyrics, but structure, tempo, key, timbre, and so on. Then, depending on the topic of investigation, the next step after attentive analysis of the qualities of individual songs may be intertextual interpretation—exploring how the meaning of a musical composition is shaped by its relation to other songs, a band or artist's output, the genre of which the song is a part, other media and artistic forms, and its historical moment.

Intertextual interpretation may start with the song itself. Often, bands or artists will "cover" (record or perform their own version) a song closely associated with another band or artist. Johnny Cash's cover of Nine Inch Nails's "Hurt" is a case in point, as are Guns N' Roses's cover of "Live and Let Die" by Wings (originally recorded as part of the soundtrack for the James Bond film of the same name), The Fugees cover of Roberta Flack's "Killing Me Softly," and, of course, William Shatner's inspired version of Bob Dylan's "Mr. Tambourine Man" (google it right now if you don't know it. I'll wait). Cover songs, by their nature, are inherently intertextual—they invite comparison with their originals. In some cases, they may attempt to reproduce an earlier version of the song faithfully; in other cases, they may transform the song dramatically. Often, they are sincere forms of homage to a song or artist the new performer esteems, but not always; they may also be ironic, as when a band or artist covers a song from another genre or one typically greeted with disdain by its fans. For example, the punk band The Sex Pistols covered Frank Sinatra's standard "My Way" and country artist Joe Nichols recorded his own version of Sir Mix-a-Lot's paean to ample posteriors, "Baby Got Back." In all these cases, the way in which we respond to and interpret the songs is inextricably intertwined with our awareness—or not—of their intertextuality. If we know the earlier version, we can't help but compare the cover song with it.

In some cases, rather than performing or recording a previously existing song closely connected with a particular band or artist, composers may instead build a new song out of samples—pieces of existing recorded media. As will be discussed more fully below, the song "Paper Planes" by hip-hop artist M.I.A., for example, relies so heavily on a section of the song "Straight to Hell" by punk band The Clash that members of The Clash were credited as co-writers of the track. Kid Rock's "All Summer Long" makes substantial use of samples from Lynyrd Skynyrd's "Sweet Home Alabama" and Warren Zevon's "The Werewolves of London." In other cases, samples are used more sparingly or less obviously. Artist Jay-Z, for example, often samples jazz singer Nina Simone, including on his song "Caught Their Eyes." Sampling is by no means limited to sung lyrics—almost anything can be sampled from another song, from bass lines to horn blasts to guitar riffs to cymbal crashes. And sampling is certainly not limited to just music; sometimes, samples are snatches of dialogue from a film, television broadcast, or speech. Heavy metal artist Rob Zombie (see Fig. 6.1), for example, is fond of including samples from horror films in his songs while rap act Public Enemy famously introduced their song "Fight the Power" with a sample from civil rights activist Thomas "TNT" Todd.

The role of digital samples within song construction, therefore, needs to be addressed on a case-by-case basis. In some cases, as with the Public Enemy example, there is an obvious connection between the sampled material and the political emphasis of the song—the samples therefore reinforce the ideological message present. In other cases, the samples are meant as kinds of "Easter eggs" or inside jokes for fans who grasp the reference points. Horror movie fans who can identify Rob Zombie's samples not only can feel pleased with themselves but also experience a closer connection with the artist with whom they share a body of knowledge. In still other cases, the point is a kind of ironic juxtaposition of samples taken from a variety of different genres and media.

The Beastie Boys 1989 album *Paul's Boutique* is famously composed almost entirely out of samples, as is DJ Shadow's 1996 *Endtroducing*. Although the role of sampling needs to be considered on a case-by-case basis, sampling by its nature, however, is a form of intertextuality that shapes the meaningfulness of a given song for those who appreciate the reference points.

Fig. 6.1 Rob Zombie

From Song to Album

Thinking of a song as a kind of semiotic sign, its meaning is not only influenced for us by its characteristics and qualities, but also by its **syntagmatic** and **paradigmatic** relationships—that is, its relationships to other songs and to its place in a given genre. In some cases, how we understand a song is influenced for us by its position on and relationship to other songs on an album—is it the lead-off track? The final track? A "deep cut" in the middle? Is it the only slow song on an album of otherwise up-tempo rock songs? Is it the one instrumental on the album? The only one with a guest vocalist? The only song that plays with the conventions of genre on an album that is otherwise consistent—say, by unexpectedly getting weirdly a bit bluegrass on an emo release? We also might think about the role of the song—and the album it is on—in relation to the musical history of a particular band or artist. Is it the hit off of the artist's debut? Is it associated with a particular period in the artist's career? These are syntagmatic connections—intertextual connections that inflect the meaning of a song in light of its position on an album or connection to an artist or band's body of work.

From Song to Genre

We can also think about intertextual interpretation in terms of paradigms, which here we'll think of in relation to genre. A musical genre is a category of music that groups songs with shared characteristics together. Genres are often broad and can have many subgenres—more specific categories within the larger umbrella category. For example, rock music, as a genre, can be subdivided into many smaller genres, ranging from heavy metal to punk to alternative rock to surf rock. Hip-hop as a genre can be divided into subgenres including crunk, freestyle, trip, and breakbeat. Musical artists and bands are typically associated with a particular genre. This is primarily due to the qualities of the music they compose and perform, but is also influenced by factors such as aesthetics and marketing.

Intertextual interpretation of a song in relation to genre is a comparative process that examines the qualities of a song in relation to the characteristics that define a genre connected to the song or the performer. Analysis may conclude that a song is paradigmatic, which means that it is representative of a particular genre; alternatively, analysis may conclude that the song in some ways deviates from expectations for that genre.

Analysis may similarly conclude that a song is representative of the generic output of a given artist or band or is a generic departure. As will be developed in the sample essay below, an interesting example of a song that invites intertextual interpretation in relation to genre is American rapper Lil Nas X's ubiquitous 2018 hit "Old Town Road," which fuses rap with country. The song invited controversy when *Billboard*, the organization that tracks musical popularity in the US, removed it from the "Hot Country Songs" chart after determining the song lacked sufficient markers of country music to be included in that category.

From Song to History

Intertextual interpretation of a song may finally move beyond the construction of a song and its connections to other songs to consider its various histories, which include the history of the song itself, its connection to the history of a particular band or musical artist, its connection to social history, and its connection to our personal history. The history of a song has to do with who wrote it, how it came to be recorded, where and when it was performed or played, and what it has been used for. For example, a song that famously used to be heard at sporting events is Gary Glitter's "Rock 'n' Roll, Part 2,"—better known as the "Hey" song. A consideration of the history of the song would start by noting its 1972 release on an album called *Glitter*. It became associated with pumping up the crowd at sporting events in the 1980s. It began to fall out of favor in the early 2000s after Gary Glitter was convicted of downloading child pornography, but then was used in a high-profile way in 2019 in the film *Joker* as character Arthur Fleck (Joaquin Phoenix) dances down a staircase. What one knows about the history of a song and the artist who wrote or recorded it influences the way in which that song is meaningful for that person.

Gary Glitter's "Rock 'n' Roll, Part 2" also serves as an example of how songs can become intimately interconnected not only with the history of a particular performer, but social history. "Rock 'n' Roll, Part 2" is part of the history of professional sports—as are songs such as

Ozzy Osbourne's "Crazy Train" and C&C Music Factory's "Everybody Dance Now" (music at professional sporting events seems trapped in a kind of time warp). Some songs become indelibly connected with particular moments in time or social movements and help us to touch the structure of feeling of a specific historical moment: Sam Cooke's "A Change is Gonna Come" (1964), Edwin Star's 1969 "War," and Kendrick Lamar's 2015 "Alright" are all protest songs, for example, connected with the 1960s Civil Rights movement, anti-Vietnam sentiment, and BLM respectively.

Thinking about the social histories of particular songs also shifts our attention away from a consideration of the formal qualities of individual songs and the relations of songs to other songs and genre and toward the ways different audiences respond to and make forms of music meaningful. In thinking about the significance of particular songs, albums, and artists, we need to bear in mind *who* listens, when, how, and under what conditions. Genres are simply categories of music that group together songs that share particular qualities; however, genres are also connected to particular cultural traditions and marketed to specific demographics defined by race, ethnicity, age, sexual orientation, and so on. Some genres are associated with particular events—marches, for example, are associated with formal military events and parades. Some genres are marked by region—Latin music, for example, is directly associated with music that comes from Spanish and Portuguese-speaking parts of the world. And some genres are associated with—and marketed to—people of particular ethnicities. Soul music, for example, which originated in the 1950s and 1960s with performers such as Ray Charles and Sam Cooke leading the way, developed out of traditional African American gospel and rhythm and blues music and remains closely connected to an African American audience despite significant inroads into other demographics.

We also have to consider not only who listens, but how and where. Listening to a band at a concert in an amphitheater is a very different experience from listening on headphones while one exercises—one is a highly communal experience, while the other is solitary. Listening while dancing at a nightclub is very different from listening at home on an expensive home theater set-up. One invites the body into motion, the other encourages a more sedentary experience. The wheres and hows are additional factors that inflect how music becomes meaningful to us—and are important aspects of one final intertextual category: our personal associations with specific songs.

At the start of this chapter, I asked you to consider a bit your personal musical history. We gravitate toward genres of music and specific performers and songs for many reasons. We are introduced to music by family and friends who will play a major role in our taste formation and with whom we may associate particular songs or styles—a father who loves jazz, for example, or a friend who was deeply into techno; music may be included as part of our education; we hear it in movies, on TV, as part of videogames, via streaming services, and so on and we may find ourselves humming the theme song from a sitcom we enjoyed as teenagers or a favorite film from when we were growing up. Music often marks important life events: the first dance with a partner or at a wedding, graduation from high school, songs enjoyed with friends, songs associated with break-ups and other events that stir powerful emotions. We connect songs with where we were and how we were feeling at particular moments—the excitement of a first concert, the solidarity of a sporting event or political rally, the song in our headphones when we achieved a personal milestone or received some unhappy news. The lyrics of songs may "speak to us"—catch us just right at particular moments in our life. These associations, idiosyncratic as they may be, nevertheless become intimately intertwined with the songs, which become powerful triggers for reflection—sometimes nostalgic, sometimes melancholic or bitter. We can even think about a changing relationship to a song: one that we hated as a child because a parent always played it that we now love for the exact same reason: it reminds us of someone for whom we have a deep connection.

> **YOUR TURN:** Think about the way a song relates to your personal history. How did it become meaningful for you?

Performance

As this chapter has outlined, approaching popular music from a scholarly perspective is far from simple as there is potentially a great deal to consider: the songs themselves; their relationships to other songs, the artist, their genre, and other genres; and their histories—the history of the song, its connection to social history, and its role in personal histories. Of course, what aspects of a song's structure, relationships, histories, and reception one considers depends on the nature of the investigation being pursued. One other important factor that must be taken into consideration when evaluating how a song conveys meaning is something that, strictly speaking, is not an aspect of the song itself, but that is nevertheless difficult to disentangle from it: its performance. Put simply: it is one thing to hear a song by Elvis or Prince or Beyoncé or Shakira or Lady Gaga; the experience of watching a performance of the song—either live or recorded—is another thing entirely because the visual element unavoidably influences how we respond to the musical elements. Considerations of how performance influences decoding of a musical message return us to the approaches to visual media introduced in the previous chapter and ask us to consider **technical codes** such as editing, sets, choreography, lighting, effects, color, and, of course, sound.

These technical codes then feed into **conventional representational codes**, among the most important of which in the twenty-first century, as discussed in chapter 4, is **authenticity**—the perception on the part of consumers of popular music that the song is a sincere representation of the performer's skill and/or personal beliefs and feelings. This seems rather straightforward but can in practice be more complicated as there are different strategies to convey authenticity. However, in both live settings and recordings (both recordings of live performances and music videos) authenticity is conveyed primarily via the emotive intensity of the singer and the virtuosity of the musical performers.

Sample Essays

Because popular music, like other forms of pop culture, feels dated quickly, any attempt in a book such as this to be current is doomed from the start. (By the time the book reaches your hands, what was popular while I was preparing this has gone from hot to not.) For that reason, the two sample essays included here, both prepared specifically for this textbook, focus on songs notable for their popularity when they came out and for particular features discussed in this chapter. In "'M.I.A. Straight to Hell?' Intertextuality and Popular Music," Konrad Sierzputowski examines the complicated intertextuality of the 2007 hip-hop track "Paper Planes" by M.I.A., while in "Whip That Porsche: 'Old Town Road' by Lil Nas X," Gina Arnold explores the complicated negotiation of genre performed by Lil Nas X's 2018 hit.

"M.I.A. Straight to Hell?" Intertextuality and Popular Music

Konrad Sierzputowski

What is text? One could say with certainty: sentences combined to create meanings. This answer is of course correct, but it is not sufficient. Text, as a concept, is much more than novels or poetry. Text is all you can read and interpret, which is not solely constrained to letters, sentences or phrases, but rather it is something that can be created through pictures (comic books) or sounds (music), and because reading can be recognized as a process of understanding, "reading a text" signifies understanding its meaning, indeed a complex process. For this reason, interpretation is a form of intellectual work, a task where the reader needs to ask questions that can have more than one answer. There is not only one truth hidden in the text because no text exists in a void. Each text is connected to the world through geopolitical conditions in which it was created and its meaning is a product of the dynamic relationship between past and present, between the author and the reader, in relation to other texts. Texts are complex, vast, and exciting, which is why literary and cultural theorists propose so many different methods of interpreting them. One of those concepts, useful to understand the relation between different texts is called "intertextuality."

The concept of intertextuality was introduced by the Bulgarian researcher Julia Kristeva in her book, *Desire in Language: A Semiotic Approach to Literature and Art,* in 1966. Her innovative ideas were inspired by the works of Russian intellectual Mikhail Bakhtin and by French semiotician Roland Barthes's theory. According to Kristeva in her essay "Word, Dialogue, and Novel," intertextuality existed as a universal phenomenon that elucidates the communicative interconnections between a text and other texts and between a text and its context. As she wrote in her book, intertextuality maintains that a text is "a mosaic of quotations; any text is the absorption and transformation of another" (37). Her concept of intertextuality is useful in examining the mutual relations between various texts and the contexts in which these texts were created. The main goal of intertextual analysis is to find and extract the textual borrowings (clichés, quotes, references) to recreate the process of producing the text. This is made possible by the fact that "meaning" is not a passive, static, and immanent feature of the text but rather the main effect of dynamic powers clashing between culture, the author and the reader. It is possible to see any text as a mosaic, where each meaningful element in one text is a part of the text preceding it.

How does it work in practice? Comparative and close readings are necessary methods to recognize and examine the relationship between texts. This is also possible with non-literary texts, as is done with movies when particular scenes are interpreted as quotes or **parodies**. In order to better understand the conditions of the relationship between two non-literary texts, I suggest a "close reading" of the musical piece by M.I.A. [see Fig. 6.2], "Paper Planes," where it is not the lyrics but rather the sound that is the main locus of intertextuality.

"Paper Planes" is a song written and recorded by British hip-hop artist M.I.A. for her second studio album, *Kala* (2007). Its lyrics, inspired by M.I.A.'s own difficulties in obtaining a visa to work in America, satirize

US immigration discourse. Since the popular music archive is full of songs about immigration struggles that could be easily compared to M.I.A.'s songs, it is possible to see potential intertextuality already on this level. However, a more interesting interpretation lies in the particular music structure. The first ten seconds of music feature a very characteristic set of sounds combined in a melody, which, from a formal point of view, is an interpolation of English rock band The Clash's 1982 song "Straight to Hell." Interpolation means that either the whole melody or just portions of it from a previously recorded song are recreated in a new recording, rather than just taken as a sample from the previous piece. In this way, we have two songs for which the beginning is based on the same melody. Without any doubt, we can assume that M.I.A.'s decision was intentional in order to create an intertextual bond between "Paper Planes" and "Straight to Hell." This bond between the two songs can also be witnessed at the level of the lyrics. Like many songs by The Clash, the lyrics of "Straight to Hell" decry injustice: they reference the shutting down of steel mills in Northern England and its social effects, while also considering the alienation of non-English-speaking immigrants in British society. The song also targeted the abandonment of children in Vietnam fathered by white soldiers after the war. While these are distant themes, they share postcolonial melancholy, guilt, and disagreement with injustice.

Fig. 6.2 Hip-Hop Artist M.I.A.

While The Clash presented an outsider perspective, M.I.A. as a Tamil immigrant has a chance to speak from the inside. The intertextual bond works as a "call and response" structure. By introducing a fragment of a politically meaningful song into her own work, she performs postcolonial deconstruction from her own immigrant perspective. That is how meaning is created during the process of interpretation. When The Clash sings about immigrants in Britain, M.I.A. speaks up on the matter herself, giving her own song a testimonial character as an immigrant who now lives in London. That is how the relation between those two texts is intertextual: M.I.A. incorporates a reference to a different text and enriches it with her own experience. Thanks to the intertextual bond between those two songs, the reader/listener can engage in a more complex analysis of critical postcolonial interventions in popular music.

Works Cited in the Sample Essay

Kristeva, Julia. *Desire in Language: A Semiotic Approach to Literature and Art*, edited by Leon S. Roudiez, translated by Thomas Gora, Alice Jardine, and Leon S. Roudiez, Columbia UP, 1980.

——. ."Word, Dialogue, and Novel." *The Kristeva Reader*, edited by Toril Moi, Columbia UP, 1986, pp. 34–61.

M.I.A. "Paper Planes." *Kala*, XL Recordings / Interscope, 2007.

Whip That Porsche:
"Old Town Road" by Lil Nas X

Gina Arnold

In a 2007 essay entitled "Why Does Country Music Sound White? Rage and the Voice of Nostalgia," Geoffrey Mann argued that the reason that country "sounds" white is because it relies on tropes of an idealized past. Mann identifies a number of sonic identifiers, such as acoustic and stringed instruments, southern accents, twang, and lyrical interests rooted in conservative values, that together create a style of music that relies on nostalgia as its dominant mode. "The narratives of loss these songs relate take several forms in country music," he writes, "but in general, they valorize things like a return to 'simplicity,' moral clarity, social stability and cohesion, small-scale community and a 'slow pace,' honesty, loyalty, tradition—all of which are usually framed as in decline" (Mann 79). The point, he says, is that the "good old days" that country music songs are often set in are also the days before *Brown vs. Board of Education*, the days before Civil Rights. Hence, "the songs of a racialized and mythic 'used to' sound a present in which whiteness makes sense retroactively, calling white people to their whiteness" (Mann 83). Inevitably, he concludes, a call to such a past does not hail African Americans: rather, black audiences often prefer music, which, like Dr. King's famous speech on the steps of the Washington Monument, calls to an idealized future.

Mann's conclusions about country music make sense as far as they go, but he forgot Jacques Attali's famous stricture that music is a herald, "for change is inscribed in noise faster than it transforms society" (Attali ix). And when a 19-year-old Atlanta artist called Lil Nas X dropped the song "Old Town Road" onto SoundCloud in late 2018, that herald was tolling its message as loud as an old church bell. A loping, funny, and impossibly catchy song about a guy riding a horse to his hotel, the song, which avowedly belonged to a niche genre called "country-trap," flew up *Billboard*'s country charts only to be yanked off them and re-labeled "R & B" merely due to the race of the singer.

That gesture, by *Billboard*, created a public kerfuffle, but the truth is that "Old Town Road" is emblematic of more than just a racially motivated mess-up: it is also the poster-child for how popular music success works in the age of social media, i.e., completely outside the mainstream music industry. The song used a track purchased anonymously on the Internet for $30 alongside a sample from the Nine Inch Nails song "34 Ghosts IV," used imagery from the video game *Red Dead Redemption*, was picked up as TikTok's Yeehaw challenge, and finally, rose so fast in the hearts and minds of listeners that radio stations had to download the audio from YouTube to catch up with its popularity. After a re-mix was released that featured a rap by country music star Billy Ray Cyrus [see Fig. 6.3], it eventually became the longest running #1 single in the history of *Billboard*'s singles chart.

Fig. 6.3 Lil Nas X and Billy Ray Cyrus in "Old Town Road"

One thing that may have helped "Old Town Road" was the controversy surrounding what genre it belonged to: apparently, people hadn't noticed until then that genres were racially segregated, ideological categories invented and institutionalized by the music industry both to stratify and sell music. In the same way that the invention of cell phone cameras exposed police brutality that had always been there, "Old Town Road" made the silliness and hypocrisy of this system entirely visible. The truth is that all American music, including country, shares a legacy that is thoroughly multi-racial. In her article, "She's A Country Girl Alright," Kim Mack highlights the fact that old-time string music, and later outgrowths, such as bluegrass and country, have long and important black histories. The banjo, for instance, is an instrument of African American origins, or what Rhiannon Giddens calls "a hybridization of African construction and tune systems and European adaptation and adoption" (Mack 145). And while rap music's roots can be located not only in impoverished black communities but in one specific black community, the South Bronx in the early 1970s, it too has numerous ties to every style of music, regardless of the race of its makers.

Even so, "Old Town Road" is perhaps the zenith of that hybrid, highlighting all the factors that make rap and country more similar than different. In fact, as Joshua Clover pointed out in his article "The High Rise and the Hollow," country and rap are "best enemies" one rural, one urban, but both the beloved narratives of the American working class. Clover dubs the racial ideologies that undergird rap and country part of "the fantasy life of American genre, wherein the two great indigenous forms signify an entire arrangement of the nation in which black urban and white rural life are set against each other." He continues,

> No matter that this circumstance has never truly existed; it remains the dream of the nation, the nightmare from which we cannot awaken, freezing into place the two endlessly debated, endlessly ignored political communities, the black proletariat warehoused as surplus in the cores of deindustrialized cities, and the much-bruited "white working class" sharpening their resentments out in Trump country. The musical genre system more broadly has succeeded by mobilizing this world picture. "Old Town Road" succeeds by trolling the entire fantasy.

Clover goes on to read "Old Town Road" alongside three important movies of 2018–19, Jordan Peele's *Get Out*, Spike Lee's *BlacKkKlansman*, and Boots Riley's *Sorry to Bother You*, all of which get their tension from placing a white voice in a black body. By so doing, all three films, and "Old Town Road" as well, insist that race is a social construct, but in "Old Town Road," this conceit may be said to be elevated to its purest vision, as we watch Billy Ray Cyrus *rap* and Lil Nas X—seated on a horse—*sing* country. As the most widely disseminated of the four artifacts and the one that has told us the most about the ways that old media institutions like print, radio, and records have for better or worse shaped people's consciousness into racially segregated categories, the song stands as an inflection point in the social and cultural imaginary of America, tipping the concept of racial authenticity right out the window.

Works Cited In The Sample Essay

Attali, Jacques. *Noise: The Political Economy of Music.* Vol. 16, Manchester UP, 1985.

Clover, Joshua. "The High Rise and the Hollow; Hip-Hop on Horseback against Billboard Apartheid." *Commune Magazine*, vol. 5, Winter 2020, https://communemag.com/the-high-rise-and-the-hollow/.

Lil Nas X. "Old Town Road." Released independently, 2018.

Mack, Kimberly. "She's A Country Girl All Right: Rhiannon Giddens's Powerful Reclamation of Country Culture." *Journal of Popular Music Studies*, vol. 32, no. 2, 2020, pp. 144–61.

Mann, Geoff. "Why Does Country Music Sound White? Race and the Voice of Nostalgia." *Ethnic and Racial Studies*, vol. 31, no. 1, 2008, pp. 73–100.

Suggested Assignments

1. Perform a close analysis of a song of your choice, attending to both what it says and how it says it. Start by observing its formal features and then consider how these aspects correspond to lyrical content.

2. Use one of the critical approaches introduced in chapter 3 to explore how a song encodes ideological messages for listeners to decode.

3. Create a reflective essay that examines the importance of a particular song, album, or artist to your life. In what ways and why did the song, album, or artist achieve the impact that it did on you?

Additional Suggested Reading

Bennett, Andy, Barry Shank, and Jason Toynbee. *The Popular Music Studies Reader*. Routledge, 2005.

Frith, Simon. *Performing Rites: On the Value of Popular Music*. Harvard UP, 1996.

George, Nelson. *Hip Hop America*. Penguin, 2005.

Greil, Marcus. *Mystery Train: Images of American Rock and Roll*. Plume, 2008.

Hubbs, Nadine. *Red Necks, Queers, & Country Music*. California UP, 2014.

Lawrence, Tim. *Love Saves the Day: A History of American Dance Music Culture*. Duke UP, 2004.

Middleton, Richard. *Voicing the Popular: On the Subjects of Popular Music*. Routledge, 2005.

O'Brien, Lucy. *Shebop: The Definitive History of Women in Rock, Pop, and Soul*. Penguin, 1996.

Theberge, Paul. *Any Sound You Can Imagine: Making Music/Consuming Technology*. Wesleyan, 1997.

van der Merwe, Peter. *Origins of the Popular Style: The Antecedents of Twentieth-Century Popular Music*. Oxford UP, 2002.

Wald, Elijah. *How the Beatles Destroyed Rock n' Roll: An Alternative History of American Popular Music*. Oxford UP, 2011.

Walser, Robert. *Running with the Devil: Power, Gender, and Madness in Heavy Metal Music*. Wesleyan UP, 1993.

Wilson, Carl. *Let's Talk About Love: Why Other People Have Such Bad Taste*. Bloomsbury Academic, 2014.

CHAPTER 7

COMICS

*This chapter was prepared in consultation with
Justin Wigard, Michigan State University*

With Great Power Comes Dangerous Capes

What do you think of when you hear the words "comics" and "comic books"? Did you read comic books as a kid? Do you still read them today?

If so, then you aren't alone. North American sales of comics and **graphic novels** in 2019 exceeded $1.2 billion US dollars (Comichron). However, as with other forms of pop culture, the popularity of comics curiously has often been construed as antithetical to value or complexity. The history of comics studies, in fact, in some ways runs parallel to the history of popular culture studies in general. Throughout much of the twentieth century, comics were generally dismissed as simplistic reading material for children. That perspective, however, has increasingly been challenged as scholars have explored how we make sense of comics as well as their cultural significance. While some comics are, indeed, for kids—as are some books, TV shows, and movies for that matter—some are also amazingly sophisticated (although these are sometimes separated out and referred to as graphic novels). And, whether the target audience is children, adults, or both, not only does interpreting comics require a special set of learned strategies, but like other pop culture artifacts and practices, comics come loaded with **ideological messages** that ask readers to accept a particular picture of how the world works.

How Do You Read a Comic Book?

Our beginning point with comics—as with any pop culture object, form, or practice—is to get a handle on what we're dealing with by asking what is this thing and what makes it tick? For many, the word "comics" probably calls to mind one of two things: comic strips and/or comic books. Comic strips, such as those traditionally found in newspapers, are typically short sequences of drawings, usually organized in inter-related *panels*, that tell a short, generally humorous, story. In some cases, these stories are serialized—spread across a number of strips published sequentially. In other cases, individual strips stand alone, although, as in long-running strips such as *Calvin and Hobbes* and *Garfield*, they make use of recurring **themes** and characters.

In contrast to comic strips, which tend to be relatively short in length and a small part of something else, such as a newspaper or website with other content, comic books have historically stood alone as discrete objects and often develop longer narratives, although they can also be anthologies of shorter tales. And, although comic books can come in many forms ranging from crude underground compendiums of comic strips to sophisticated graphic novels with high production values, they are perhaps most immediately associated in the West with the kinds of works that became popular in the 1940s and 1950s during what has been called the Golden Age of Comic Books: colorful panels printed on cheap paper combining text and image to tell an exciting story, and chiefly marketed toward kids. It was during this period that many familiar superheroes were introduced to the world through comic books, including Superman, Batman, Captain Marvel, Wonder Woman, the Flash, and Aquaman. While we still often associate comics with superheroes—an association reinforced in the twenty-first century by the proliferation of big-budget cinematic **adaptations**—the range of subject matter that can be addressed in comic form is, of course, much broader. Scott McCloud in *Understanding Comics*—a wonderful introduction to comics written itself in the form of a comic—defines comics as "juxtaposed pictorial and other images in deliberate sequence, intended to convey information and/or to produce an aesthetic response in the viewer" (20).

Whether in strip or book form and whether consisting of simplistic storylines for young readers or complicated, extended narratives for adults, comics require interpretation and this necessitates learning a set of **decoding** strategies. As with watching TV or listening to popular music, once we learn these strategies, they become second nature and not something we tend to consciously consider unless we run into something that resists those strategies. Let me show you what I mean. Compare the two images, Figs. 7.1 and 7.2, below. What does each mean when pointed at the head of a comic book character?

Figs. 7.1 and 7.2 Word and Thought Bubbles

If you have some conversance with comics, you probably answered that the first would indicate what a character is saying while the second would indicate what a character is thinking. But how did you know that? The answer is that the *speech balloon* and the *thought bubble* above are **semiotic signs** governed by the conventions of comics. After we learn the **code**, we no longer have to stop and think about it.

As with a consideration of music or television, it is helpful when approaching comics to have available a shared vocabulary with which to discuss their composition. This allows us to discuss the features of comics with some degree of specificity. To begin with, comics consist of *panels*—sometimes called frames or boxes. Each of these boxes tells a piece of the story. Panels are often surrounded by a *border* that separates one panel from another; however, a panel can sometimes take up an entire page or lack a border. The spaces between panels are referred to as *gutters*. Most comics include some combination of images and text, although the extent to which either dominates an individual panel can vary greatly. (It is possible to have a comic that lacks text entirely; however, if it lacks images entirely then it isn't a comic.) Text is generally introduced in one of two ways indicated above: either through a *balloon* or *bubble* connected to a character (the little part directed at the character is sometimes called a *pointer* or *tail*) or through a *caption*, which consists of words in a box separated from the rest of the panel, often serving as the voice of a narrator. The shape of speech bubbles and thought balloons can be manipulated to express emotion, while captions can also include *onomatopoeia*—words that mimic sounds like (see Fig. 7.3):

Fig. 7.3 Onomatopoeia

Figs. 7.4 and 7.5

There are many other visual conventions of comics that convey information that readers decode to understand what is happening. What's going on, for example, in Figs. 7.4 and 7.5?

Again, if you are familiar with comics, you likely realize that the horizontal lines behind the representation of the man running indicate that he is moving quickly, while the wavy cloud associated with the skunk indicate that it is stinky. Motion lines and stink lines are familiar conventions of comics that we as readers learn to understand. Like most signs, the connection between **signifier** and **signified** is arbitrary. Once established however, the connection is reinforced by repetition.

YOUR TURN: If you are familiar with comics, can you think of other conventions of comic illustrations like motion or stink lines that convey sensory information or establish mood?

Much of what's involved in learning to read comics is the process that McCloud refers to as **closure** in which we, as readers, make connections between the words and images within individual panels, and then connect different panels to one another. McCloud puts it elegantly when he writes that "comics panels fracture both time and space, offering a jagged, staccato rhythm of unconnected moments. But closure allows us to connect these moments and mentally construct a continuous, unified reality" (67). Because we are familiar with comics, we automatically connect these individual panels in Fig. 7.6:

Fig. 7.6 Closure as Represented in Scott McCloud's Understanding Comics

This is what McCloud refers to as "aspect to aspect" transitions as the four panels present us with different aspects of one scene. As readers of this comic strip, we connect the panels across the gutters. We recognize as well that the wavy lines above the pot indicate heat, that the "chop! chop! chop!" is the sound being made by the knife, that the woman depicted in the third panel is the one doing the chopping, and that the "tik tik tik" sound in the fourth panel is the sound of the timer. All of these connects are as a result of closure—the way we've come to understand visually distinct signs (signifier = wavy lines, signified = heat), and to comprehend the **syntagmatic** relationship between individual panels.

McCloud actually describes six types of panel-to-panel transitions, each of which requires more active participation on the part of the reader to make connections than the preceding ones:

- *Moment-to-moment* transitions show us a progression of basic movements. Imagine three comic panels showing the same figure riding a horse toward us from a distance, getting closer to us in each one.
- *Action-to-action* transitions show us a sequence of actions. Imagine three panels with our rider on her horse in the first, then drawing her gun, then shooting it.
- *Subject-to-subject* transitions between panels stay within the same scene but vary the focus. Imagine our rider on her horse shooting, then imagine a panel of the bullet heading toward us surrounded by motion lines, then imagine the concerned face of an onlooker to the scene.
- *Scene-to-scene* transitions move us across time and/or space. Imagine our rider shooting her gun, then a funeral, then a solitary mourner at the grave. If we decode the sequence as intended, we recognize that the three panels show us a sequence of related events at different times and places.
- *Aspect-to-aspect* transitions, as in the cooking example above, show us different elements of a scene occurring at the same moment. Imagine three panels of our rider, the first showing her hat, the second her spurs, and the third her hand on the reins.
- And then there are transitions McCloud calls *non sequiturs* in which there is no logical relation between a panel and the one that precedes it. So, imagine our rider on her horse, then a panel showing a satellite in space, and then a third with just a fork.

YOUR TURN: Working with print or online comics, see if you can find examples of the different types of transitions outlined above.

When you stop to unpack it, there is actually a lot going on when one reads comics. We first have to decode individual panels, attending to the interrelation of image and text. And, as McCloud also points out, there are different ways that text can relate to image: in some cases, the words do the most work in conveying the meaning; in other cases, the images primarily convey the ideas. Sometimes words and images work together to convey the same idea, but then there are instances, which McCloud refers to as "parallel combinations" (154) where words and images follow different paths. And, in contrast to reading literature, the *color* and *style* of images—the way the images are presented—also play a significant role in creating *atmosphere* and *mood*. Whether something is crudely drawn or exquisitely detailed, in black and white or in vibrant color, sharp or fuzzy, and so on shape how we interpret panels and the feelings they evoke from us. So, we start with decoding the individual panels, and then readers of comics have to make connections between panels. As with English print text, this often involves reading comic panels from left to right one line at a time in descending order; however, this isn't always the case. In some instances, panels can be laid out in non-linear ways that require readers to make conscious decisions about the order panels will be addressed (some interesting scholarship exists on this—see, for example, del Rey Cabero).

> **YOUR TURN:** Again working with either print or online comics to which you have access, look for examples of comics that complicate the familiar process of reading English-language prose from left to right in descending lines. What introduces the complications and what cues in the comic panels guide you in understanding the order in which to read them?

The end result is something that is surprisingly complicated. Like other forms of communication, comics can be thought of as a semiotic system in which senders **encode** meaning using the codes and conventions of the medium for decoding by readers on the other end. If readers successfully decode the intended meaning of a message—and, as we discussed in the chapter 5, there are always possibilities for misfires—readers are then put in the position of determining whether they embrace the intended meaning (the **dominant / hegemonic** position), have a "yes, but" qualified response (the **negotiated** position), or reject the intended meaning (the **oppositional** response). What this reveals is that, as is the case with consumers of other forms of popular culture, readers of comics are far from being passive "couch potatoes." They are instead engaged in active processes of interpretation as they derive meaning from the texts in front of them.

Comics and Ideology

Interpretation of comics begins with making sense of individual panels, which can be thought of as being like individual scenes within a movie or TV show. In the same way that a television show or movie connects scenes to express ideas and/or tell a story, the reader of comics connects panels to decode more complicated messages. In narrative forms of comics such as comic strips and comic books, the panels taken together convey a story, which can be short and simple or lengthy and complicated. In keeping with stories in general, we can explore comic book stories in terms of their plot, conflict, theme, **motifs**, characterization, setting, atmosphere, and so on. We can consider the point of view from which the story is told (typically first person or third person), as well as the author's tone and style—conventional forms of literary analysis. And then, as discussed above, we can consider the role that images play in creating meaning as well. All of the elements of narrative comics, both text and image, culminate in ideological messages about how the world is or should be.

As was noted at the start of this chapter, comics for a long time were mostly dismissed as unsophisticated entertainment for children. However, comic books did attract some significant attention in the mid-1950s when a psychiatrist named Fredric Wertham published an infamous book (infamous at least among comic book fans) called *Seduction of the Innocent* that connected comic books to juvenile delinquency. With a particular focus on horror comics and crime comics of the 1940s and 1950s, but also with an eye toward superhero comics, Wertham analyzed violent and gruesome scenes arguing that such depictions encouraged similar behavior in children. Wertham also made claims about hidden sexual themes in comics, such as that Batman and Robin were homosexual partners who found their "Lesbian counterpart" (192) in Wonder Woman. Wertham even found fault with Superman, who he characterized as un-American because he imposes his will through force (34).

Superman

Wertham's concerns, as possibly outlandish as they may sound to us today, resonated with some in 1950s America. Parents were alarmed and a US Congressional inquiry was launched to take a closer look at comic books and the comic book industry. In response, the Comics Magazine Association of America established the Comics Code Authority (CCA) in 1954 as a form of industry self-regulation. The process, which was voluntary, had publishers submit comics in advance of publication to the CCA, which screened them according to its set of criteria that banned depictions of violence, gore, and sexual inuendo. If the comic passed muster, it received a CCA seal of approval. The code, which was updated a number of times during the second part of the twentieth century, wasn't abandoned completely until 2011.

I've summarized this part of comics history not just because it is an interesting story (and it really is an interesting story—something that might be fun to research in greater depth), but because Wertham, for all his hysterical claims, did perceive something essential: comics, just like all other narrative forms, convey ideological messages through their representations of their characters and the worlds they inhabit. Wertham's study, it needs to be pointed out, had serious problems— among them that he claimed comics caused behavioral disorders with little evidence and, according to Carol L. Tilley, he "manipulated, overstated, compromised, and fabricated evidence" for his claims (Tilley 386). However, his study did raise some interesting questions that might still be worth considering. For example, he raised the question of what effect impossibly proportioned female characters might have on the developing self-image of girls and what effects images of violence and gore might have on young readers. There's nothing wrong with asking these kinds of questions—and asking them makes clear something important: despite the fact that comics are often associated with fantasy and science fiction, they nevertheless remain tethered to the "real world" as they inevitably participate in naturalizing certain ways of thinking even as they may call into question other perspectives. Answering questions of how actual readers interpret, understand, and are influenced by comics—or any other popular culture medium—is, however, tricky in part because it involves collecting and interpreting data in responsible ways. In some cases, answering questions such as these require longitudinal studies that collect data from the same population across a period of time; in other cases, it involves surveys with sufficient sample sizes and safeguards to ensure that one's conclusions are meaningful.

The constraints of a course on popular culture may prohibit undertaking larger studies or surveys. However, what we can do—as with movies, TV, and other narrative forms—is to consider the ways in which the

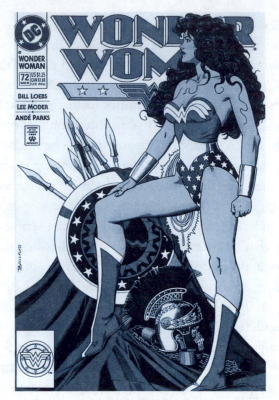

Wonder Woman

elements of individual comics work together to convey ideological messages for readers to decode and accept, question, or reject. For example, Wertham's questioning of representations of female bodies in comics can be the beginning point for a **feminist** analysis of those representations. While we can't say what effect these representations have on actual consumers of comics without carefully gathering data (beyond our own personal experiences that is), what we can do as a beginning point is to look at the representations in comics and propose that the heroic proportions of characters such as Wonder Woman create an unrealistic standard of beauty for women against which real women (not to mention those with darker skin) can never measure up. Alternatively, one could undertake a **Marxist** analysis of various comic books, considering the role that class plays (e.g., the privileges that Bruce Wayne's vast wealth affords Batman versus the villainous plutocrats who try to exploit and oppress the masses in Gotham City). Any of the critical approaches outlined in chapter 3 can be used as lenses through which to explore the ideological messages conveyed to readers through comics.

YOUR TURN: Representations of women with unrealistic proportions and representations of violence are two areas worth considering when thinking about comics (and other popular culture forms). Can you think of other possibly problematic issues associated with comics that could similarly serve as starting points for discussion and analysis? On the flip side, can you think of any positive forms of representation that work to counter long-standing stereotypes?

Comics Questions

As with our approaches to other popular culture forms, we can generate a list of questions to enable a consideration of what and how particular comics mean. These questions will follow a trajectory similar to other lists in this textbook that begin with specific questions about the characteristics of particular comics and then proceed to larger connections.

Qualities

- What is the medium of the message? Is it a print form or a digital form? Is it included as part of another publication (such as a newspaper or website) or does it stand alone?
- Is it in color or black and white?
- How would you characterize the production values? If it is a print form, is it a glossy graphic novel or cheap paper?
- If there is a narrative, is it one continuous story or is it broken up into parts?

Codes

- **GENRE**. What genre does the message belong to? (e.g., superhero, horror, crime, erotica, "slice of life," etc.). What generic markers make this clear?
- **CONVENTIONAL REPRESENTATIONAL CODES**. What types of settings and characters are present? How would you summarize the plot? What role does dialogue play?
- **TECHNICAL CODES**. Here is where the comic-specific questions come into play—What kinds of relations exist between text and image in specific panels? What kinds of transitions are employed between panels? Does one read the comic in a conventional linear way or does the comic require readers to figure out how panels are connected? How do the qualities of color and line in individual panels, larger sections, and the work as a whole evoke **affective** responses from readers and participate in conveying meaning?
- **IDEOLOGICAL CODES**. What are the larger themes of the work? What picture of the world does the work naturalize? What should the ideal viewer of the work think and feel having completed reading it? How does the work either reinforce or contradict **social codes** of its moment?
- **METATEXTUALITY**. Does the text play with the conventions of genre or adhere to them uncritically? Does it foreground its own status as a text in any way, calling attention, for example, to itself as a comic?

Intertextual Questions

- **CONTEXT**. What kinds of knowledge does decoding the text as intended require? For example, is the comic part of a particular comics universe? Is it part of a series? Does it require knowledge of a particular history, social group, or lifestyle? How is the text a reflection of its particular historical moment? If the text being considered is an older one, how does its decoding today compare with that of its moment? That is, is it received differently today due to shifting social codes or has its meaning remained stable?

- **ALLUSION**. Does the text reference or allude to other works either in the same medium or other media?
- **SYNCHRONIC COMPARISON**. How does the text's style, themes, and ideological messages compare to other works of its genre produced at around the same moment?
- **DIACHRONIC COMPARISON**. How does the text compare or contrast with similar works from earlier periods, demonstrating trends or a lack of development?

Audience

- Is the text intended for a particular audience? If so, how does the text signal this and what marks the intended audience? Where was the work produced and how was it marketed?
- How have different groups—e.g., men / women, old / young, people of color / white, cisgender / LGBTQIA+, wealthy / not wealthy, religious / non-religious, and so on—responded to the text and what aspects of the text have shaped their responses?

Comics and Adaptation

A word needs to be said here about comic book adaptations for film and television such as HBO's *Watchmen* series, the *Avengers*, *X-Men*, various *Batman* films, and spin-offs such as 2019's *Joker*, 2018's *Black Panther*, and so on, which are one primary means through which contemporary audiences encounter comic book characters. Adaptations need to be addressed in medium-specific ways, bearing in mind the specific **affordances**—qualities and characteristics—of that medium. Put differently, the experience of watching a film is not the same as reading a book or comic book because the qualities of the medium shape the messages sent (the medium is the message!).

YOUR TURN: Thinking about adaptation from comic book to film or television, what can comic books do better than film and TV and vice versa? Why?

Despite needing to address adaptations in relation to the specific qualities of the medium into which the **source text** has been adapted, adaptations are by their nature inherently **intertextual**. Because they are adaptations, the way in which they are decoded will depend on what the viewer already knows about the characters, story, and the world in which the story is set. And where comics have been adapted multiple times, as with the different versions of Batman, including the television series starring Adam West that ran from 1966 through 1968, the Tim Burton films, and Christopher Nolan's *Dark Knight* trilogy, intertextual comparison becomes inevitable as the latest iteration is compared to preceding ones in the same and different media. As a consequence, adaptation allows us interesting insight into changing cultural contexts. While one needs to be very, very careful about making large generalizations based on one TV series or film (or even a trilogy of films), one can examine texts in light of what stands out about their individual qualities and seek to make connections with other works that start to reveal patterns suggesting an emerging **structure of feeling**.

YOUR TURN: To what extent do you think the fidelity of an adaptation to a source text—in this case, the comic book being adapted—should be used as a yard stick against which to assess the success of the adaptation?

Sample Essay

In the sample essay authored for this textbook below, Justin Wigard explores the comic book series *Black Panther* in relation to the idea of Afrofuturism.

Black Panther and Afrofuturism

Justin Wigard

Originally coined by Mark Dery in 1993, Afrofuturism is "speculative fiction that treats African-American themes and addresses African-American concerns in the context of twentieth-century technoculture—and, more generally, African-American signification that appropriates images of technology and a prosthetically enhanced future" (180). Within popular culture, Afrofuturism is speculative fiction that reimagines African-American history (past, present, and future) through advanced technology, art, and culture, a description that finds strong purchase in the comics of Marvel superhero Black Panther. Debuting in *Fantastic Four #52* in 1966, Black Panther is often noted as being the first black superhero in mainstream American comics. While Black Panther has gone through waves of popularity since his inception, he saw a resurgence in popularity with Christopher Priest's run on the character in the late 1990s, and then most notably with the film *Black Panther* (2018), which drew inspiration from the comic iteration of *Black Panther* (2016) written by Ta-Nehisi Coates and illustrated by Brian Stelfreeze. Early in Coates and Stelfreeze's comic, we are told that "the African nation Wakanda is the most technologically advanced society on the globe" due to its possession of a rare and valuable fictional mineral called "Vibranium." This detail prompts a consideration of the Afrofuturistic themes of *Black Panther* and, as Wanzo has discussed in relation to the film, particularly how it imagines a future free from white colonization as a consequence of technological prowess and access (see Wanzo). Liberation, as imagined by the comic, depends on technological mastery.

Walter Greason notes that the fictional space of Wakanda, the homeland of Black Panther, represents Afrofuturistic ideals of being free from white colonization and rising to fiscal and technological prosperity due to the abundance of Vibranium in the ground under and around Wakanda (#WakandaSyllabus). Coates and Stelfreeze utilize the visual affordances of the comics page to convey this advanced infrastructure, visualizing this wealth and advanced technological capacity through scenes of futuristic flying vehicles equipped with multiple wings and silent jets. In a panel of Coates and Stelfreeze's *Black Panther #1*, for example, a gyroplane seemingly hovers in mid-air before dropping off Wakandan king T'Challa—who is also the superhero Black Panther—to a meeting with his mother, another high-ranking official in the Wakandan government. Upon T'Challa's entering this meeting, the room itself announces "Soul-Stalker Interface Initiated" as a colorful interface emerges out of thin-air. The combined audible announcement and visual interface demonstrates that technology is not only interlaced through the very rooms of Wakandan buildings but naturalized as such. Manifesting first within the comic for T'Challa, this same interface infrastructure is depicted within a later panel, in the hands of a Wakandan rebel outside the government buildings, which denotes a pervasiveness to this technology. Gone are concerns over technological literacy or underfunded infrastructures, instead demonstrating that T'Challa is not the only Wakandan citizen with access to technology, but that everyone has this access. Through the lens of Afrofuturism, Wakanda's fictional existence acts as a call for similar technological access and futurity for other African nations.

T'Challa has monarchal power to govern over his people and, as Black Panther, superheroic power to defend his people, both of which stem from the same advanced technological source: Vibranium. A fictional metal that is notable for its ability to store, harness, and expend kinetic energy, Vibranium gives rise to new and unprecedented technological potential as evidenced by T'Challa's Black Panther suit. Historically, the suit has always been interwoven with Vibranium, but Coates and Stelfreeze utilize the affordances of the comics medium to show this, rather than make it explicit through textual narration. Comics scholar Scott McCloud talks about the unique comics element of "closure," the interpretive act of the reader making sense of narrative events between panels and closing the gap by filling in these events (63). In the first of a three-panel sequence, Wakandans are fighting each other; in the second, T'Challa's face is half-covered in blue-black material interlaced with purple circuit board-like lines; in the third, Black Panther's mask is complete, the Vibranium circuitry becoming one with the outward appearance of the suit (Coates and Stelfreeze 7) [see Fig. 7.7]. Comics closure demonstrates that Black Panther's suit is technologically advanced such that it is always with him until he has need, then it grows outward around him; he is empowered by technology at all times, and thus, able to act at any given moment.

Fig. 7.7 T'Challa Looks Out over his People before Donning his Black Panther Cowl, the Vibranium Suit Morphing around his Face

The following page again visualizes this technologically infused power when Black Panther runs into swaths of brainwashed Wakandan miners who swarm the superhero, seemingly overwhelming him in a moment of uprising and rebellion before Black Panther provides just a glimpse of this power. One particular panel at the bottom of page 8 depicts the superhero hunched under the weight of several miners who are all grasping at him, attempting to restrain Black Panther (8). The green tint to miners' clothes and eyes again marks them as influenced and hostile while highlighting the blue-black costume of Black Panther,

Fig. 7.8 Black Panther Leaps into the Fray, Armored in the Technologically Advanced Supersuit

*Fig. 7.9 Now Imbued with Kinetic Energy,
Black Panther Disrupts the Rioting Wakandans*

making his superheroic body the focal point. On turning the page, we are treated to a new perspective, presumably from Black Panther's own vantage point as a superheroic hand laced with Vibranium and crackling with energy hurls one miner into the sky before unleashing kinetic energy that scatters the rest of the miners. Black Panther's body is lit with technological circuitry that illuminates his hands and feet, all of which crackle with that same energy [see Figs. 7.8 and 7.9]. In this page, as throughout the series, Black Panther is the living embodiment of the imagined future of Afrofuturism, a Black superhero empowered through futuristic technology to defend his country and lead his people, even as his throne is being challenged.

Works Cited in the Sample Essay

Coates, Ta-Nehisi and Brian Stelfreeze. *Black Panther: A Nation Under Our Feet Book 1*. Marvel Entertainment, 2016.

Dery, Mark. "Black to the Future: Interviews with Samuel R. Delany, Greg Tate, and Tricia Rose." *Flame Wars: The Discourse of Cyberculture*, edited by Mark Dery, Duke UP, 1993, pp. 179–222.

Greason, Walter. "Introduction to the #WakandaSyllabus." *AAIHS*, 19 June 2016, www.aaihs.org/introduction-to-the-wakanda-syllabus/.

McCloud, Scott. *Understanding Comics: The Invisible Art*. HarperCollins, 1993.

Wanzo, Rebecca. "And All Our Past Decades Have Seen Revolutions: The Long Decolonization of *Black Panther*." *The Black Scholar*, 19 Feb. 2018, https://www.theblackscholar.org/past-decades-seen-revolutions-long-decolonization-black-panther-rebecca-wanzo/.

Suggested Assignments

1. Perform a close reading of a particular comic panel or page. What relationships exist between text and image? If relevant, what kinds of transitions between panels are present? What roles do color and shape play in conveying meaning?

2. Use one of the critical lenses introduced in chapter 3 to analyze the ideological messages present in a particular comic strip or comic book.

3. Research the history of a particular comic book, comic strip, or comic book character. How has the **text** changed over time in response to changing cultural expectations and circumstances?

4. Create your own short comic strip (you don't need to be a brilliant artist to do this!). Then, using the terminology introduced in this textbook, consider the formal qualities of your comic strip, as well as the ideological messages you encoded through them.

Works Cited in the Chapter

"Comics and Graphic Novel Slates top $1.2 Billion in 2019." *Comichron: Comics History by the Numbers*, https://www.comichron.com/yearlycomicssales/industrywide/2019-industrywide.html.

del Rey Cabero, Enrique. "Beyond Linearity: Holistic, Multidirectional, Multilinear and Translinear Reading in Comics." *The Comics Grid: Journal of Comics Scholarship*, vol. 9, no. 1, 25 Mar. 2019, http://doi.org/10.16995/cg.137.

McCloud, Scott. *Understanding Comics: The Invisible Art*. William Morrow, 1994.

Tilley, Carol L. "Seducing the Innocent: Fredric Wertham and the Falsifications that Helped Condemn Comics." *Information & Culture: A Journal of History*, vol. 47, no. 4, 2012, pp. 383–413.

Wertham, Fredric. *Seduction of the Innocent*. 1954. Main Road Books, 2004.

Additional Suggested Reading

Abate, Michelle Ann. *Funny Girls: Guffaws, Guts, and Gender in Classic American Comics*. UP of Mississippi, 2019.

Alaniz, José. *Death, Disability, and the Superhero: The Silver Age and Beyond*. UP of Mississippi, 2014.

Duncan, Randy, Matthew J. Smith, and Paul Levitz. *The Power of Comics: History, Form, and Culture*. Bloomsbury Publishing, 2015.

Grant, Barry Keith and Scott Henderson, editors. *Comics and Pop Culture: Adaptation from Panel to Frame*. University of Texas Press, 2019.

Hatfield, Charles. *Alternative Comics: An Emerging Literature*. UP of Mississippi, 2009.

Karasik, Paul and Mark Newgarden. *How to Read Nancy: The Elements of Comics in Three Easy Panels*. Fantagraphics Books, 2017.

McCloud, Scott. *Understanding Comics: The Invisible Art*. HarperCollins, 1993.

Robbins, Trina. *From Girls to Grrrlz: A History of Women's Comics from Teens to Zines*. Chronicle Books, 1999.

Sousanis, Nick. *Unflattening*. Harvard UP, 2015.

Whitted, Qiana. *EC Comics: Race, Shock, and Social Protest*. Rutgers UP, 2019.

CHAPTER 8

GAMING

Prepared in consultation with Justin Wigard,
Michigan State University

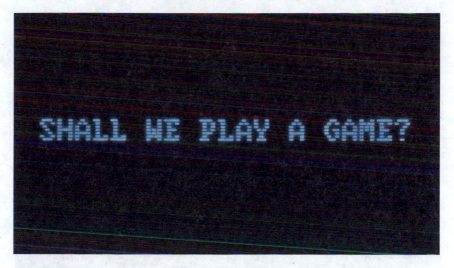

The Question Put to Matthew Broderick's character, David Lightman, in
Wargames *(1983), One of the First Films to Represent Videogaming*

When I say "gaming," what comes to mind for you?

Is your first thought videogames such as *Fortnite*, *Call of Duty*, or *Bioshock*? Or did role-playing games such as *D&D* or *Vampire: The Masquerade* occur to you? It is always possible that you are a tabletop game fan, so you thought of *Monopoly* or *Scrabble* or maybe checkers or chess or other boardgames. Or that you thought of card games like solitaire or blackjack or even (if you have younger siblings or babysit or have kids of your own) Go Fish. Or dice games like *Yahtzee*. Or puzzles. If you are James Bond, then maybe your first thought was "games of chance," like roulette or poker or (for Bond purists) baccarat. It seems a little less likely that sports were the first thing to pop into your head, but gaming could certainly accommodate playing soccer, shooting hoops, tossing horseshoes, and engaging in other sports. You might even have thought of the kinds of games we typically associate with kids: hide and seek, kick the can, jacks, tag, and so on. Since gaming at its most basic is a structured form of play that we usually engage in for entertainment, the category can encompass a lot. Games can be played alone or with others, by amateurs or professionals, face-to-face or online, by kids or adults. They can involve luck or strategy—or often both to different degrees. They can be educational and involve acquiring a particular skill set, engaged in for exercise, or simply exhilarating.

Now, another question: Do you think these different forms of gaming have anything in common? What connections, if any, can you make, for example, between pinball, *Bioshock*, duck duck goose, and *D&D*?

You might suggest that what they all have in common is that they are played for fun. This would mean then that they are distinct from *work*, which is labor that one undertakes for reasons other than (or

James Bond Participating in High-Stakes Gaming

in addition to) enjoyment, often as a means to procure needed goods and services, either directly or indirectly. Relatedly, you might say that playing a game is an end in itself—we play games for the enjoyment of playing the game, not as a means to some other end. Gaming in this sense might be construed as unproductive or frivolous. ("Stop playing games and get to work!") These are reasonable suggestions (so well done to you!). But then there are some people who play games professionally as a means to earn a living (professional athletes and Esports players, gamblers ... James Bond). And sometimes games *are* a means to an end as with games that promote literacy, teach one to fly planes or diagnose illness, help older people retain mental agility, and so on. Of course, professional athletes may still play for "the love of the game," and those playing games as part of learning or training may still enjoy the games, but in these cases, it is also a form of work.

There have in fact been quite a few attempts to try to pin down the **sign** "game" and figure out just what makes a game what it is. The French sociologist Roger Caillois, for example, proposed six characteristics in a 1958 work called *Men, Play and Games*:

- We choose to play games; it is not obligatory
- Games are played at particular times, separate from other activities
- Games include an element of chance; the outcome is uncertain
- Games are non-productive; they don't accomplish anything useful
- Games are rule governed
- Games involve make-believe or pretending in a different reality

Some of these characteristics seem questionable. Is a game still a game if you are forced to play it? Can't one play a game while also doing something else at the same time (i.e., "multi-tasking")? And there are lots of games that do accomplish useful things—educators increasingly incorporate games in the classroom for precisely this reason. The "make-believe" part is also perhaps a little "dicey," but we can think of it as agreeing to abide by the rules of the game, which are different from the rules that govern our lives outside of the game.

A leaner definition for what a game is has been offered by Kevin Maroney, who in a piece for *The Games Journal* argues straightforwardly that "a game is a form of play with goals and a structure" (Maroney). *Structure* for Maroney includes not just the rules, but the way the gaming universe is set up—what it means to play the game in the first place. The *goal* is to win the game—an objective that can take a variety of forms ranging from besting an opponent to completing one's personal goals to finishing a story section, and that can be accomplished either competitively or cooperatively. *Play*, for Maroney, has three different **connotations**: first, it means that players participate actively and the actions they take or decisions they make can alter the outcome of the game (if you don't get to do anything or if what you do doesn't make a difference, Maroney doesn't consider this playing the game—instead, it is something "inflicted" on you (Maroney); second, it means that games (as Caillois suggests) involve an element of pretending. Games "are far from reality and occur completely within a bounded game space. If they aren't, they're no longer games—they're life" (Maroney). And, third, play means that games are—or at least are intended to be—for fun. Maroney acknowledges that games can serve other purposes; however, "in the end, if it isn't fun, it's not a game; it's training or therapy" or just a waste of money (Maroney).

> **YOUR TURN**: Do you find Maroney's definition of what a game is to be sufficient? Is there anything you would add or delete?

Pop Culture and Gaming

Like Maroney, I'm inclined to keep our definition of what a game is as broad as possible and I think Maroney's three elements of gaming provide a sound basis for thinking about what makes something a game: a structure (rules and a kind of imagined world in which they apply), a goal, and play in the sense of active participation, imagination, and enjoyment. I would add from Caillois that for a game to be a game, there has to be some element of chance or conflict to be overcome involved—if you can't lose (or can't win), then it isn't really a game. (Maroney, to be fair, does gesture toward this when he mentions in his discussion of play that actions taken by players should matter in determining the outcome.) The operative question now becomes: what does it mean to approach games and gaming from a pop culture perspective? Once again adapting the model of television studies proposed by John Fiske (see chapter 5) to a new category of inquiry, we can focus our attention on three different aspects of games and gaming: the formal qualities of games; their **intertextual** relationships with other games, other forms of entertainment, and with a given **culture** more broadly; and on socially situated players and the act of playing. Put differently, we can ask: what is this game, how does it relate to its various contexts, and how do different gamers make sense of it? Where this will culminate, as always, is with the **ideological messages** conveyed by particular games and the ways in which they are **decoded** by socially situated players.

Formal Qualities

So, we start with the thing in front of us—a particular game. The approach adopted throughout this textbook may seem methodical—and it is—but before we can really determine what and how something means, we need to take stock of just what it is and how it is put together. Our first question, therefore, is: what kind of game is this? To answer that, we can then look to how the game is played and the tools needed to play it. Using these two criteria, a preliminary distinction can be drawn between sports and non-sports, with sports being games involving competitive physical activity and non-sports being games that do not involve competitive physical activity. (I'll come back to Esports below.) Non-sport gaming then can arguably be subdivided into three primary categories based on the equipment needed to play them: videogames, tabletop games, and live-action role playing games (LARPs) (see Fig. 8.1). Videogames are electronic games involving some player interaction with technology (an *interface* of some kind) that allows a user to control game play. This may be a joystick, controller, keyboard, motion sensor, and so on. Videogames can then be subdivided depending on their type of computer system or *platform*—arcade game, console game, PC games, mobile game, and so on. Tabletop games is a broad category on its own, but all tabletop games require a flat surface (or digital approximation) to manipulate the equipment that constitutes the game, which may include boards, dice, cards, and other tools. LARPs are games in which players portray characters in a fictional setting as a kind of improvisational theater. While LARPs technically require no equipment apart from players and a space in which to play, many do involve a set of rules or shared player's handbook, as well as costumes and props.

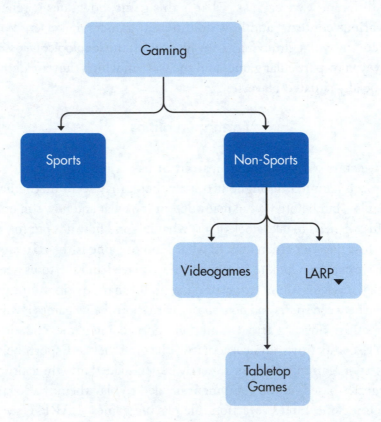

Fig. 8.1 A Taxonomy of Gaming

Non-sport game categories can then themselves be subdivided according to several different criteria, including *gameplay* **genre**, *conventional genre*, number of players, duration, and form of conflict or competition. Gameplay genre has to do with the action and objective of the game: a fighting game is still a fighting game regardless of whether it takes place in space, under the sea, in an arena, in the old west, or in an urban setting. It is the same with shooter games, sports games (thinking here in terms of video games in particular), survival games, strategy games, and so on. I am distinguishing gameplay genre here from conventional genre, which refers to established categories of literature, film, and television, such as fantasy, science fiction, horror, mystery, romance, pornography, adventure, crime, western, and so on. All games will fall into a gameplay genre. Only some games will also fall into a conventional genre. For example, videogames such as the *Silent Hill* and *Resident Evil* franchises can be categorized as survival (gameplay genre) horror (conventional genre) videogames. *Risk*, in contrast, is a kind of strategy boardgame (gameplay genre) that draws on the war (conventional) genre. *Clue* is also a kind of strategy game (gameplay genre) that draws on the detective (conventional) genre. Basketball as conventionally played doesn't fall into a conventional genre; laser tag, in contrast, just might.

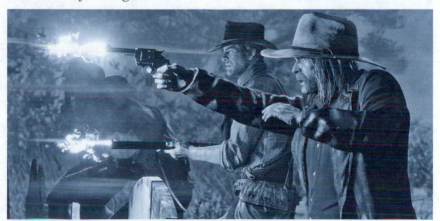

The Red Dead Redemption *Series are Videogames Making use of Conventions of the Western Genre*

Number of players is a straightforward parameter, but makes a huge difference in how games are played and how players experience them. Games can involve one person, a restricted number, or an unlimited number. Solitaire—as per its name—can be played by one player; many boardgames require at least two but are capped at 4 or 6; some massively multiplayer online role-playing games (MMORPGs) such as *World of Warcraft* and *Final Fantasy* can involve many thousands of players. While single-player games require the player to be the sole arbiter and to make all decisions, multiplayer games foster social interactions and may require collaboration—and changing the number of players can alter the dynamic significantly (try adding a third person to a light-saber duel!). *Fortnite Battle Royale* involves up to 100 players and allows for players to go it alone, team up, or form squads (usually 3 or 4 players).

Duration is also relatively straightforward and refers to how long it takes to complete the game from start to finish. Games with a strictly limited duration are constrained by time, available resources, and/or a rule restricting the overall number of actions a player may take in the course of the game. Many sporting events, for example, have a fixed duration—say, two thirty-minute halves or three twenty-minute periods—while the boardgame *Ticket to Ride* ends when all the available pieces have been played. Games with an open duration can continue until the overall objective or goal is completed, the players lose, or everyone loses patience (I'm looking at you, *Monopoly*). Open-duration games in some cases are possibly endless in practice (you could play forever and never beat the game or achieve the goal), but our working definition of a game as something with a goal or objective means that all games must have a theoretical endpoint. Some games, such as *D&D*, may seem limitless in terms of duration, but in reality, rely on sequential goals or campaigns—once one objective has been met, the players turn their attention to a new one. Only an activity without an actual goal has a truly limitless duration. This then might exclude from our consideration as games open-ended *sandbox* games featuring worlds that can be explored freely and without any apparent goal, such as *Minecraft* and *Animal Crossing* (more about this below).

YOUR TURN: If a game can't be won or lost, do you consider it a game?

Form of competition gets a little more complicated. In single-player games, the competition will always be player vs. game, which means that the player's objective is to overcome the forces that seek to retard the player's progress—this may be a computer algorithm, it may be luck, or, in the case of some physical activities, it may be physics. When games involve more than one player, there are three possible competitive configurations:

1. In player(s) vs. player(s) games such as chess, players compete against one another and the outcome is decided entirely by the skill of the players. Temporary strategic alliances or teams are possible in some player(s) vs. player(s) games.

2. In cooperative games, players work together against the game to achieve game objectives, and either the players win or the game wins.

3. In player vs. player vs. the game, players compete against one another, but actions can also be affected by luck and/or elements of the game. For example, in games of chance such as poker or games involving dice, players compete against one another but an element of luck outside the player's control is involved. This may be the case in videogames as well in which the algorithm introduces unexpected challenges or rewards. As with player(s) vs. players(s), temporary strategic alliances and teams are possible.

What I've outlined above is essentially a taxonomy, or system of classification, for gaming. As with most taxonomies, there can be hybrids and complications. For example, a rhythm game like *Dance Dance Revolution* with a significant element of physical exertion combines sports elements with videogaming. My distinction between sports and non-sports results in categorizing things such as laser tag and kick the can as sports, while electronic sports (Esports), despite "sports" as part of the name, is competitive videogaming. And then there is again the question of whether something is a game if it can't be won or lost—this taxonomy says no. Is *The Sims* a game? Is *Minecraft* in its creative mode? What about a puzzle? What do you think?

YOUR TURN: What are other ways games could be categorized? Create your own taxonomy of games or of a particular division of games.

Here then is a list of preliminary questions to ask concerning the formal qualities of a game—these are the things that make the game what it is and distinguish it from other games:

Structure and Play

- What equipment or tools does one need to play the game?
- How is the game designed? If it is a videogame, what *platform* is it for and what kind of *interface* is utilized?
- What does the game look like and how would you characterize its aesthetic?
- Does the game involve sound and/or music? If so, how would you characterize the sound and music?
- What general category of gaming does it fall into? (I.e., sports / videogame / tabletop / LARP / hybrid)
- What gameplay genre does it fall into?
- What does the game narrative involve?
- What kind of world does the game construct? Does it fall into a conventional genre?
- Is the duration of the game fixed or open?
- To what extent does luck determine the outcome of the game, as opposed to skill or strategy?
- How does one play the game? Does it require physical exertion as part of gameplay?

- What are the rules of the game? Are they explicitly stated or learned by players as they go? How do the rules organize the game or gameplay? Can the rules be bent, broken, or transformed? If so, what happens as a consequence?
- What is the overall goal or objective? How does one win the game?
- Does it require participants to possess any particular skills or abilities?
- How many people are needed to play the game? Is there a limit on the number of people?
- Are teams or collaborations possible or required?
- Is it cooperative or competitive?
- Does the game require you to have an **avatar** of some kind?
- How is the game packaged? How much does it cost?

Intertextual Relationships

To consider a game intertextually is to move beyond a close analysis of its formal qualities and consider how it relates to other games of the same type (**paradigmatic** relationships), how it relates to games of different types, how it relates to other forms of amusement more broadly, and how it is connected to its overall cultural context. The filters that one applies for purposes of comparison depend a good bit on what aspect of the game one wishes to focus on. For example, tennis is part of the paradigm "sport games played with racquets." In keeping with our discussion of **semiotics** in chapter 2, the meaning of one element of the paradigm is shaped by its differences from other elements that could be substituted—so our understanding of the meaning of tennis is shaped by its differences from racquetball, squash, badminton, ping pong (AKA table tennis), and so on. One can similarly ask how the videogame *Bioshock* differs from other entries in its first-person shooter gameplay genre, such as *Doom Eternal*, *Call of Duty*, *Halo*, and so on, or how tabletop role-playing games such as *D&D*, *Call of Cthulhu*, and *Vampire: The Masquerade* compare. This comparison could range widely and include gameplay elements, conventional genre, difficulty, duration, graphics and music (for videogames), and so on. Focusing on the differences among games in the same category helps to identify what makes a particular game mean in the way that it does.

Intertextual consideration of games can also apply to games of different types. For example, taking tennis as a starting point again, one could explore the odd systems of scoring that pertain to different sports—tennis's 15-30-40-game system, football's extra point / two-point conversion / safety / field goal / touchdown system, basketball's 1-point / 2-point / 3-point system, and so on. Alternatively, one could consider how one game has been **adapted** into another gaming medium—say how professional football compares with its videogame representation in *Madden NFL*. Or, as we will discuss in more detail near the end of this chapter, one can compare the different ideological messages conveyed by different games—say the differences between competitive and cooperative games or games in different gaming genres that nevertheless all have as a goal the accumulation of wealth and resources.

From here then, intertextual consideration of games and gaming can expand still further outward. One can consider the process of **adaptation** for example: how have games such as *Clue*, *Silent Hill*, *Sonic the Hedgehog*, and *Resident Evil* been adapted into films? How have narratives in other media such as literature, film, and television been adapted as games? And how have existing games been tied into other media such as the *Fortnite* edition of *Monopoly* or the *Star Wars* edition of *Sorry!*? One can consider the representations of gaming in other media, such as *D&D* in *Stranger Things*, *World of Warcraft* on *South Park*, videogames in general in *Ready Player One* and the *Wreck-It Ralph* films, and the whole genre of sports films. And one can consider how a game or a type of game relates to its own historical moment and shifting historical contexts. Collegiate and professional sports, for example, have long histories of excluding women and people of color—and many still do on the levels of coaching and administration. *D&D* famously created a kind of moral panic in the 1980s connected to broader cultural concerns about shifting social mores, rising rates of divorce, and corruption of youth (see "The Great

1980s Dungeons & Dragons Panic"). The proliferation of first-person shooter games could be considered in the context of American military action in the Middle East (see Mirrlees)—and violent videogames in general have repeatedly come under scrutiny as possibly desensitizing players to violence and contributing to youth delinquency and overall levels of cultural violence.

Thinking intertextually, here is a list of questions that can be used to investigate games:

- Who designed the game and for what company? What other games has the designer created and the company released and how does this game compare to those?
- If the game involves music, who created the music? What genre does the music fall into? How does the music compare to other releases by the artist or band? How does it compare to music in similar games?
- How does a particular game compare and contrast with other games in the same gameplay genre and, if relevant, conventional genre? What formal features does it share with other, similar games that

could be substituted in its place? What formal features, if any, make it stand out? This can include game aesthetics (how something looks); gameplay features such as duration, narrative, and objectives; and incidental features such as price.

- If the game is part of a conventional genre such as horror or science fiction, how does it reference or **adapt** elements associated with that genre? How, for example, does the tabletop role-playing game *Call of Cthulhu* make use of American author H.P. Lovecraft's Cthulhu Mythos? How do games based on the works of J.R.R. Tolkien adapt his Middle-earth novels?

- Thinking intertextually, how does a game or type of game in one gaming division or subdivision compare to a game or type of game in another category in terms of formal qualities, participation and audience, marketing and target audience, history, cultural significance, ideological messages, and so on?

- How and to whom has the game been marketed? How have marketing strategies shifted over time?

- Is the game tied in to or connected with something outside of gaming, such as a film, TV show, celebrity, or product?

- How has the game been represented in or adapted to other media?

- How has the game's design changed over time and what has driven those changes? Videogames, for example, often have multiple editions. How do later editions compare with earlier editions and what forces shaped the changes that were implemented?

- How is the game connected to cultural trends or issues at a particular moment in time?

Socially Situated Playing

It's fine to consider the formal qualities and intertextual relationships of particular games and types of games, but obviously what makes games what they are is the fact that they are played (and even sometimes enjoyed) by people—specific people in particular times and places. The next set of questions one can ask concerning games and what and how they mean therefore deals with the actual conditions of gameplay: who plays, when, where, why, how often, under what conditions, and so on. Relatedly, one can also consider marketing and **fandom** practices—how companies target particular audiences for games and how players celebrate their enjoyment of the games they play.

Game Players

Some of these questions, it must be pointed out, are difficult to answer without in fact surveying actual players and gathering sociological data (and research agendas such as these often need clearance from institutional review boards, so check with your instructor!). In the absence of such data, one can draw on published accounts and data, as well as one's own personal experiences. How much research material you will find on a particular game or type of game will vary greatly depending on how long it has been around, how popular it is, and whether or not there have been controversies associated with it. A good deal of the published literature on games and gaming focuses on sports, such as histories of baseball and football that address the challenges women and people of color have faced in order to participate as players and spectators.

The demographics of videogame playing have also been of interest to researchers, so some data is available on this topic, such as a 2017 Pew Research Center study that broke down videogame participation by **sex**, race, age, and level of education (see Brown). And references to gameplaying abound in **popular press** articles and biographies, such as Mark Barrowcliffe's *The Elfish Gene: Dungeons, Dragons and Growing Up Strange* (2009) and Stefan Fatsis's *Word Freak: Heartbreak, Triumph, Genius, and Obsession in the World of Competitive Scrabble Players* (2002). Looking ahead to the section below on ideology, there have also been some excellent studies on racism, sexism, homophobia, and other forms of bigotry both within the gaming world and within games themselves. This includes what has come to be called "Gamergate"—the ways in which videogame developers Zoë Quinn and Brianna Wu, as well as media critic Anita Sarkeesian, were targeted by coordinated campaigns of harassment starting in 2014 for their critiques of sexism within gaming and the gaming industry (see Dewey).

If you are dealing with a more recent game or type of game, however, or something relatively obscure, demographic data on who plays may be harder to come by. In such instances (again, unless you are prepared and approved to conduct sociological investigation), you may be forced to rely on your own experiences of gameplay. Depending on the type of project you are developing, personal reflection can often be both appropriate and useful—as long as it is framed properly as your individual experience from which you are not attempting to extrapolate large generalizations!

> **YOUR TURN:** Think in terms of your own experience with games and gaming. What types of games appeal to you most and why? Do you have a favorite game? If so, what makes the game your favorite?

Connected to the issues of who plays particular games are the ways that games are marketed to specific populations, as well as the ways in which players make use of the game beyond the confines of actual game play. A consideration of marketing would look at where and how a game is advertised and made available for purchase—factors that will obviously influence who seeks out a game and has access to it. Part of the "how" of marketing would consider the age, sex, and race of those represented in advertising materials, which can communicate either explicitly or implicitly for whom the game is intended by its creators. A consideration here as well is the game's purchasing model—that is, whether the game is a physical object purchased once, a game based on a "microtransactional" model in which the game might be free to download but users can make in-app purchases, a subscription model, and so on. And, dovetailing with the consideration of fandom in chapter 10, a full consideration of the pop culture significance of a particular game or type of game could also include what fans do with the game beyond actually playing it—this could include how games are celebrated at pop culture, comics, and gaming conventions (including **cosplay**), gamer **fan fiction**, newsletters, and even fan-made game modules and worlds.

Gaming Cosplay. Used by Permission.

The following is a list of questions one can ask in relation to socially situated game players:

- Who plays (or played) a particular game or type of game and who is excluded from game play? This may include age, race, ethnicity, sex, **gender** identity, socio-economic situation, nationality, religion, physical ability, level of education, and so on.
- Where and under what conditions is/was the game played? This may include whether it is played at home or a park or an arena, whether it is played by oneself or at parties, whether it is played online or in a physical space, whether it is played during the day or at night, and so on.
- With whom does one play? Is it solitary, a family game, a MMORPG?
- How and to whom is the game marketed?
- What social practices do gamers engage in around the game outside of game play?

Ideology

What should people look like? How should men and women act? How should we treat one another? Who and what should we desire? Who should we fear? Who should enforce the rules? How should we resolve conflict? What should our relationship with the natural world be? What constitutes success?

Consideration of the formal qualities of games, their intertextual relations, and the ways games are played by particular people in specific times and places culminates in analysis of ideological messages: how a game is played, the kinds of interactions it structures, and the overall goals and objectives of a game work together to convey and naturalize ideas about how the world is and should be. In this sense, games are always from the pop culture scholar's perspective "serious fun"—they are played for enjoyment but inevitably reinforce or challenge prevailing ways of thinking about the world. For example, thinking in terms of

Lara Croft from Tomb Raider *(1996) and Kratos from* God of War
*(2005) Showing Off Their Physiques in Early Versions
of the Respective Games*

economic structure, the majority of games—both sport and non-sport—
are built on a competitive model in which there can be only one winner
(either an individual or a team) rather than a cooperative model in which
the players all work together to achieve a particular objective. Further,
many competitive games involve competition for acquisition of scarce
resources and the accumulation of wealth. Such games both reflect
and reinforce the economic **base** of the cultures that manufacture and
market them: **capitalism**. Indeed, many games both for kids and adults
involve money, buying, and selling. This is the whole basis of *Monopoly*,
for example, as well as *Payday* and a variety of games marketed to kids
as tools to teach them how to manage their money (because what kid
wouldn't go crazy for a game called *Managing My Allowance?*). Not
content simply to teach players that the accumulation of wealth is the
best gauge for success, *The Game of Life* (sometimes just called *Life*)
makes clear what life consists of: school, profession, marriage, home
ownership, kids, pets, and retirement!

> **YOUR TURN:** Thinking of a game with which you are familiar,
> what would you say its "values" are? That is, what does it mean to
> win the game and how does one succeed?

Games can also be considered in terms of how they reinforce or challenge stereotypes related to race, gender, sexuality, physical ability, and so on. To what extent, for example, are people of color included at all as players, characters, avatars, or in game design and marketing? If non-white ethnicities are included, how are they represented—as principle characters, sidekicks, comic relief, or enemies to be blown up? Similarly, how are men and women included or represented? If women are present, are they depicted with impossible Barbie doll proportions and presented merely as objects to be looked at or conquer, or do they have some agency? And are the male characters simply avatars of **toxic masculinity**, shooting anyone and anything that impedes their progress and taking what they want? That games can convey messages on such topics is clear, for example, in the case of the *Grand Theft Auto* franchise, which has not only been accused of glamorizing violence, but has been criticized for misogynistic representations of women, including prostitutes that players can not only pick up, but kill. Some very interesting work has been done by media scholars in relation to videogames in particular and their ideological messages. Tanner Mirrlees argues in a discussion

Soldiers in the Videogame America's Army

of the videogame *Medal of Honor*, for example, that "war justifies the making of war games, and war games—in turn—legitimate dominant forms of warfighting" (242). Souvik Mukherjee, looking at a different videogame called *Age of Empires*, has made use of **postcolonial theory** to explore the game's use of stereotype and attitude toward imperialism.

It is important to be wary of simplistic correlations: playing *Assassin's Creed* is no more likely to turn players into professional assassins than playing *Madden NFL 20* will turn them into professional football players. And people are not simply programmable robots who automatically adopt a **dominant / hegemonic** position in relation to all the messages beamed at them by games and other media. Yes, some people may well adopt the militaristic position advanced by war games such as *Medal of Honor*, although there are likely other forces in their lives reinforcing this position as well. Other people, however, may occupy a **negotiated** position and play the game but with mixed feelings about "militainment" (Mirrlees 243). Still others may adopt an **oppositional** position in relation to the messages of the game and choose to quit or not to ever start playing.

> **YOUR TURN:** Thinking of a game you currently enjoy or have played at other points in your life, what ideological messages does the game *encode*? Have you ever had a negotiated or oppositional response to a game? If so, what provoked this response?

Games, arguably, are often ideologically most productive not where they are flashy or controversial, but rather where they simply reinforce ideas that are accepted as "normal" or "common sense" within a particular context. *Of course* the winner is the one with the most money at the end of the game. *Of course* players compete against each other. *Of course* men should act aggressively and women are there to be looked at (assuming they conform to well-established standards of beauty). And what's not present is equally vital because representation matters in shaping social norms. So if people of color and differently abled and elderly people just aren't there at all, and the game simply assumes that heterosexual desire is the only form of sexual attraction that exists in the universe, the white cisgender able-bodied young adult is reinforced as the standard against which every other body is judged (and, in some respect, found wanting). Just like other forms of media, games encode ideological messages—some intentional on the parts of their creators, some unintentionally reflective of the assumptions and logic that prevails in a given time and place. And just like other media, games can be analyzed using the various critical lenses introduced in chapter 3 to help us understand how the meaning of a game or type of game is shaped by—and in turn participates in shaping—larger understandings of what the world is and how it works.

Sample Essays

The following two essays provide examples of scholarly approaches to games and gaming. In Justin Wigard's "*Minecraft* and Worldbuilding," written for this book, Wigard focuses on the idea of "worldbuilding" in videogames, contrasting the popular game *Minecraft* with other games that offer fewer opportunities for players to participate in the act of world creation. Matthew Thomas Payne and Michael Fleisch's contribution, in contrast, adopts a **Marxist** approach to the first-person-shooter science fiction game *Borderlands*, showing how it is easier for us to imagine the end of the world than an end to capitalism.

"*Minecraft* and Worldbuilding"

Justin Wigard

The concept of worldbuilding is, as Mark J.P. Wolf notes, one that is pervasive throughout popular culture; it is an act of "wayward speculation, conjuring new wonders, strange terrors, and [exploring] the unexplored byways of beckoning vistas" (1). Within popular culture, worldbuilding manifests in imagined worlds that are imbued with meaning themselves or that act as reflections of the real world. However, Marta Boni argues that worldbuilding is not just dependent upon the creator of that fictional world, but is "also dependent upon their explorers who, in turn, become world-builders" (10). Eddie Paterson, Timothy Simpson-Williams, and Will Cordner push this idea further to say that video games not only feature worldbuilding, but the various elements of video games (mechanics, storytelling, player interactions, audio-visual design) naturally lend themselves to worldbuilding (xviii). As one of the best-selling video games of all time (see Chiang), *Minecraft* is entrenched in popular culture due in no small part to its innovative featuring of worldbuilding as its primary mode of gameplay. *Minecraft* is a sandbox game where "players can build creative structures, creations, and artwork on multiplayer servers and single player worlds" (*Minecraft Wiki*). Within the game, players explore a procedurally generated world comprised of blocky, simplistic visual elements and have access to tools with which they can build anything, as seen in players' constructions of to-scale football stadiums, imagined and futuristic worlds, and even functional computers. By procedural generation, I mean that each player's world in *Minecraft* is not only unique, but builds itself as it goes, a particularly powerful **affordance** for video games. As Kevin Schut notes, "procedural generation offers something new in comparison to older media: functionally limitless imaginary worlds.... [D]ue to procedural generation, software can continue to produce something indefinitely given the appropriate hardware resources" (429–30). Through its core gameplay of building the world via exploration, mining, and crafting, *Minecraft* operates not only as a game uniquely situated to worldbuilding, but one that fosters worldbuilding as its primary mechanic, goal, and outcome. *Minecraft's* primacy of worldbuilding as core gameplay, therefore, gives players an unprecedented amount of agency over their gameplay experience, and this control is central to why *Minecraft* has become one of the most popular video games ever created.

Within *Minecraft*, the most immediate action that players take is one of movement-based exploration, whether exploring the ever-expanding vistas or exploring for resources. Every new game begins with its own unique world seed, a numerical identifier that correlates to the unique composition of the world the player inhabits. To move is to, initially, explore, fostering a sense of mapping out one's conception of their unique world, discovering wide expanses of seas, or perhaps a series of hills and valleys, maybe even a seemingly shallow chasm that leads to a pit of lava! Because *Minecraft* is, as noted, a procedurally generated video game, as the player explores, the world unfolds before them, such that neither they nor the game system itself knows what exists just out of sight. In order to play the game's default mode, "Survival," the player must explore the world for resources to survive, whether laterally as players explore the infinite horizon, or vertically as they dig deeper into ground, but this mode of exploratory play necessarily leads into every other gameplay action, from mining to crafting to building, and even to combat.

Mining and crafting, parts one and two in *Minecraft*'s portmanteau title, are essential actions for worldbuilding within the game, as one must *mine* resources in order to *craft* game objects. On first loading into a new game world, players immediately see any number of potential resources, but have no tools. Here, players initially use their hands to carve out the environment, destroying trees and rocks to get crude wood or stone, then building successively stronger tools like stone pickaxes or iron shovels that expedite the process. The cycle is such that if players don't craft new tool upgrades, they can't proceed through harsh or otherwise impassable environments, nor can they build constructions or wonders as they see fit. This inherent combination of mining, crafting, and exploration means that players mold the world as they play, morphing a premade imaginary world into one fitting their own imagined schemes and plans, enacting a constant cycle of setting—and achieving—goals. Each decision to chop down a tree, build up a shelter, or abandon a cavern, correlates to players participating in acts of worldbuilding.

Minecraft is not solely a single-player game wherein one works toward personal goals or intrinsic ones, but also a game with multiplayer modes that can include other players. This extends worldbuilding out through several ways achieved via play-based interactions. First, players can build the world together: they can collaborate on construction and mining, explore shared spaces, and traverse hostile environments. Worldbuilding can also become an act of social negotiation and potential competition: if only one block of a rare source is revealed, say, a block of valuable diamond ore, which player earns it—the one who discovered it or the one who has greater need of it? Competition may begin infusing and spilling into these acts of worldbuilding such that, if conflict arises (or even if conflict doesn't), players may potentially utilize destructive items to catastrophically and irrevocably destroy a shared world, tearing it apart through tools like dynamite available within the game. Of course, *Minecraft*'s nature as a video game means that if a world has been thoroughly mined, explored, even destroyed beyond recognition, a new one can be started within seconds via the "New Game" function and old ones can be replaced or rewritten. While this destructive act of players literally dismantling the shared world's environment, structures, or creations may seem counterintuitive, it builds out the narrative of the world: one shared *Minecraft* server may be devoted wholly to player-vs.-environment and constructive gameplay, while another shared multiplayer world may be tinged with nonsensical actions; the choice is relegated to the players. Put another way, *Minecraft* not only offers a virtual space for players to construct worlds individually or communally, but the power to do so through its core gameplay, for better or for worse.

This is not to say that the onus of worldbuilding is placed wholly on the player(s). Since the default game mode of *Minecraft* is Survival, players face hostile and mobile non-playable creature ("mobs"), and as players plumb the depths for rarer resources, they will encounter increasingly difficult and strange enemies. Through building out their world, players may discover portals to "The Nether," a strange and dark hellscape that is home to, among other monstrosities, the game's primary antagonist: the Ender Dragon, a gargantuan black dragon that flies around spewing purple fireballs. Players could, in theory, play infinitely without ever discovering the Ender Dragon, much less defeat the monster, but the implementation of in-game "Achievements" awarded for milestone actions encourages players to build out the world and, eventually, confront the Ender Dragon.

These achievements begin early and are awarded often: "Taking Inventory" is awarded for opening the inventory, while "Hot Topic" is awarded for constructing a furnace. While players proceed through the world, the embedded goals push players towards completing more complicated or difficult tasks, including defeating the Ender Dragon to unlock the coveted "The End" achievement. The persistent anchors of elements like in-game achievements and a common antagonist ensure that the player always has goals to strive for, but only should the player make the choice to pursue them. In this way, the player has autonomous control over the story of their world, pursuing in-game achievements should they choose or going about their own intrinsic aims.

Minecraft, an open-ended sandbox game built around procedural generation, has entrenched itself in popular culture through centering worldbuilding as its primary mode of gameplay. Part of *Minecraft*'s enduring popularity stems from the unique formal qualities of the video game medium: by providing infinite and unique space with tools for shaping the environment, *Minecraft* acts as a platform for emergent worldbuilding only achievable through play. Whereas the vast majority of other video games and game developers build the worlds themselves, *Minecraft* gives an unprecedented amount of control over the game to players who decide what to do, choose what stories to tell, and how they do so. The significance is not just that *Minecraft* provides the potential for infinite possibilities, but that *Minecraft* affords players the agency to play in whatever manner they can imagine, provided they do so in pixelated cubes.

Works Cited in the Sample Essay

"About *Minecraft*." *Minecraft Wiki*, Gamepedia, 4 Sept. 2020, https://minecraft.gamepedia.com/Minecraft_Wiki.

Boni, Marta. *World Building: Transmedia, Fans, Industries*. Amsterdam UP, 2017.

Chiang, Helen. "Minecraft: Connecting More Players Than Ever Before." *Xbox Wire*, Xbox/Microsoft, 18 May

2020, https://news.xbox.com/en-us/2020/05/18/minecraft-connecting-more-players-than-ever-before/.

Paterson, Eddie, Timothy Williams, and Will Cordner. *Once Upon a Pixel: Storytelling and Worldbuilding in Video Games.* CRC Press, 2019.

Schut, Kevin. "Hello Game's No Man's Sky." *The Routledge Companion to Imaginary Worlds*, edited by Mark J.P. Wolf, Routledge, 2017, pp. 425–32.

Wolf, Mark J.P. *Building Imaginary Worlds: The Theory and History of Subcreation.* Hoboken: Taylor and Francis, 2012.

"Borderlands: Capitalism"

Matthew Thomas Payne and Michael Fleisch

It has been said that it is easier to imagine the end of civilization than it is to imagine the end of capitalism. As with much received wisdom, the origin of this aphorism is up for debate; some point to Marxist cultural theorist Fredric Jameson, others ascribe it to the philosopher-provocateur Slavoj Žižek, and still others credit cultural historian H. Bruce Franklin. Yet, importantly, the claim itself is hardly contested. The idea that capitalism can survive calamities ranging from giant asteroids to nuclear fallout resonates because it conforms to our shared imaginary popularized by post-apocalyptic fiction. Indeed, numerous fictional worlds have been decimated by natural disasters, leveled by bombs, or invaded by hostile aliens. Consider television's *Jericho, Falling Skies, Battlestar Galactica*; cinema's *Mad Max, Waterworld, Children of Men*; or the video game universes of *Fallout, Rage*, or *The Last of Us*. Despite the cataclysmic events that have befallen these realms, and for all the social and environmental upheaval that make them distorted versions of our own world, what endures in some distilled form is capitalism, an economic system of private ownership predicated on the accumulation of goods and mediated by a marketplace of exchange, all of which is propelled by conditions of scarcity, a desire for profit, and inescapable competition.

This, too, is the case for the *Borderlands* series of video games. In *Borderlands* (Gearbox Software, 2009) and *Borderlands 2* (Gearbox Software, 2012), the player is an adventurer seeking riches on the ravaged and dangerous planet of Pandora. In the years preceding the player's arrival, Pandora's mineral resources attracted waves of fortune seekers and corporations. After extracting what they could, these groups abandoned their facilities and released the criminals who were used as forced laborers. Pandora's remaining settlers were left to fend for themselves, competing for survival against the planet's indigenous monsters and the now-liberated criminal population.

The player is thrust into these harsh and unforgiving conditions with the primary goal of finding "The Vault," a legendary treasure trove of money, guns, armor, and assorted technologies. Along the way, players earn money and level up their characters and weapons until they are finally equipped to face the game's nastiest enemies. The sequel introduces more characters and settings, but the endgame remains the same: dispatch innumerable enemies en route to discovering and accumulating hidden treasures. The series showcases capitalism's excesses and its underlying logic in multiple ways. Narratively, Pandora's history is one of unchecked exploitation on a planetary level, a point consistently raised by the world's rusted ruins and its corporations' aggressive branding and advertising. Procedurally, the games require players to engage in endless cycles of item accumulation and marketplace exchanges. The drive to efficiently maximize in-game economic advantage finds its most fulsome expression in some players' pursuits of advantageous programming glitches and exploits. These unauthorized "solutions," and the backlash against using them, reveal that capitalism, as rendered and performed in the *Borderlands* community, is itself an uneven gamified system founded on exploitation and power imbalance.

The series has been a hit with gamers and critics alike, spawning the spinoff *Borderlands: The Pre-Sequel* (2K Australia, 2014); a graphic adventure game, *Tales from the Borderlands* (Telltale Games, 2014); a feature film that is in development as of 2018; and a commitment from Gearbox to create another installment. The franchise has been widely praised for its cooperative-preferred gameplay and for the darkly sardonic humor of its narrative campaigns. Conceived as a *"HaloDiablo"* mash-up, these games combine the perspective and frenetic action of a first-person shooter (FPS) with the leveling-up and item-collection systems of a role-playing game (RPG). The gratuitous gun violence is tempered by cartoonish, cell-shaded graphics that—according to the developer's visual design team—give the games an "ill-mannered whimsy."[1] Furthermore, the games' procedural content generation systems add gameplay variation and tiered incentives to the otherwise repetitive quests and combat activities.[2] These content algorithms spawn an assortment of shields, guns, and items, virtually ensuring that no two treasure chests or loot boxes contain the same goodies. *Borderlands 2*'s promotional campaign boasts of "87 bazillion guns," a clearly tongue-in-cheek gesture toward the practically infinite combinations of gear and loot to be discovered.[3]

Yet this marketing hyperbole gestures at a substantial design challenge: how to guard against creating repetitive and rote tasks that lead to a sense of "grinding." Although the games' mechanics keep enemies at appropriate levels of difficulty to promote a balanced sense of experiential "flow"[4]—the enemy is rarely too easy (leading to boredom) or too difficult (leading to anxiety and frustration)—there is a great deal of noncombat content begging to be played. That is, although primarily pitched as a "role-playing shooter"—a term coined to describe the first *Borderlands*'s unique mix of gameplay styles—much fun comes from contemplative, nonfrenetic moments of gathering, buying, selling, and trading items.

Hidden behind the comic-book veneer and cartoonish gunplay one finds an ostensible action franchise built on gamified file management. *Borderlands* is a game of data defragmentation supported by an ideological commitment to economic liberalism and private property. As a file-management FPS, *Borderlands* cycles fragging (slaying enemies to reap rewards) and defragging (economizing one's inventory), with each activity driving and reinforcing the other. The successful player painstakingly optimizes the endless inundation of guns, armor, and class specific skills to unlock a variety of combat effects and benefits. Weaker items are traded or sold away to allow for the acquisition of marginally better goods. Indeed, in these protracted moments, this FPS franchise is better conceived of as a first-person spreadsheet.

To understand *Borderlands* simply as an action-oriented role-playing shooter is to elide some of its most basic, capitalistic pleasures—both sanctioned and unsanctioned. The games' rendering of laissez-faire capitalism engenders pleasures of accumulation by maximizing one's return-on-(playtime-)investment through the strategic management of in-game assets. This is the "right" way to play the game. There are likewise unsanctioned pleasures to be had by circumventing those systems with exploits and glitches. Thus, these games present a case study in a designed system of capital and how its users engage in *and* work around that system.

To illustrate how the *Borderlands* games reflect, internalize, and articulate reigning beliefs about free market capitalism, we discuss the repetitive cycling between the fragging that begets item accumulation and the decision-making that defrags one's limited inventory space. Next, we explore how the accumulation of property implicitly invites players to discover shortcuts to transform otherwise banal file management into the efficiently sublime. By attending to the designed trading systems, as well as gamers' pursuits of shortcuts, we demonstrate that Pandora is a post-apocalyptic wasteland that has been ravaged and exhausted by capitalism in appearance only. Instead, it should be seen for what it truly is: an idealized and thriving playground of late capitalism, a place where maximizing wealth accumulation remains the game's primary focus and where subverting the game's established economic system violates the letter but adheres to the spirit of capitalism's law.

Gun-based combat and the micro-management of one's inventory and skill tree dominate the gameplay of *Borderlands*. As limited inventory space is filled by loot collected from bested enemies and completed quests, gamers make repeated trips to the vending machines that dot Pandora's landscape. These colorful machines are used to buy and sell guns, armor, grenades, and various class-specific upgrades.[5] Not only are they critical to the game's leveling and asset management processes, but because vending machines are insulated from enemies by a safe remove, these sites also function as social hubs for players trading gear and tips. Checking for daily specials, re-upping on ammo, selling less effective items, and so on constitute a necessary pre- and postfight routine; one needs to gear up before a big battle and unload postconflict spoils. These vending machines serve as veritable water coolers for collective strategizing on optimizing character builds and synchronizing complementary skill sets. Over time, the repetitive vending machine meet-ups transform into social rituals (see figure 20.1).

Figure 20.1 A player carefully optimizes the inventory options.

Gameplay repetition should not be confused with ritual. Through an iterative, trial-and-error process players make sense of a game's rules and play mechanics. Repetition is key for establishing the pattern recognition that is the foundation for successful gameplay: green mushrooms give Mario extra lives; power pellets turn *Pac-Man*'s ghosts into vulnerable blue targets; completing a horizontal row of blocks clears a line in *Tetris*. But pattern recognition does not necessarily give rise to meaningful and ritualized play. All game rituals involve repetition, but not all gameplay repetitions carry ritualistic meanings. As Alison Gazzard and Alan Peacock note, "[w]hile repetition is necessary within the game world, repetition that steps beyond function and is understood as ritual provides the player with a significant moment in the logic of the game."[6] A game's ritual logic is a culmination of repetitive actions that bring about some essential transformation. Gameplay repetition offers information about what is possible, whereas gameplay ritual offers insight into the deep play structure representing broader cultural beliefs and social values.

Conceived along a spectrum, some repetitive activities are more functional or "automatic" in nature (i.e., necessary to make the game work) while others involve "conscious awareness" that imbue them with special meaning not found with the rote activities.[7] Counterintuitively, the automatic acts in *Borderlands* are the battles, whereas the plotting data management tasks are more ritualistic. Fighting and optimizing inventory are both repetitive and complementary actions. The better the gamer is at selecting the right items at the vending machines, the better equipped they are to fight enemies. And because Pandora is a perilous world full of numbers and multipliers that parade as colorful enemies and loot boxes, *Borderlands* grants gamers the visceral pleasure of immediately seeing the effects of their optimization efforts through quantified, aestheticized feedback: cascading rainbow numerals of drained hit points. Capitalism kills, beautifully.

What then is the ritual logic of *Borderlands*? What are those repetitive actions that, taken together, constitute a normative framework for understanding how Pandora functions as a fictional world while also revealing something about our own? Frequenting the vending machines in *Borderlands* is necessary for leveling up. As players review their inventories, a wealth of gaming information is shared between them: "Who needs a high-damage shottie?" "Is your assassin focusing on the rogue or gunslinger skill tree?" "How in the hell do you kill Skagzilla?" Information may be shared at any point, but the fact that it commonly happens in the safe spaces around vending machines transforms these sites into marketplaces for the exchange of items and gaming capital (see Mia Consalvo's chapter in this collection). The vending machine-based rituals of *Borderlands* present capitalism as a rules-based system that rewards incremental grinding and equitable economic exchange. When played "properly," *Borderlands* is a virtual lesson in the meritocratic virtues of capitalism and the Protestant work ethic, a post-apocalyptic American dream modeled through an interactive ritual logic. But this is not the only way to play the game. Indeed, how does one win at the game of capitalism? An obvious solution: one cheats.

If *Borderlands*'s ritual logic issues from the metered transmission of authorized, rules-based data, then it is a system begging to be hacked. As gamers repeatedly tear through *Borderlands*'s story campaigns in increasingly difficult playthroughs, they begin looking for alternative incentives beyond the narrative developments they have already experienced. Superlative item hunting becomes, for many, the enduring motivation for play; the pursuit of the most elusive, highest-level items evolves into a new, emergent endgame.

The *Borderlands* player community evidences passionate differences of opinion regarding their interpretations of what constitutes exploits and if and how these shortcuts should be utilized. Elite gamers up to speed on the latest discoveries thanks to YouTube and social media typically believe that these hacks fall into one of several categories: results of developer-intended design, unintended effects that nevertheless adhere to the game's parameters, clear software malfunctions, and cheat scripts uploaded by users. Moreover, the online discourse concerning these exploits tends toward moral positioning, the preceding list ordered by decreasing community acceptance, which maps precisely to perceived alignment with the developers' intent. This promotes a model of the producer-consumer dynamic along a spectrum of socio-moral norms, where the gamer community self-polices according to the rules they believe the developers want them to follow. Thus, any "cheating" becomes less about one's *own* gaming experiences and more about whether players who have "worked hard" to earn the top items truly have the most power versus those with whom they are not in contact—those who have "gamed the system." This oppositional framing mirrors the labor-versus capital power struggle at the heart of many critiques of capitalism; is there greater potential for growth by grinding out a slowly improving bare survival (labor) or by leaping to access exceptional items (capital)? Who would you rather be: the dutiful gamer who maintains the sanctity of capitalism's magic circle of meritocracy or the "cheater" who games the system for personal reward, including showcasing the cracks in the system?

The best-known *Borderlands 2* exploit involved a marriage of legendary items: "The Bee" amp-damage shield (which added a large amount of damage to every fired projectile) and the "Conference Call" shotgun (which randomly fires between 5 and 77 pellets). Gamers quickly discovered that a single player could defeat nearly invincible super-bosses in just a few seconds. Within two weeks of release, the exploit had grabbed the attention of Gearbox CEO Randy Pitchford, who tweeted, "... Bee shield is so getting nerfed."[8] One month later, a patch required for online play dramatically weakened The Bee and similar amp-damage shields. Addressing the inevitable backlash, Pitchford again took to Twitter: "Bee was broken. Not nerfed enough, [in my opinion]. Some of you like broken games—I get it."[9] Gearbox has frequently rebalanced other aspects of gameplay with similar patches, usually igniting similarly passionate responses. "Hacking" bugs in programming code to produce a better outcome for one's character or team presents capitalism as a "meta" game, one where—instead of fighting more monsters for marginally better loot—players engage in complex but illicit innovating of the game itself. Meanwhile, Gearbox "corrects" its titles with patches while fans loyal to authorial intent take to discussion boards to shun and shame peers who manipulate its systems.

The core generic challenge in post-apocalyptic games is surviving with very little. The dramatic tension and, indeed, the fun of these titles come from managing a scarcity of resources. The ritual logic of *Borderlands* asks players to balance the pros and cons of a given character build and equip gear against the demands of a quest and the makeup of their party; *Borderlands* is a first-person spreadsheet in need of constant adjusting and balancing. Yet the state of artificial scarcity created and perpetuated by the franchise—a hostile environment defined by scant goods (despite the digital capacity to remedy any such shortage)—incents players to seek out exploits and glitches that offer elegant gameplay shortcuts.

Borderlands's content generation algorithms are calibrated (and recalibrated via patches and updates) to give players *just enough* of an edge to incentivize additional play while enterprising gamers find ways to beat the system. And although nearly all games, by necessity, keep overpowered objects from players to engender balance and a sense of challenge, few titles are so thoroughly imbued with a kind of neoliberal play economy where the design logic expresses an underlying market ideology.

Culturally and economically speaking, *Borderlands* is an exceedingly American game series. Pandora is a frontier-style, free-market universe populated by adventurers who dutifully grind hour after hour in pursuit of the next level. Once dedicated gamers complete the story missions and reach their level cap, they can continue the fight to collect and then display rare items to showcase their gaming acumen. But the circulation of tips that produce such digital goodies carries with it a radical gesture that belies its subversive counterplay; there is more than just "cheating" afoot.

Capitalism's ideological power is partly owed to its ability to appear neutral and natural and not as it is—a set of contingent and exploitative social conditions that mediate our relationships to one another and to our world. Similarly, the gameplay rules of *Borderlands* model capitalism as a cyclical fantasy of commodity accumulation in a never-ending pursuit of satisfying a perceived lack. But the calming balm of the next-best gun offers only temporary relief. The game's progression mechanic is a "bait and switch" trick that models capitalism's relentless spirit of perpetual accumulation. Gameplay satisfaction is fleeting in *Borderlands*. One can never have enough stuff, and there is always more stuff to be had.

The ritual logic of *Borderlands*'s gameplay effectively conditions and supports character customization and optimization, a drive that is simultaneously perpetuated and satisfied by the franchise's vibrant fan community. But the pervasive discussion board theme of "proper" game-play-turned-morality arguments, in tandem with Gearbox's frequent updates, sanction and forbid certain gameplay practices in service of maintaining a perfect relationship between utility and rarity on Pandora. This is the mythic and idealized state of meritocratic capitalism. With every newly discovered exploit, scarcity is revealed as but one possible universal precondition, and the existence of alternatives is incrementally reconfirmed, at least until the next patch; ironically, the game inadvertently reveals the truth that there is not a singular, natural capitalism but multiple, socially engineered capitalisms and that exploitations are not outside the system but are inherent to its nature.

In closing, it is worth asking, "What does it mean—culturally, ethically—that even in a cartoonish role-playing fantasy game, light-years removed from our own reality, that capitalism persists? Are *Borderlands* players who condemn others for gaming the system protecting Gearbox's rules of play, or those that govern free market capitalism? What will it take to reimagine the rules and rituals of the digital sandbox?" Perhaps the next *Borderlands* installment will feature a Pandora that privileges user creativity over the algorithm, user freedom over developer control, creative abundance over capitalistic scarcity. But, alas, as someone once said, that's a pretty hard world to imagine.

Notes

1   Aaron Thibault, "Postmortem—Gearbox's Borderlands," *Game Developer* 17, no. 2 (February 2010): 27.

2   Julian Togelius, Emil Kastbjerg, David Schedl, and Georgios N. Yannakakis, "What Is Procedural Content Generation?: Mario on the Borderline," in *Proceedings of the 2nd International Workshop on Procedural Content Generation in Games*, June 28, 2011 (Bordeaux France: ACM, 2011), 3.

3   The developer has not shared the exact number of guns *in Borderlands 2*. However, the first *Borderlands* title holds the Guinness World Record for most weapons at a staggering17.75 million. See Wesley Yin-Poole, "How Many Weapons Are in Borderlands 2?," *Euro gamer*, July 16, 2012, www.eurogamer.net.

4   Jeanne Nakamura and Mihaly Csikszentmihalyi, "The Concept of Flow," in *Handbook of Positive Psychology*, ed. Charles R. Snyder and Shane J. Lopez (New York: Oxford University Press, 2002), 89–105.

5   Jacob Brogan, "Why Did this Guy Collect 500 Screenshots of Soda Machines in Video Games? Because He Is a Genius," *Slate*, October 21, 2016, www.slate.com.

6   Alison Gazzard and Alan Peacock, "Repetition and Ritual Logic in Video Games," *Games and Culture* 6, no. 6 (2011): 505.

7   Gazzard and Peacock, "Repetition and Ritual Logic," 505–506.

8   Randy Pitchford (@DuvalMagic), "@Addy John_V Bee shield is so getting nerfed," Twitter, October 6, 2012, 12:38 PM, https://twitter.com/duvalmagic/status/254666987479904256.

9   Randy Pitchford (@DuvalMagic), "Bee was broken. Not nerfed enough, IMO. Some of you like broken games - I get it," Twitter, November 14, 2012, 7:38 AM, https://twitter.com/DuvalMagic/status/268709452096610304.

Further Reading

Consalvo, Mia. *Cheating: Gaining Advantage in Videogames.* Cambridge, MA: MIT Press, 2007.

Kline, Stephen, Nick Dyer-Witherford, and Greig de Peuter. *Digital Play: The Interaction of Technology, Culture, and Marketing.* Montreal: McGill-Queen's University Press, 2003.

Mandel, Ernest. *An Introduction to Marxist Economic Theory.* New York: Pathfinder, 2005.

Suggested Assignments

1. Research the history of a particular game and explore how the game and/or its marketing has changed over time. What forces have shaped the changes?

2. Use one of the critical lenses introduced in chapter 3 to explore the ideological messages encoded in a particular game or genre of gaming.

3. Explore how a game has been adapted into a different medium or how a narrative from a different medium has been adapted into a game. What does this process of adaptation reveal to us about the limitations and possibilities of the two different mediums?

4. Using Henry Jenkins's idea of **textual poaching** from chapter 4, explore fan practices in relation to a particular game or category of gaming.
5. Design your own game and explain the ideological messages you would encode in it and how these would be conveyed.

Works Cited in the Chapter

Barrowcliffe, Mark. *The Elfish Gene: Dungeons, Dragons and Growing Up Strange.* Soho Press, 2009.

Brown, Anna. "Younger Men Play Video Games, But So Do a Diverse Group of Other Americans." *Pew Research Center*, 11 Sept. 2017, https://www.pewresearch.org/fact-tank/2017/09/11/younger-men-play-video-games-but-so-do-a-diverse-group-of-other-americans/.

Caillois, Roger. *Men, Play and Games.* 1958. Translated by Meyer Barash, University of Illinois Press, 2001.

Dewey, Caitlin. "The Only Guide to Gamergate You Will Ever Need to Read." *The Washington Post*, 14 Oct. 2014, https://www.washingtonpost.com/news/the-intersect/wp/2014/10/14/the-only-guide-to-gamergate-you-will-ever-need-to-read/.

Fatsis, Stefan. *Word Freak: Heartbreak, Triumph, Genius, and Obsession in the World of Competitive Scrabble Players.* 20th ed., Penguin Books, 2002.

"The Great 1980s Dungeons & Dragons Panic." *BBC News*, 11 Apr. 2014, https://www.bbc.com/news/magazine-26328105.

Maroney, Kevin. "My Entire Waking Life." *The Games Journal: A Magazine About Boardgames*, May 2001, http://www.thegamesjournal.com/articles/MyEntireWakingLife.shtml.

Mirrlees, Tanner. "*Medal of Honor* (Militarism)." *How to Play Video Games*, edited by Matthew Thomas Payne and Nina B. Huntemann, New York UP, 2019, pp. 242–49.

Mukherjee, Souvik. "*Age of Empires* (Postcolonialism)." *How to Play Video Games*, edited by Matthew Thomas Payne and Nina B. Huntemann, New York UP, 2019, pp. 157–64.

Payne, Matthew and Michael Fleisch. "Borderlands: Capitalism," *How to Play Video Games*, edited by Matthew Thomas Payne and Nina B. Huntemann, New York UP, 2019, pp. 165–73.

Additional Suggested Reading

Flanagan, Mary and Helen Nissenbaum. *Values at Play in Digital Games*. MIT Press, 2014.

Juul, Jesper. *Half-Real: Video Games Between Real Rules and Fictional Worlds*. MIT Press, 2011.

Malkowski, Jennifer and TreaAndrea M. Russworm. *Gaming Representation: Race, Gender, and Sexuality in Video Games*. Indiana UP, 2017.

Michael, David R. and Sandra L. Chen. *Serious Games: Games That Educate, Train, and Inform*. Muska & Lipman/Premier-Trade, 2005.

Payne, Matthew Thomas and Nina B. Huntemann, editors. *How to Play Videogames*. New York UP, 2019.

Quinn, Zoe. *Crash Override: How Gamergate (Nearly) Destroyed My Life, and How We Can Win the Fight Against Online Hate*. PublicAffairs, 2017.

Salen, Katie and Eric Zimmerman. *Rules of Play: Game Design Fundamentals*. MIT Press, 2004.

Schell, Jesse. *The Art of Game Design: A Book of Lenses*. 3rd ed., CRC Press, 2019.

Schreier, Jason. *Blood, Sweat, and Pixels: The Triumphant, Turbulent Stories Behind How Video Games Are Made*. Harper Paperbacks, 2017.

Shaw, Adrienne. *Gaming at the Edge: Sexuality and Gender at the Margins of Gamer Culture*. University of Minnesota Press, 2015.

Taylor, T.L. *Watch Me Play: Twitch and the Rise of Game Live Streaming*. Princeton UP, 2018.

Upton, Brian. *The Aesthetic of Play*. MIT Press, 2015.

CHAPTER 9

SOCIAL MEDIA

*Prepared in consultation with Anirban K. Baishya
of the Communication and Media Studies
Department at Fordham University*

Social Media

Several times in this textbook on popular culture, I have mentioned a phrase very familiar to media students and scholars: "the medium is the message." As discussed in chapter 5 on television and film, the expression was coined by communications scholar Marshall McLuhan in his 1964 book *Understanding Media: The Extensions of Man*, and, put simply, it refers to what he calls the "character" of a medium—the nature and characteristics of a channel of communication, its **affordances**—and how that medium's character shapes the **messages** that it conveys. There is no better way to illustrate this claim than to consider different forms of social media, which we will think of broadly as forms of electronic communication—websites and apps—that allow users to share information.

Take Twitter for example. For most Twitter users, messages (called "tweets") are limited to 280 characters. This parameter obviously influences how users compose messages—what and how Twitter users tweet is shaped by the qualities and constraints of the Twitter platform. TikTok in some ways is the video equivalent, limiting the length of videos to no more than a minute. These limitations on length are part of the character of Twitter and TikTok and require users to tailor their messages accordingly. The medium shapes the message. The ephemerality of Snapchat messages shapes messages in a different way—knowing that something will disappear after it has been seen or after a prescribed period of time (which is what differentiates Snapchat from many other social media platforms) influences what users feel at liberty to say. Instagram is more image-based, so users are channeled into uploading images, which can be altered using a variety of filters and effects. What we say and how we say it is shaped by the character of the medium through which we say it.

The affordances—qualities and properties—of a social media platform also dictate how we interact and with whom. On Twitter, users can choose to follow someone and reply to their tweets (unless and until they get blocked). Because users of Twitter choose who to follow and to whom to respond, exchanges on Twitter are famously aggressive. On Facebook, in contrast, one has greater control over the audience for one's messages—posts on one's own page can be public, limited to friends, or tailored to a particular audience and, unless a post is public, one must be "friends" with the person making the post to reply.

> **YOUR TURN**: To accept a "friend request" on Facebook is simply to agree to allow someone to see and respond to posts on one's page limited to friends. It is a curious kind of friendship when you think about it. Why do you think Facebook decided to call it "friending" and do you think this practice influences how we think of friends in general?

Facebook also provides a limited set of emojis that responders to a post can use to signal their reaction: like, love, laugh, wow, sad, angry, and the newest, care. This is a good demonstration of the principle that you can choose everything but your choices.

Emojis

YOUR TURN: What emojis would you add to the list of possible Facebook responses? And how would the inclusion of your emojis change the character of Facebook?

Self-Presentation

An important area of interest for those who study social media is the relationship between individuals and various communities online. One beginning point for such a consideration is with self-presentation: the way in which an individual user of social media constructs an impression of themselves to share online. On some digital platforms, this may start with choosing a username and/or selecting an **avatar**—an image that represents you. Avatars can be pictures of the user, other icons (such as a celebrity, animal, or geographic feature), or something abstract. Self-presentation then encompasses the content a social media user chooses to share, including *selfies* and other photographs, videos, status updates and other types of posts, **memes**, repostings of content created by others, news articles, and so on.

Shared content intentionally or unintentionally participates in creating an online identity or persona for other social media users—and raises interesting questions about **authenticity**. On the one hand, users of social media may feel that social media platforms permit them to present a "truer" picture of themselves to the world than they are at liberty to do so in their day-to-day interactions in the physical world. On the other hand, there is a pronounced social media tendency to "accentuate the positive"—that is, to highlight the good things that have happened while omitting the negative, and to present the most impressive picture of the user possible. While not necessarily "inauthentic," skewing heavily toward the positive is certainly one-sided, and some users of social media have, as a consequence, described themselves as feeling depressed by or jealous over the apparent *bon vivant* lifestyles of others (see, for example, Altman). It is easy to feel inadequate, jealous, or sad when all the stories and images that fill up your social media feed are of vacation pictures from far-flung places or success stories!

YOUR TURN: Thinking in terms of your social media avatar, username, and/or the content you share on a particular social media platform, what impression of yourself do you seek to cultivate and how? Do you present yourself differently on different formats? And do you consider your social media presence as a more or less authentic reflection of your "true self"?

From Self-Presentation to Community

Attention to the ways one curates online content to construct an impression of oneself for others inevitably shifts us from thinking about self-presentation to a consideration of how and with whom one interacts online—that is, we shift from thinking about individual users of social media to the audiences they reach and their participation in online communities. Social media participation, of course, serves a range of functions and permits a variety of different types of communication. Users can stay in touch with family and friends, search for relationship partners, explore interests, promote their ventures, and find entertainment. A good deal of social media interaction, however, takes place within groups—communities of social media users sharing a particular connection, interest, orientation, or philosophy. The focus of groups can include just about anything from German Shepherd lovers to yoga enthusiasts to those who went to the same high school or who hate brussels sprouts, and the size of groups can range from a few people to millions.

Almost by default, social media groups are to some extent *homophilic* in the sense of linking people with similar interests—you're more likely to join a Nicholas Cage fan group if you like Nicholas Cage than if you don't know who he is or hate him (and if you love brussels sprouts, you are probably not going to join a group for those who hate them unless your purpose is to *troll* them with pictures of your latest brussels sprout creations). This, of course, is also how groups work in the physical world as well, and there can certainly be much to enjoy in interacting with people who share with you a background, interest, passion, hobby, experience, and so on. Social media groups, however, can sometimes facilitate potentially dangerous *filter bubbles* in which particular **ideological** perspectives are reinforced through repetition and the absence of competing viewpoints. Conspiracy theories and extremist views thrive in such environments. If someone believes, for example, that the US moon landing in 1969 was faked, or that the 9/11 attacks were orchestrated by the CIA, or that vaccines cause autism (spoiler: it wasn't, they weren't, and they don't), it is easy to find groups online composed of members who share the same views, and hearing others voice an idea that you believe or are at least open to can strengthen you in that belief—if all one hears are their own views parroted back to them, those ideas assume the solidity of truth. Again, this is not unique to digital environments. Hate groups sadly exist in the non-digital world, as do groups committed to conspiracy and crackpot theories. Social media platforms, however, make it much easier for such groups to form, share materials, and coordinate.

I hasten to add that it is important to acknowledge the flip side to this as well: social media platforms can also enable collective action and progressive social activism. The anti-government protests and uprisings referred to as the Arab Spring that started in 2010, as well as the #MeToo and BLM movements, were in many respects products of the social media age as social media enabled coordination and the spread of information. While social media activism often takes the form of what has been called "slacktivism," low-intensity engagement in which one's support for a cause is expressed through signing an online petition or clicking a button, it is nevertheless the case that every modern political movement that seeks to gather people together or get them out into the streets now includes a social media component.

YOUR TURN: To what extent are you trapped in a social media filter bubble? How often do you see posts that challenge your beliefs or present points of view that differ from your own?

Going Viral

According to the January 2019 *We Are Social* report, a whopping 3.5 billion people actively use social media—that's 45 per cent of the world's population ("Digital in 2019"). The extensive reach of social media that has been harnessed by political and civil rights movements has also created the conditions for two other related phenomena: *social media influencers* and *virality*. A social media influencer is someone with a large audience, a message, and a tall soapbox from which to shout it to the world. The idea of an "influencer," of course, isn't new. Politicians and celebrities have often played these roles, using the mediums of print, radio, and television to reach large audiences—we still have advertisements and commercials on network television featuring "celebrity spokesmodels" who try to convince us to use a particular shampoo or donate to a particular cause. The rise of social media, however, has democratized the potential pool of influencers. One no longer needs to be famous first in another medium to have access to a large audience of followers. Instead, through blogs, videos on platforms such as YouTube and Instagram, podcasts, and social media posts, individuals can develop a following. Some rise to the level of *mega-influencers* with more than a million followers; others, sometimes referred to as *micro-influencers*, cultivate a specialized niche with a following of somewhere between 1,000 and 50,000 followers. Influencers are generally knowledgeable on a particular topic and present information in an engaging way. As with becoming a celebrity in more conventional media though, such as music, TV, and film, achieving success as a social media influencer also often involves useful connections, clever promotion strategies, and an element of luck.

The success of social media influencers is related to the phenomenon of *virality*—the rapid spread of a social media message (post, meme, image, story, etc.) from person to person and group to group. Perhaps more than anything else, the possibility of something "going viral" on social media highlights what differentiates social media from other mediums of communication. Within literally a matter of seconds, social media content created by platform users can reach thousands or even millions of other users. This can become problematic when *context collapse* occurs. In face-to-face interactions, or even in online interactions with a limited group, we generally know with and to whom we are speaking and adjust our presentation of self and tone accordingly. But when a message is going out to thousands and thousands of people, that becomes impossible. Sophie Goodman describes the challenge as "like trying to comfortably chat with your mother, bar buddy, work colleague, and ex-boyfriend at the same time" (Goodman). The **dominant / hegemonic** response to a tweet, post, or image tailored to a particular audience can be flipped on its head and become **oppositional** when it is received by users with different views.

> **YOUR TURN:** Describe a negative response you have had to a social media post that likely resulted from context collapse.

Another feature of the social media age is the prominence of memes. Memes begin their lives as images or short animated or video sequences. The most common feature is an image with a witty caption or catch-phrase, often with an **intertextual** element—famous ones feature the character Boromir (Sean Bean) from Peter Jackson's 2001 *Lord of the Rings: The Fellowship of the Ring* explaining that "one does not simply

Fig. 9.1 A Heckin Good Meme

walk into Mordor"; Ned Stark from *Game of Thrones* (also, coincidentally, Sean Bean) telling us to brace ourselves for winter; Dos Equis beer's "most interesting man in the world" who doesn't always do something or other, but does it with *éclat* when he does; sad Keanu Reeves; and so on. Others are built around a funny or interesting character or scene—a grumpy looking cat, a baby with a clenched fist and determined mien, a distracted boyfriend and aggrieved girlfriend, a portrait of a curiously jovial eighteenth-century gentleman, and so on. These images then become memes when they are shared widely and can even seep into the broader popular culture consciousness as when the misspellings and broken English of memes featuring dogs and cats find themselves repeated outside the heckin context of the Internet (see Fig. 9.1).

YOUR TURN: What memes show up most frequently in your social media feeds? What do you think is responsible for their popularity?

Fake News

Another social media issue related to the speed with and extent to which content can be distributed is the phenomenon of *fake news*. Fake news refers to the deliberate posting of disinformation with the intention of misleading recipients of the message, who are then influenced to think and/or act in particular ways and who often then repost the message, facilitating its spread. As with the ideas of filter bubbles and influencers, fake news absolutely isn't a new thing. Disinformation campaigns have long histories, going all the way back to the ancient world. In the early part of the twentieth century, it was called *yellow journalism*. Later, it was referred to as *tabloid journalism*. Sensationalist and dishonest stories often have found audiences both because of their often-outrageous

Twentieth-Century Tabloid "Fake News"

nature and due to what is often called **confirmation bias**—the tendency to favor information that supports one's beliefs or values. If someone already suspects that aliens landed in Area 51 in New Mexico and that the government is covering it up, they will be more inclined to seek out, respond favorably to, and share "reports" that support this position.

Several aspects of social media, however, have amplified the problem fake news has always presented. First, social media *algorithms* advance the spread of fake news by channeling dubious content to those ready to receive and spread it. Social media algorithms are formulas that prioritize what content appears in a social media feed based on certain parameters. In some cases, users can manipulate the parameters of the algorithm—for example, by choosing "most recent" stories over "top stories" on Facebook so that you see the newest posts rather than those that have received the most "likes." But algorithms also function to channel content to users that, based on users' social media histories, they are likely to receive favorably. This is enormously important to online advertising and marketing—you've probably noticed that if you visit a commercial retailer's website, for example, you'll find advertisements for that retailer and related ones showing up in your social media feed. This is also part of *data mining*, by the way—the collection of data about individual social media users and larger social media trends, often for purposes of marketing. Social media algorithms, however, don't just try to find the advertisements that are most likely to appeal to users; they will also channel content based on social media activity. If someone is interested in paleontology and visits a lot of social media sites related to dinosaurs, they're more likely to have articles about paleontology show up in their feed. And, alas, if someone is convinced that survivors of mass shootings are really "crisis actors"—people paid to pretend to be survivors to promote a particular political agenda—and visits social media sites related to conspiracy theories, social media algorithms are likely to funnel information of a dubious nature to them that will solidify these views—often with sensationalist "clickbait" headlines or salacious images that encourage one to follow a link ("you won't believe what happened next!").

The problem of fake news on social media has further been amplified by the phenomenon of **deepfakes** in which someone's image in a picture or video is convincingly altered through sophisticated technology. While this can be done to comic effect, as when actor Jim Carrey's face replaces that of Jack Nicholson in the film *The Shining* (see Fig. 9.2) or Nicholas Cage's face replaces, well, just about everyone's, deepfakes can also be used to pernicious effect when the image being altered makes it appear that someone is participating in illegal, immoral, or embarrassing activity. Some deepfakes, for example, have featured the likenesses of female celebrities engaged in sexual activity. Others have targeted politicians, in some cases making them appear to say things they did not in fact say. Deepfakes, as with fake news stories in general, often play to users' confirmation bias, and their sophistication can make them difficult to identify.

Fig 9.2 A Deepfake Image Replacing Actor Jack Nicholson's Face in The Shining *with that of Actor Jim Carrey*

Swipe Left: Social Media Behavior

We've been talking throughout this chapter about how the affordances of social media shape its content. The medium is the message. However, what we've also been observing is that the character of social media platforms not only influences what people say and how they say it, but indeed how they think and act—and, as with all mediums of communication, this can be for both good and ill. Social media can certainly facilitate connections among individuals and allow people who might not otherwise have ever come in contact to exchange views and become friends. However, the relative anonymity of social media discourse and the absence of face-to-face interactions have also fostered negative interactions such as *trolling* and *cyberbullying*. Internet "trolls" post provocative comments with the intention of eliciting anger from other social media users. Cyberbullies use electronic forms of communication to send threatening or demeaning messages. And then there are the comments sections following many online news publications—if there is a better angel to human nature, it is noticeably absent from such forums.

YOUR TURN: Thinking now about social media platforms in general and ones you are familiar with in particular, how common are trolling and cyberbullying? What about the platforms you are familiar with permits or fosters these kinds of interactions, and what do you think can be done to address these problems?

Interpreting Social Media

Because our lives today are so intimately intertwined with social media, any consideration of contemporary popular culture needs to think in terms of what and how these apps, sites, posts, and practices mean, how they shape our thinking, and how we can use them in meaningful and productive ways. The idea of "interpreting" a social media platform in light of its qualities and meanings may, however, seem less familiar to you than thinking about the meaning of narrative works such as books, TV shows, and films where the ideological messages perhaps seem more straightforward; this to a certain extent has to do with educational training more than anything: we're often taught through English courses and other classes how to think about the meaning of what we read and watch; there tends to be less emphasis (if any at all) on the platforms we read and watch those narratives on, the contexts in which we read and watch those things, and the ways we consume them. (You've likely read lots of books in your life—but did you ever stop and think about what it means to read a book and what books mean in general?) The process we'll follow in considering the meaningfulness of forms of social media will be similar to that used to address other forms of popular culture in this textbook. We'll ask questions—lots of them—that begin with the thing itself and its qualities, move on to how users use the thing, think about its meaning in a broader context, and then inquire into the ways the thing naturalizes certain understandings of the world while, perhaps, calling into question other ways of thinking.

Qualities

When thinking of the significance of social media apps or sites, the place to begin is with a consideration of the qualities of the app or site itself, with an eye toward the types of messages and behaviors it requires, encourages, permits, discourages, and prohibits. Among the questions one may ask are:

- What are the stated purposes of the site or app? What other purposes does it have? What is it used for? How does it seek to achieve its purpose(s)?
- What is the app or site's business model? How does it seek to generate revenue?
- How is the app or site constructed? What does it look like, what functions does it permit or prohibit, and how does one navigate it? What is the "experience" of using the app or site like?

- How does the app or site differentiate itself from other similar apps or sites?

Users

- Who are the app or site's primary users? In what ways does the site or app target particular populations? Are particular populations intentionally or unintentionally omitted or excluded?
- How do users interact with each other using the site or app? Who "talks" to whom, about what, when, and in what ways? How does the site organize, direct, police, or manipulate users?
- What assumptions are built into the site or the app about users, their abilities, and their preferences? What assumptions do users bring to the site or app?
- What data does the app or site collect about its users? What does it do with that data?
- How do users build boundaries around themselves on these sites? Do they post their information or updates on the app or site treating it like private space, even though the site or app is publicly viewable, or owned by a corporation?

Messages

- Who generates content and of what types? How is content distributed, by whom, and to whom? If some content is user generated, in what ways does the site or app constrain or influence user-generated content?
- What is content used for and by whom? How long is content available? What makes content on the site or app more or less valuable or enticing?
- What distinguishes content on the app or site from content on similar apps or sites?

- What behaviors does the site or app reward, permit, discourage, or prohibit? What rules—stated or implicit—govern how users interact with the site and each other?
- How are users rewarded or punished for their ways of using the site? How is power distributed on the app or site?

Histories and Contexts

- Who created the app or site? How has it developed and changed over time? Have there been controversies or conflicts related to its design, developers, or use?
- How has the app or site been represented in other media? In what ways has it been incorporated into popular culture outside of social media?
- How has the app or site been utilized as part of social movements? How does it reflect the concerns or preoccupations of its historical moment? In what ways has it in fact helped shape its historical moment?

Ideology

- What *values* does the app or site implicitly or explicitly endorse? Are there conflicts between the stated goals of an app or site and how it actually functions?
- In what ways does the site or app reconfirm or challenge established ways of thinking?

These last questions concerning ideology may be particularly difficult to think about in relation to social media apps and sites, but they are also extremely important questions to consider. What do the social media apps we use ask us implicitly or explicitly to accept about, among other things, privacy, private property, social class and wealth distribution, race, **gender,** and sexuality? To what extent are such sites implicated in replicating and reinforcing existing forms of oppression and exclusion?

Can social media apps be used to challenge forms of oppression while also turning their CEOs into .com billionaires? In the two short readings created for this textbook that follow, communications scholar Anirban K. Baishya offers examples of how one might begin to think about the social significance of Instagram and selfies.

Sample Essays

"Unpacking the Selfie"

Anirban K. Baishya

The word "selfie" was incorporated into the *Oxford English Dictionary* in 2013. The *OED* describes the selfie as "a photograph that one has taken of oneself, esp. one taken with a smartphone or webcam and shared via social media" (*OED*). But, if the selfie is a photograph of the photographer themselves, then why not just call them self-portraits? After all, photographers have been taking photographs of themselves much before the advent of social media. For instance, in his ongoing project *Every Day*, photographer Karl Baden has been photographing his face daily since 1987 (Baden). Clearly, photographers photographing themselves is not new. However, as art critic Brian Droitcour points out, what is new is the possibility of "distributing it on a network almost immediately." Similarly, media scholar Katrin Tiidenberg defines selfies as "self-representational, networked photographs" (21). Thus, a selfie is a photograph, but it is also something more. It is innately connected to the emergence of social network sites, as well as camera-enabled, networked handheld devices such as cellphones.

Most people imagine the selfie to be a picture of one's face. But what about images of the photographer's feet, or images that are hashtagged as "#selfie" but have no human presence? Should they not be considered "selfies"? Tiidenberg points out that any photograph that is "self-referential" can be a selfie (21). Within this expanded definition we can think of selfies as ways of self-presentation—a carefully curated process in which the selfie-taker makes conscious choices with regards to framing, angle, embellishment (text and filters for example) and hashtags and decides what elements of their lived experience they should present. Thus, selfies are reflective of what sociologist Erving Goffman calls "impression management" (8).

Comparing human society to a stage, Goffman says that individuals try to control a situation by managing how others perceive them. "Frontstage" behavior is where individuals act most formally, while in the "backstage" such formality can be dropped (Goffman 78). Selfies can have both front-stage and backstage aspects. For instance, you may try to appear at your best if you upload a selfie on a social media account that is accessible by employers or family (frontstage). On the other hand, you may exchange "ugly" selfies with your closest friends on Snapchat (backstage). So, we can consider selfies to be inherently *performative*—they are images cur-ated for specific audiences. In corollary, we can also consider selfies to be "cumulative self-presentations" (Rettberg 35) or similar to "postcards [and] diary entries" (Westley 380)—i.e., they build a profile of the user's identity when seen as part of a series.

Sometimes selfies may be taken to document one's presence in a particular place or time; they may feature just one person, or sometimes a group (for example, Ellen DeGeneres's now famous "Oscar Selfie"). No matter what the occasion and regardless of whether they feature one or more persons, selfies are a social, communicative form. This communication can take place through hashtags, embedded text or sometimes without any additional elements—think for example, of a selfie you may send to a friend with just a funny expression on your face, or with an added smiley or sticker. Such communicative practices are called "phatic com-munication" which "serves the purpose of maintaining and defining social relationships" rather than conveying a very specific message (Sarjanoja et al. 2013). As media scholar Paul Frosh puts it, a selfie "inscribes one's own body into new forms of mediated, expressive sociability with distant others" (1621). So, the selfie always imagines a world of onlookers and we partake in its communicative potentials even when we are not certain of what we want to say through the image.

Contrary to what has been said here, public discourse about the selfie has often tended to be negative. Selfie takers are often portrayed as narcissistic or lacking "culture." However, as students of **culture** we must be careful about rushing into such conclusions. What is important to note is that selfie-taking puts the control over the production of self-images into the hands of every person with a camera-phone. In contrast to previous historical modes of image-making such as oil-painting portraiture and studio photography, taking selfies does not require expertise. Advancements in technology have wrested the production of images away from the few and placed them in the hands of the many or the "planetary majority" (Mirzoeff 62). Selfies then, are not only one of this era's most popular cultural forms, but also layered images from which we can learn about ourselves and our society.

Works Cited in Sample Essay

Baden, Karl. "EVERY DAY … CONFUSING ART AND OBSESSION SINCE 1987." http://kbeveryday.blogspot.com/.

Droitcour, Brian. "A Selfie Is Not a Portrait." *CultureTwo*, 24 Oct. 2013, https://culturetwo.wordpress.com/2013/10/24/a-selfie-is-not-a-portrait/.

Frosh, Paul. "The Gestural Image: The Selfie, Photography Theory, and Kinesthetic Sociability." *International Journal of Communication*, vol. 9, 2015, pp. 1607–28.

Goffman, Erving. *The Presentation of Self in Everyday Life*. Random House, 2008.

Mirzoeff, Nicholas. *How to See the World: An Introduction to Images, from Self-Portraits to Selfies, Maps to Movies, and More*. Basic Books, 2016.

Rettberg, Jill. *Seeing Ourselves Through Technology: How We Use Selfies, Blogs and Wearable Devices to See and Shape Ourselves*. Palgrave Macmillan, 2014.

Sarjanoja, Ari-Heikki, et al. "Small Talk with Facebook—Phatic Communication in Social Media." *AcademicMindTrek '13:*

Proceedings of International Conference on Making Sense of Converging Media, 2013, pp. 118–21, https://doi.org/10.1145/2523429.2523449.

"selfie, n." *OED: Oxford English Dictionary*, Jan. 2018, https://www.oed.com/view/Entry/390063?redirectedFrom=selfie.

Tiidenberg, Katrin. *Selfies: Why We Love (and Hate) Them*. Emerald Publishing, 2018.

Westley, Hannah. "Reading the Self in Selfies." *Comparative Critical Studies*, vol. 13, no. 3, 2016, pp. 371–90.

"Doin' It for the Gram: Instagram and Aesthetic Capitalism"

Anirban K. Baishya

Like "Xerox," for photocopying, and more recently "Google" for web searches, Instagram has become synonymous with contemporary digital visual culture. Simultaneously a company, a platform, an app, a social network and a form of digital practice, Instagram was co-founded by Kevin Systrom and Mike Krieger in 2010, and acquired by Facebook in 2012. As phones become more like computers, apps like Instagram have become the bridge between the "black box" of algorithms, and the welcome embrace of mobile UX design—what Jeremy Morris and Susan Murray call the "aesthetic mode of selling digital objects" (6). This sets Instagram apart from software like Adobe Photoshop that also bridges code and GUI (Graphic User Interface), but without the intuitive user experience of the cellphone.

Instagram can be seen as an extension of long developments in photographic technology. Alicia Chester draws connections between Instagram and the Polaroid's shared drive to "produce instantaneous photos created to share with friends and family" (10). Instagram also emulates the Polaroid's square picture format (Manovich 41, Chester 11) and its original logo invoked the Polaroid OneStep camera before it was changed in 2016 (Chester 10). But Instagram's networked nature accelerates the social functions of photography far beyond its analog predecessors, providing the photo-taking, editing and distribution apparatuses in one platform (Manovich 18). Further, it simplifies image-editing for the lay-user through easy to use control over exposure, contrast and sharpness and its range of filters allows users to endow a certain "look" on their images. While such filters make our everyday reality look different or special, the repetition of such filters in imaging apps and camera phones nullifies this defamiliarization effect and filters themselves become "a cliché" (Rettberg 26). Think for example, of the hashtag "#nofilter" on Instagram which is meant to negate the Instagram's filter aesthetic. The #nofilter hashtag highlights the constructed nature of what is considered to be "authentic" online. While filters invite users to "creatively document a life lived well," the machinic effort to create the look of authenticity through nostalgic, analog-look filters, belies authenticity itself (Salisbury & Pooley 12). The authenticity-effect is central to social media's culture of self-branding which "significantly extends the potential for fame and celebrity" (Khamis et al. 6). Thus, Instagram is also embedded in a neoliberal market, where authenticity often works as capital.

Instagram's visual aesthetics are also centrally tied to Internet celebrity, marketing and influence. Take for instance the phenomenon of "Rich Kids of Instagram" (RKOI), a special subset of Internet celebrity in which fame is "achieved almost solely by flaunting wealth on the internet" (Abidin 22). In this case, Instagram becomes reflective of class positions, and the visual display of wealth is seen as an almost natural thing to do. If this is a "marketing" of the aestheticized self, there are more direct ways in which Instagram converges with the market. Elisa Serafinelli notes that Facebook's ownership of Instagram has changed its status from that of "a mere photosharing platform into a business machine that relies on the power of visual communication" (100–101). Consequently, not only do users attempt to "emulate brands' images," but "companies and brands are increasingly including the use of Instagram in their marketing plans" (Serafinelli 101). This has led to a new class of users—influencers, who "attract and maintain a sizable following [...] which can be used as conduits of information to amplify messages" (Abidin 71). Of course, influencers are not limited to Instagram alone, but it is a major platform for the Internet influencer industry globally. For such influencers, "the sequence aesthetics takes priority over any individual photos" (Manovich 129)—i.e., Instagram's grid-visuality becomes both an aesthetic and a business model.

Of course, we should not assume that Instagram is not used in other ways. Family snapshots, travel photos, selfies and pictures of mundane moments suffuse the Instagram landscape. However, we must remember that while Instagram ostensibly offers users the freedom to make and display such images, it also limits what can be seen or shown on the platform. For instance, Instagram's no-nudity policy implies that showing the "body is intolerable and inappropriate," a rhetoric that is "often used for fat- or trans-shaming" (Olszanowski 87). Although users—many of them artists, fat-positivity activists and queer/trans visibility activists—do find ways around such limitations, Instagram's profit-driven, corporate structure draws a boundary around visual expression that may challenge or question normative standards. Thus, what Manovich calls Instagram's propensity for "aesthetic visual communication" (41), is also a form of aesthetic capitalism—one where images and control over visibility often hold the key to upward social and financial mobility.

Works Cited in Sample Essay

Abidin, Crystal. *Internet Celebrity: Understanding Fame Online*. Emerald Publishing Limited, 2018.

Chester, Alicia. "The Outmoded Instant: From Instagram to Polaroid." *Afterimage*, vol. 45, no.5, 2018, pp. 10–15.

Khamis, Susie, et al. "Self-branding, 'Micro-Celebrity' and the Rise of Social Media Influencers." *Celebrity Studies*, vol. 8, no. 2, 2017, pp. 191–208.

Manovich, Lev. *Instagram and Contemporary Image*. Manovich. net, 2017, http://manovich.net/index.php/projects/ instagram-and-contemporary-image.

Morris, Jeremy Wade and Sarah Murray. *Appified: Digital Culture in the Age of Apps*. University of Michigan Press, 2018.

Olszanowski, Magdalena. "Feminist Self-Imaging and Instagram: Tactics of Circumventing Censorship." *Visual Communication Quarterly*, vol. 21, no. 2, 2014, pp. 83–95.

Rettberg, Jill. *Seeing Ourselves Through Technology: How We Use Selfies, Blogs and Wearable Devices to See and Shape Ourselves*. Palgrave Macmillan, 2014.

Salisbury, Meredith and Jefferson D. Pooley. "The #nofilter Self: The Contest for Authenticity among Social Networking Sites, 2002–2016." *Social Sciences*, vol. 6, no. 1, 20 Jan. 2017, 10; https://doi.org/10.3390/socsci6010010.

Serafinelli, Elisa. *Digital Life on Instagram: New Social Communication of Photography*. Emerald Publishing Ltd., 2018.

Suggested Assignments

- APP DESIGNER. Imagine you are an app designer and are going to develop your own social media app. What would its purpose be? What features would it include? How would it differ from existing apps and how would yours be an improvement?

- SOCIAL MEDIA AND SOCIAL UNREST. Focusing on BLM, the Arab Spring, #MeToo, or other social movements, explore how social media platforms have been used to facilitate social activism.

- CRITICAL THEORY. Adopt one of the **critical theory** approaches introduced in the first part of this textbook and use it as a lens through which to consider the ideological messages conveyed by a particular social media platform.

- BOTS, TROLLS, BUBBLES, FAKE NEWS, AND DEEPFAKES. Dig deeper into some of the challenges users of social media confront, considering what causes the behavior and how it might be addressed.

- DATAMINING AND PRIVACY. Explore the ways social media apps gather data about users and what they do with it.

Works Cited in the Chapter

Altman, Connor. "Social Deception: Managing Social Media Jealousy."
    Forbes, 10 Oct. 2017, https://www.forbes.com/sites/
    payout/2017/10/10/social-deception-managing-social-
    media-jealousy/#5cc243cd52b7.
"Digital in 2019." *We Are Social*, https://wearesocial.com/
    global-digital-report-2019.
Goodman, Sophie. "How Real Are You on Facebook?" *Sapiens:
    Anthropology / Everything Human*, 6 Apr. 2016, https://www.
    sapiens.org/technology/social-media-and-identity/.
McLuhan, Marshall. *Understanding Media: The Extensions of Man*. 1964.
    The MIT Press, 1994.

Additional Suggested Reading

Baym, Nancy. *Personal Connections in the Digital Age*. Polity, 2010.
boyd, danah. *It's Complicated: The Social Lives of Teens*. Yale UP, 2014.
Castells, Manuel. *Networks of Outrage and Hope: Social Movement in the
    Internet Age*. Polity, 2015.
Noble, Safiya Umoja. *Algorithms of Oppression: How Search Engines
    Reinforce Racism*. New York UP, 2018.
Phillips, Whitney. *This Is Why We Can't Have Nice Things: Mapping the
    Relationship between Online Trolling and Mainstream Culture*. The MIT
    Press, 2015.
Roberts, Sarah T. *Behind the Screen: Content Moderation in the Shadows of
    Social Media*. Yale UP, 2019.
Shifman, Limor. *Memes in Digital Culture*. The MIT Press, 2014.
Vaidhyanathan, Siva. *Antisocial Media: How Facebook Disconnects Us and
    Undermines Democracy*. Oxford UP, 2018.
van Dijck, José. *The Culture of Connectivity: A Critical History of Social
    Media*. Oxford UP, 2013.

CHAPTER 10
FANDOM

Prepared in consultation with Amanda Firestone,
University of Tampa

A Star Trek Fan

"Most people are fans of something" note the editors of the first edition of the scholarly collection of essays titled *Fandom: Identities and Communities in a Mediated World* (1). You are probably a person (or at least a bot with a vested interest in maintaining your disguise). So, what are you a fan of?

Before you answer though, the question requires us to back up a step and to ask what it means to be a fan. Media scholar Henry Jenkins—who has been mentioned numerous times across this textbook and really is the guru when it comes to scholarly approaches to **fandom**—observes that the meaning of the word is broad and can be used "to describe anyone who forms an intense bond with a particular property, whether or not they share those feelings with anyone else." "Sometimes," he continues, "being a fan means nothing more than pressing 'like' on some Facebook page" (Jenkins, "Fandom" 16). Maybe so, but there are fans and then there are *fans*—which Jenkins, of course, acknowledges. With this in mind, Jenkins goes on to distinguish individual fans of something from a fandom, which he defines as a **participatory culture** whose "members engage with a broad array of different media objects but who share traditions and practices built up over many years" (Jenkins, "Fandom" 16). A fan may be someone who clicks "like" on Facebook, but a fandom is a type of *community* consisting of fans who interact with one another in relation to a particular **text** or practice.

The key feature of fandom as described by Jenkins is that it is *participatory*, which means that fans act not only as media consumers, enjoying a given book or movie or TV series or band on their own, but interact with one another and are themselves *content creators* of media that engages **intertextually** with the **source text**—the fandom's focus. Fans in this sense don't just watch, read, look, or listen; they make and do things as a consequence of reading, watching, looking, or listening to a source text that they share with each other. Backing up slightly, a participatory culture, according to Jenkins, is one with:

1. Relatively low barriers to artistic expression and civic engagement
2. Strong support for creating and sharing one's creations
3. Some type of informal mentorship whereby what is known by the most experienced is passed along to novices
4. Members who believe their contributions matter
5. Members with a degree of social connection with one another (Jenkins et al. 3)

Members of participatory cultures interact with one another, share information, and create media content with more experienced members guiding newbies to some extent.

Fandom as a form of participatory culture takes a variety of shapes. It can involve media creation in the form of **fan fiction** (or fanfic), fan art, and fan videos (fanvids); it can involve performances such as **cosplay** and **filk** songs; and it involves interaction through forms including online groups, newsletters, conventions, meetings, and other interpersonal interactions. In the twenty-first century, the majority of fan creations are posted online as part of what Tisha Turk has described as a "gift economy" (Turk), which means they are made available or exchanged for free. Practically speaking, this avoids copyright entanglements but, beyond this, the gift economy is also a way to step outside processes of **commodification**—enjoyment becomes the primary goal rather than profit.

> **YOUR TURN:** What forms of fandom are you familiar with? Do you participate in a fandom or other form of participatory culture? What is your perception of various types of fandom?

Fan Fiction

Fan fiction (or fanfic) consists of stories about fictional characters or a fictional world written by fans of a work or series. Fan fiction is thus a process of developing and extending an existing fictional world—it is a form of appropriation or, in Henry Jenkins's terms, **textual poaching**, that uses established characters and/or an established world to develop new stories (see Jenkins, *Textual Poachers*). As such, it is inherently intertextual. As a contemporary phenomenon, fanfic arguably finds its basis in *Star Trek* fandom. Beginning in the 1960s, fans of the program began writing their own stories using the series's characters and settings. Long ago in those pre-Internet days of yore, these stories were included in *fanzines*, non-professional and non-official print publications, which were mailed to other fans and circulated at conventions. Interestingly, as

Francesca Coppa has written, the vast majority of *Star Trek* fanfic was written by women—90 per cent of it by 1973 (Coppa). While some of these stories created new plotlines for Captain Kirk (William Shatner), First Officer Spock (Leonard Nimoy), Dr. McCoy (DeForest Kelley), Lieutenant Uhura (Nichelle Nichols), and the rest of the characters in keeping with the format of established plotlines, others reimagined the relationships between the characters, depicting more explicit sexual encounters than the television series would permit or inventing same-sex romances between Kirk and Spock and/or other characters. The fanfic practice of reassigning sexual orientation to characters **coded** as heterosexual and pairing them in same-sex relationships has come to be referred to as *slash* fic, from the diagonal line used to separate the names, as in Kirk/Spock (pronounced Kirk slash Spock). While slash originally referred to homosexual pairings of either **sex**, male/male stories became so numerous that a separate category, *femmeslash*, was coined for female/female stories. Other works of fanfic (*Star Trek*-related and otherwise) may develop minor characters more fully or introduce new ones.

> **YOUR TURN**: Why do you think women would have been so involved in developing *Star Trek* fanfic? What possibilities does fanfic present for expanding on or *reimagining* an existing narrative?

Creators of **fanfic** are inevitably in the position of negotiating between the twin polarities of **canon** and **headcanon**. Canon—which comes from the idea of a list of books accepted as genuine and authoritative (e.g., the "Western canon" of "essential" books)—refers to what fans generally agree "actually" happens in a given work. Harry Potter goes to Hogwarts, for example, Darth Vader is Luke's father in *Star Wars*, and Lord Walder plots a massacre on *Game of Thrones*. Headcanon, in contrast, is a fan's creation, which can involve creating a backstory for a character, giving characters new habits or inclinations, altering the relationships between characters, and so on. Sometimes, headcanon may directly contradict canon; other times, headcanon teases out a subtext present or suggested by canon. If headcanon becomes generally accepted by fans, it can evolve into *fanon*—commonly accepted traits or beliefs that started in fanfic. Alternatively, contradictory or inadvertent headcanon may be rejected (sometimes harshly) by fans. And then there is always the possibility of being delightfully *Jossed*, which occurs when a fan creates an explanation for a character's behavior in canon, only to have the text's creator come back and explain it in a different way later on—writer/director Joss Whedon is famous for this, hence the term Jossed.

Whereas early **fanfic** was distributed via *fanzines*, contemporary fanfic is primarily circulated online on sites devoted to fanfic and through groups associated with particular media properties. Not surprisingly, the volume of fanfic associated with a given work maps onto overall popularity, so there are significant quantities, for example, of *Harry Potter*, *Twilight*, and *Lord of the Rings* fanfic. Some fan communities, however, such as those associated with Joss Whedon's creations or the various *Star Trek* series, have been more prolific in this respect than others.

Fan Art and Fanvids

Fan art, like fanfic, is the creative extension of an existing fictional universe on the part of fans and, as with fanfic, fan art is typically neither commissioned nor licensed by the creators and copyright holders of the work from which fan art is derived. Fan art can take many forms ranging from paintings and drawings of characters to sophisticated computer-generated animations, maps, banners, and collages. Fan art can hew closely to how a character or world is represented on screen, illustrated in a book, or described in a text, or can seek to reimagine the appearance of a character, scene, or world—and, as with fanfic, fan art can depict alternate universes, plucking characters from their settings in the source text and placing them into entirely new ones. Fan art can also fill in details left ambiguous in a text, such as how the narrator of the long-running podcast, *Welcome to Night Vale*, looks.

Harry Potter *Fan Art by Kate Carleton, katecarleton–illustrations.com*

Fanvids are somewhat different from **fanfic** and fan art in that creators **remix** existing footage by editing together clips and scenes from movies and TV shows. These are then typically set to music (Henry Jenkins discusses, for example, a *Star Trek* fanvid set to Nine Inch Nails's song "Closer"; see Jenkins, "How to Watch") and uploaded to a streaming platform such as YouTube. Fanvids can function as tributes to a character or source text—for example, choreographing Deadpool to Fall Out Boy or mixing together the most touching moments from Robin Williams's career—and end up feeling like movie trailers or Academy Award retrospectives; alternatively, they can be more comedic, can draw out a subtext present in the source text (often a romantic one), or can in the way of fanfic suggest a new inclination through clever editing.

Fan Performance: Cosplay and Filk

Cosplay, which is a shortened form of costume play, is a kind of fandom performance in which participants dress up as specific characters from a source text. Cosplay, of course, is not new. Costumes have been associated with Carnival events such as Mardi Gras, as well as with holidays such as Halloween and events such as masquerade balls, for millennia. Contemporary fandom cosplay, however, arguably finds its roots most directly in the practice of fans dressing up as characters at science fiction conventions (or cons) (see Raymond). *Star Trek* conventions, for example, have featured cosplay since their beginnings in 1969. Cosplay as an aspect of fandom—as with fandom more generally—has experienced rapid growth since the 1990s and is now a common feature of fan conventions in general, some of which involve cosplay contests, as well as on social media. Tangential to science fiction and fantasy, and unusual,

Elder Scrolls Cosplay

if not unique, in relation to cinema, cosplay has formed a central part of *Rocky Horror Picture Show* fandom since fans began dressing up for showings in the late 1970s (see Weinstock); and, although participants might not recognize it as such, cosplay forms a visible component of sports fandom, with some fans wearing costumes and/or body paint to events—fans of the Oakland Raiders in particular were notable for their cosplay enthusiasm (see Silver).

Rather than dressing up, filk involves singing; filk is a **genre** of folk music generated by fans of fantasy, science fiction, and horror. Or, as Jeff Suwak puts it in a light-hearted overview, "Filk is where music and science-fiction-and-fantasy geekery collide" (Suwak). Filk music often takes an existing song and alters the lyrics—Leslie Fish's "Banned From Argo" is an original composition from 1977 written in a blue grass style that pokes fun at (you guessed it) *Star Trek* as it weaves a silly story about the bawdy hijinks of the *Enterprise*'s crew on shore leave. Filk music—the name of which finds its origins in a typo that caught on (see Gold)—originated in late night singing at science fiction cons (presumably with appropriate libations), and then, as cons associated with science fiction, fantasy, comics, and gaming gained prominence in the 1970s and 1980s, became incorporated as a more formal part of such events. Filk can often be playful and bawdy, offering light-hearted send-ups of its source texts, fans, and even of filk itself; however, it can also treat its subject seriously.

> **YOUR TURN:** If you were to compose a piece of fanfic, fan art, fanvid, or filk, what source text (book, film, TV show, etc.) would serve as basis and why?

Fan Community

Whether or not someone creates fan fiction, fan art, or fanvids, dresses up in a costume, or sings filk music, what distinguishes being part of a fandom from simply being a fan is the sense of participating together with like-minded others as part of a community with a shared focus. Fan interaction is central to fandom as a participatory culture, and social networks among fans allow them to express themselves in ways that may run contrary to conventions governing social interaction and self-presentation in other venues; put differently, you may not be able to dress as Harley Quinn or Thor or Hell Boy for work but, if you do it well at a comics, gaming, or fantasy/science fiction con, your efforts will be applauded. Not surprisingly, fandom as a popular culture phenomenon has expanded greatly in the age of the Internet and, as a consequence, has been normalized relative to its perception pre-Internet, when participation was often stigmatized as excessively nerdish and possibly deviant.

Harley Quinn Flash Mob, DragonCon 2019. Photographer: David Samsky. Used by Permission

Jenkins also proposes that participatory fandom can serve as a form of cultural critique through "which fans may articulate their specific concerns about sexuality, **gender**, racism, colonialism, militarism, and forced conformity" (*Textual Poachers* 283). On the one hand, this critique may come through embracing a set of values or behaviors present in the source text that are at odds with social norms. *Star Trek*, for example, was famously progressive with its casting of a racially diverse crew for the starship *USS Enterprise*, while *The Rocky Horror Picture Show* was transgressive in relation to 1970s understandings of "proper" sexuality, and fans who embrace these values show their resistance to conservative ideas regarding race, gender, and sexuality. On the other hand, participatory fandom can also critique the source text. When **fanfic** creates plotlines giving more space to autonomous female characters for example, or introduces characters of color where none was originally present, or when slash fiction adds same-sex eroticism to a source text in which it is absent (at least on the surface), fans, even as they celebrate a narrative that gives them pleasure, are expressing their personal desires for what they'd like to see in the text, in some cases highlighting the source text's limitations when it comes to depicting diversity. Fan creations in this way can function not only as homages to a beloved source text, but also as a gentle slap on the wrist, calling attention to ways that the source text fails to reflect the world certain fans would like to see.

It is important to add that, while participatory fandom can be enjoyable and exciting, fandom is not insulated or immune from social hierarchies or the kinds of sexism and discrimination that unfortunately exist within the broader **culture**. Kristina Busse has addressed what she refers to as "border policing" within fandom (Busse) and Lore Sjöberg has designed, somewhat tongue-in-cheek, a chart depicting what he calls the "Geek Hierarchy," which determines what level of fan investment is acceptable and what is excessive. At the very bottom of the list are "people who write erotic versions of *Star Trek* where all the characters are furries. Like Kirk is an ocelot or something and they put a furry version of themselves as the star of the story." Less humorously, sexism and racism within fandom have often been noted—see, for example, Hines and Pande.

Interpreting Fandom

So what are you fan of? Critical analysis of fandom is complicated by the fact that fandom encompasses such a broad range of objects and practices. However, as with other pop culture media, fandom shouldn't be addressed in the abstract. One always needs to ground one's analysis in specific examples. The place to start then is with something in particular: specific examples of fan fiction or fan art, fanvids or filk songs, particular fan websites or cons, examples of cosplay, and so on. These will be your **primary texts** and are what will allow you to build larger arguments, although one also must be careful about deriving large generalizations on the basis of a limited set of examples. We start therefore, as in the other chapters of this textbook, with the thing itself.

Qualities

- What is this thing before me? Is it a song or video or social media site? If so, the questions included as part of the units in this textbook on popular music, film/TV, and social media may apply.
- Is it a piece of fan art? If so, who or what is represented? What medium is it in? How would you characterize the style? Is it black and white or in color? Professional looking or less polished?
- If it is cosplay, who or what is represented by the costume? How would you describe the costume?
- If it is a convention or other event, what is its nature and purpose? Where and when is it held? Who attends? Is it big or small? What kinds of meetings and activities take place?

Intertextuality

As outlined above, fandom is by nature inherently intertextual. Fans are always fans *of something*, so objects and practices are always guided by or in relation to the source text. Among the questions one may ask, therefore, are the following:

- What source text is referenced by the fan creation or activity? Of what genre is it a part? To what extend is it considered a representative or anomalous example of its genre? What sets the source text apart from other, similar works?
- To what extent does the fan creation or activity adhere to canon? That is, does the creation or activity attempt to replicate or keep within established confines of the source text or does it innovate? If it departs from canon, in what ways does it do so?
- Thinking **paradigmatically**, how does a fan creation or performance compare to other, similar creations or performances?
- Thinking **syntagmatically**, what is the context for the fan creation or activity? Where is it included, presented, uploaded, or performed? What else is going on around it?
- Who is the creator or performer of the fan text?
- Who is the intended audience for the creation or performance? What background knowledge does it assume on the part of its audience? How was the creation or performance received by its intended audience? If applicable, how has the creation or performance been received by a more general audience?
- Thinking **diachronically**, how does a fan creation or performance fit into a particular history? This may be the history of fandom of a particular source text; the history of a particular type of fandom activity or creation; the history of a particular medium; the history of a particular event, place, or group; and so on.

Ideology

Here is where we try to decide what **messages** are conveyed through fan activity and creations and the ways in which such ideas either reinforce or challenge accepted ways of thinking in a particular time and place. As with the other media addressed in this textbook, the various approaches outlined in chapter 3 in the **critical theory** toolbox can be utilized to bring into focus particular messages concerning race, gender, sexual orientation, class, age, ability, and so on. The added twist here is the intertextual aspect of fandom. In some cases, fan practice or creation will reinforce **ideological** messages present in the source text through repetition; in other cases, fan practice will intentionally or unintentionally critique ideological messages in the source text—fan practices and creations in this way can themselves be forms of criticism, highlighting racism, sexism, homophobia, and other forms of discrimination present in the source text. And, as always, both source texts and fan creations and practices can send mixed or ambiguous messages.

- What messages does the fan creation, practice, or event **encode** concerning race and ethnicity, gender and sexuality, age, physical ability and body type, class, and so on, and how are these messages encoded?
- What values, principles and/or standards of behavior does the fan practice encode and how are these messages encoded? Put differently, what does the fan creation, event, or activity tell us about how we should act, what we should do, and how we should live?
- In what ways does the fan creation or activity reinforce ideological messages present in the source text? In what ways does it intentionally or unintentionally critique or revise ideological messages present in the source text?

Sample Essay

In the following excerpted sample essay, Cait Coker explores the phenomenon of slash fan fiction in relation to the 2009 *Star Trek* **reboot** film, simply titled *Star Trek*.

Everybody's Bi in the Future: Constructing Sexuality in the *Star Trek* Reboot Fandom

Cait Coker

Star Trek fandom is notorious as one of the early progenitors of slash fiction—homoerotic romances primarily written by and for women—since Gene Roddenberry, the creator of the show and ever open to opportunities for promotion, encouraged any and all fan writing during the decade the franchise was off the air. He even coyly worked in some references to the genre in his own novelization of the first *Star Trek* feature film (see Roddenberry 6–7). The body of Trek slash literature, particularly K/S or Kirk/Spock, published from the 1970s to the current day is thus vast indeed, particularly in comparison to the "gen" or general stories which focus on traditional adventure tales and the smaller "het" fandoms comprising heterosexual romances.

When the eleventh *Star Trek* film debuted in 2009, "rebooting" what many considered to be a stale franchise, the online *Star Trek* fandom rebooted as well. It immediately attracted a new generation of writers, some of whom were familiar with the original series but many of whom were not. Thus, there were essentially two massive groups of new authors at work: a group with an intimate knowledge of *Star Trek* history, canon, and fanon, and a group of "newbies" who were either writing around the events of the 2009 film or were requesting help from older fans so they could tell new stories, but do so in a way that would be essentially recognized as "correct." Online communities spontaneously grew and developed to meet the needs for both sets of fans, including extensive support networks to share resources such as episode guides focusing on particular characters, timelines, and various Question & Answer forums.

Star Trek XI—the 2009 reboot—was the first of three films that created a loose trilogy referred to as the Kelvin universe in licensed works; early on it was referred to in fandom both as "Reboot" and as "AOS" for "Alternative Original Series" (or sometimes more literally as "Abrams's Original Series"). The Kelvin universe is also detailed further in two multi-issue monthly comics series, Star Trek Ongoing and Star Trek: Boldly Go, as well as a series of young adult novels. The series is structured around a shift in the timeline that occurs when Nero, a Romulan (one of Star Trek's alien races) from the twenty-fourth century, travels back in time over a century and a half and embarks on a plan to destroy the Federation. His ship's disruptive entry into the new timeline begins with the destruction of the U.S.S. Kelvin, setting in motion a series of events that will make Starfleet a more militarized entity, and changing the lives of all of the familiar characters from the original television series. The first film follows the young adulthoods of a very different Jim Kirk and Spock, their entry into Starfleet Academy and encounters with familiar characters and crew, and their first adventures. Eventually they are met by an elderly Spock, sometimes referred to as Spock Prime as he comes from the "Prime" or original series universe in pursuit of Nero.

Of primary interest to many fan writers were the romantic and sexual lives of the main Star Trek characters, particularly the four main protagonists of the new film: Captain Kirk, Commander Spock, Doctor McCoy, and Lieutenant Uhura. As the 2009 film also included a romantic subplot between Spock and Uhura, as well as several encounters that played off the original Kirk's womanizing for comedic effect, this rewriting of the characters by the fans functioned less as a traditional remediation for missing elements than as an expansion and explication on those elements that were already present. This study will thus focus on how Reboot fandom has adopted and adapted the **tropes** of original series fandom and added new genres to the body of Star Trek fan literature.

Rebooting Sexuality

Considering that, to date, the only source texts for Reboot fandom are the film and a handful of novels, much of Reboot fanfiction focuses on the Academy era—the period of time in which all of the characters are at Starfleet Academy together which is skirted over within the movie and in which both Kirk and McCoy and Spock and Uhura develop their relationships. Unlike the novels, the fan stories tend to focus less on the antagonistic elements of the main characters (particularly those of Kirk and Uhura) and strengthen the importance of minor characters. For instance, the green-skinned Orion Gaila, who appears for a single scene (and an outtake) in the movie and just as briefly in the franchise volumes, features regularly in fanfiction as a member of the ensemble and as the protagon- ist of her own stories [see Fig. 10.1]. In some cases, she is the romantic interest of the other characters; in most, she is a friend and confidant. As one of the few female characters, her popularity is further enhanced by the fact that the very scarcity of information about her provides the audi- ence with a *tabula rasa* for their imaginations: she can become whatever they need her to be.

Fig. 10.1 Gaila

In contrast, the main characters of *Star Trek* have nearly fifty years of information that the audience can draw on for their own creations. Thus,

Reboot fandom draws much of its characterization information from earlier source material. For example, despite the displacement of the timelines, fandom has chosen to assume that the divorce McCoy references in the film is to his original series (hereafter, TOS) wife Jocelyn Darnell (later Treadway) and that they have a young daughter, Joanna, both of whom only appear in the franchise novels (see, for example, the novels *Shadow on the Sun* by Michael Jan Friedman and *Crisis on Centaurus* by Brad Ferguson). Kirk's status as a survivor of the genocide on Tarsus IV, as referenced in the TOS episode "The Conscience of the King," has also played a larger role in Reboot fandom as a trope of unrepentantly dark stories (also known as darkfic), emphasizing his nature as a survivor and often taking a much darker spin on both the events and the character. Further, Kirk's characterization in Reboot fic is perhaps the most distant from his original incarnation, not least because of his shift from presumed default heterosexuality to a presumed default omnisexuality. In his first scene in the film, Jim Kirk, not yet in Starfleet, is hitting on Uhura in a bar. Uhura, herself a new cadet, is unimpressed with the flirtatious townie, and she shoots him down by saying she thought he was just "some dumb hick who only had sex with farm animals." To her surprise—and that of the audience—Kirk just smirks and declares, "Well. Not *only*." Uhura appreciatively laughs in surprise, and thus were a thousand tales of Kirk's sexual exploits launched.

In Alan Dean Foster's novelization of the film, written based on early scripts, Kirk's escapades are again referred to as Uhura, having discovered Gaila and Kirk in a compromising position, berates her in Orion: "You know he's been through half the cadet corps since he got here? There are rumors that not all of them were humanoid" (Foster 64). To her surprise, Kirk responds in the same language before shifting to English: "And hardly *half*. You're rounding up that number. Not that I'm not flattered, mind.... And," he added as he made his exit, "they were *all* humanoid—I think" (Foster 65). In addition to providing comedic moments, these conversations construct a partial view of canonical sexual morality. In both the film and books, Kirk is depicted as essentially a cheerful manslut, happily on the prowl, as opposed to the more calculated womanizer of TOS. Interestingly, this change was greeted positively by viewers; many women, both fans and non-fans, have remarked to me that they "couldn't stand old Kirk" but they quite liked new Kirk for this reason. On the other hand, in the book Uhura is essentially attempting to "slut-shame" Kirk, not only for the (presumably high) number of partners he has had but for his *choice* of partners—not just aliens but also those aliens who are non-humanoid in appearance. Kirk's choice of defense—he *thinks* they were all humanoids—intimates an acceptance of the cultural preference for humanoids but also implies that there is the possibility for error in his history, and that that error wouldn't bother him. In other words, in the future people can possibly have humanoid panic instead of gay panic, but Kirk is unlikely to be a victim of this problem. Reboot Kirk is thus, to all intents and purposes, openly queer.

Further, two of the main conventions of Reboot fanfiction directly involve a **queered** Kirk. The first is a trope that involves the assumption of TOS Kirk/Spock (K/S) as a form of canon. In this trope, the elder Spock Prime, having succeeded in pushing the alternate Kirk and Spock together as a team, tries to encourage their romantic involvement as well. Particularly in the Kirk/McCoy fandom, this trope allows the writer to directly address for themselves the differences between the two fandoms and the histories therein. In a popular Reboot story by ceres_libera entitled "Not On My Watch," the elder Spock confronts the younger incarnation of McCoy as he prepares for the new five-year mission. After a series of interchanges with the increasingly irritated doctor, who only wants to get his supply manifest completed before they ship out, it turns out that Spock Prime wants to warn McCoy that his relationship with Kirk cannot last because of the fated love between Kirk and Spock.

McCoy points out that the younger Spock has already bonded with Uhura, and moreover, that Kirk is quite literally not the same man as the one Spock had known: blue eyes instead of hazel and possessed of a compromised immune system prone to allergies (resulting from his premature birth in space), as well as a host of physical and emotional scars stemming from an abusive childhood. The story concludes with the elder Spock's regretful acceptance that the new universe is truly *not* like that which he came from.

The second convention is more of a genre unto itself: the modern-day alternate universe (AU). Modern-day AUs make up a significant proportion of Reboot fandom, particularly in the Kirk/McCoy faction. In some cases, they can be read as an attempt to push Reboot slash into more of what we would consider genuine queer literature through writing the characters as our contemporaries; the topics of homophobia, gay pride, and the choices of living in the closet or "out" are all discussed. The genre is particularly notable considering there is no (known) equivalent in TOS fandom; TOS stories, even AUs, primarily revolved around the future rather than the present. Though many Reboot stories do take place during the *Enterprise*'s vaunted five-year mission and beyond, many take place in the here and now. For instance, lindmere's "Tallulah Falls" describes the life of a closeted Dr. McCoy, at least until he happens to meet actor Jim Kirk who is shooting a film locally. A series of plot twists lands Kirk temporarily staying with McCoy, and to his surprise, Kirk quickly discovers McCoy's real preferences.

The Evolution of a Genre

Slash or other noncanonically romantic fiction is predominantly about the readers' expectations of a romance. Those elements from the original texts—e.g., the physical closeness of actors onscreen or emotionally charged dialogue exchanges—become slashed when the viewer sees them as romantic rather than friendly or merely empathic. Indeed, the ability to "see" homoerotic elements and contents within the source texts presupposes a queer reading of the original. Wendy Pearson, in her groundbreaking essay of **queer theory** "Alien Cryptographies: The View from Queer," notes that cultural constructions of visibility are predominantly contextual. She writes that queer readings

> may set out either to reveal or to recuperate what is already in some sense a queer text, usually a product of a history in which writing as

a gay man or a lesbian was impossible or dangerous. Such queer readings also provide alternative understandings of texts that cannot be labeled gay or lesbian, since those subject positions were not available to their creators. (Pearson 25)

To fans, *Star Trek* becomes a queer text because of the strength of viewers' queered readings of it as such. Kirk's response of "not only" to Uhura's query about sex with farm animals, by virtue of not being a direct "no," provides the possibility of non-heteronormative sex and thus queers him to those viewers who do not *see* this as a profound negative. Similarly, while the film's creative team will not comment directly on or may not even themselves *see* the queer aspects of the movie's text, the reading is still extant and functions as such. The *Star Trek* franchise undoubtedly wants to maintain its designation of "family-friendly" (read: not overtly sexual, not gory, not profane) and has not successfully dwelled on controversial topics in its storylines since the original series of the 1960s. It will be interesting to see whether the franchise will ever have an "out" gay character despite two of its actors being publicly gay themselves. Because the contemporary writers cannot or will not confirm or condone queer readings, there is tension between the "real" (official) authors and the fan authors. This is the point at which queer readings become a tool not just of entertainment but, as amply demonstrated, a form of critique.

Works Cited in the Sample Essay

Ceres_Libera. "Not On My Watch." May 2010 (reposted to Archive of Our Own [AO3] December 2011), https://archiveofourown.org/works/307321.

Ferguson, Brad. *Crisis on Centaurus*. Star Trek, 1986.

Foster, Alan Dean. *Star Trek*. Simon & Schuster, 2009.

Friedman, Michael Jan. *Shadows on the Sun*. Star Trek, 1994.

lindmere. "Tallulah Falls." November 2010 (reposted to AO3 January 2012), https://archiveofourown.org/works/319643.

Pearson, Wendy Gay. "Alien Cryptographies: The View from Queer." *Queer Universes: Sexualities in Science Fiction*, edited by Wendy Gay Pearson, Veronica Hollinger, and Joan Gordon, Liverpool UP, 2008, pp. 14–38.

Roddenberry, Gene. *Star Trek The Motion Picture: A Novel*. Simon & Schuster, 1979.

Suggested Assignments

1. Create a reflective essay considering your own fan activity. Are you part of a fandom? In what ways do you participate? Why do you do it? What problems or issues have you noted within the fan community?

2. Create your own work of fanfic, fan art, fanvid, or filk music and then append an "artist's statement" explaining your intentions with the work.

3. Develop a research essay exploring the history of a particular fandom and/or the ways it is a participatory culture.

4. Perform a close reading of a fan production that analyzes its relationship to its source text. You may wish to focus on how the fan production replicates or critiques the source text's messages concerning one or more issues such as gender, sexuality, race, class, and so on.

Works Cited in the Chapter

Busse, Kristina. "Geek Hierarchies, Boundary Policing, and the Gendering of the Good Fan." *Participations: Journal of Audience & Reception Studies*, vol. 10, no. 1, May 2013, pp. 73–91.

Coker, Cait. "Everybody's Bi in the Future: Constructing Sexuality in the *Star Trek* Reboot Fandom." *Fandom Studies*, vol. 3, no. 2, 2015, pp. 195–210.

Coppa, Francesca. "An Archive of Our Own." In *Fic: Why Fanfiction Is Taking Over the World*, edited by Anne Elizabeth Jamison. Dallas, Texas: BenBella Books Inc., 2013, pp. 302–08.

Gold, Lee. "An Egocentric and Convoluted History of Early Filk and Filking." *The Fanac Fan History Project*, 1977, http://www.fanac.org/ Fan_Histories/filkhist.html.

Hines, Jim C. "Don't Look Away: Fighting Sexual Harassment in the Scifi/Fantasy Community." *Gizmodo*, 29 Aug. 2016, https://io9.gizmodo.com/ dont-look-away-fighting-sexual-harassment-in-the-scifi-1785704207.

Jenkins, Henry. "Fandom, Negotiation, and Participatory Culture." *A Companion to Media Fandom and Fan Studies*, edited by Paul Booth, 1st ed., John Wiley & Sons Inc., 2018, pp. 13–26.

——. "How to Watch a Fan-Vid." *Henry Jenkins: Confessions of an Aca-Fan*, 17 Sep. 2006, http://henryjenkins.org/2006/09/how_to_ watch_a_fanvid.html.

——. Textual Poachers: *Television Fans & Participatory Culture*. Routledge, 1992.

Jenkins, Henry, et al. *Confronting the Challenges of Participatory Culture: Media Education for the 21st Century*. The John D. and Catherine T. MacArthur Foundation, 2006, https://archive.nwp.org/cs/public/ download/nwp_file/10932/Confronting_the_Challenges_of_ Participatory_Culture.pdf?x-r=pcfile_d.

Pande, Rukmini. *Squee from the Margins: Fandom and Race*. University of Iowa Press, 2018.

Raymond, Adam K. "75 Years of Capes and Face Paint: A History of Cosplay." *Yahoo Movies*, 24 July 2014, https://www.yahoo.com/ entertainment/75-years-of-capes-and-face-paint-a-history-of- cosplay-92666923267.html.

Silver, Jake. "ESPN the Magazine Shows Iconic Oakland Raiders Fans in and out of Costume." *Bleacher Report*, 10 Oct. 2013, https:// bleacherreport.com/articles/1806524-espn-the-magazine-shows- iconic-oakland-raiders-fans-in-and-out-of-costume.

Sjöberg, Lore. "Geek Hierarchy." Brunching Shuttlecocks, 2002.

Suwak, Jeff. "Filk Combines Music and Fantasy with Geekery." *Rawckus Magazine*, 9 Feb. 2017, http://www.rawckus.com/filk-combines-music-and-fantasy-with-geekery/.

Turk, Tisha. "Fan Work: Labor, Worth, and Participation in Fandom's Gift Economy." *Fandom and/as Labor*, edited by Mel Stanfill and Megan Condis, special issue of *Transformative Works and Cultures,* no. 15, 2002, https://doi.org/10.3983/twc.2014.0518.

Weinstock, Jeffrey Andrew. *The Rocky Horror Picture Show*. Wallflower Press, 2007.

Additional Suggested Reading

Booth, Paul. *Digital Fandom 2.0: New Media Studies.* 2nd ed., Peter Lang, Inc., 2016.

—— . *Playing Fans: Negotiating Fandom and Media in the Digital Age.* University of Iowa Press, 2015.

Click, Melissa A. *The Routledge Companion to Media Fandom*. Routledge, 2020.

Duffett, Mark. *Understanding Fandom: An Introduction to the Study of Media Fan Culture.* Bloomsbury, 2013.

Gray, Jonathan, Cornel Sandvoss, and C. Lee Harrington, editors. *Fandom: Identities and Communities in a Mediated World.* 2nd ed., New York UP, 2017.

Jamison, Anne. *Fic: Why Fanfiction Is Taking Over the World.* Smart Pop, 2013.

CHAPTER 11

A FINAL ASSIGNMENT

This book has provided a framework for thinking about different forms of popular culture that finds its basis in the asking of questions. We start with questions about the thing itself and its qualities. From there, we consider its **intertextual** relations including its histories and contexts. And we conclude by asking questions about the **ideological messages** the object or practice **encodes** for socially situated consumers to **decode**.

Popular culture, however, comes in many different forms and this book has only surveyed a handful of them. As a final project, consider how you could extend the approach adopted here to a different popular form or subcategory. What questions would you ask to start thinking about Disney, for example, or advertising? What about animation or sports or even food? Using the chapters in this book as a template, develop a set of enabling questions that could serve as a starting point. Or, if you are feeling ambitious, by yourself or as part of a group, develop your own unit.

GLOSSARY

ADAPTATION. The translation of a **text** from one medium into another; for example, the movie version of a theme park ride or the novelization of a film.

AFFECT. As a noun, the psychological response something evokes.

AFFORDANCE. A quality or property of an object or medium that defines it and its possible uses.

ALIENATION. In Marxist theory, the **proletariat**'s sense of estrangement from the products of their own labor and, indeed, from the world at large as a consequence of being deprived of autonomy.

ALLUSION. An indirect reference to something; e.g., "these are not the droids you are looking for" is an allusion to *Star Wars*.

ARTICULATION. From **hegemony theory**. The process by which a person or group with specific interests connects itself to something else (a person, group, movement, concept, etc.) to achieve its goals.

ARTISANAL. An adjective describing something made in a traditional or non-mechanical way.

AUTHENTICITY. In relation to cultural practices, the sincere expression of ability, belief, and/or personality. As opposed to fakery or affectation.

AUTHORIAL INTENT. What the **encoder** of a **message** intends **decoders** of that message to understand.

AVANT-GARDE. The "cutting edge" of a particular medium; experimental creations that often challenge conventional ways of thinking and run contrary to established tastes.

AVATAR. An **icon** or image that represents a particular person in gaming or online media.

BASE. In Marxist economic theory, the economic organization of a society, i.e., its **mode of production**. The base shapes the **superstructure**.

BOURGEOISIE. From Marxist theory, the social class that owns most of society's wealth and its **means of production**.

CANON. A list of works accepted as being of the highest quality, e.g., the "literary canon." In relation to **fandom**, what fans agree actually happened in a **source text**. This is as opposed to **headcanon**.

CAPITALISM. An economic **mode of production** in which the **means of production** are privately owned rather than collectively owned by the state.

CHERRY-PICKING. The process of selecting examples that support one's position while omitting consideration of those that do not.

CLASS STRUGGLE. In Marxist theory, the contest between **bourgeoisie** and the **proletariat** for power.

CLOSURE. In relation to comics, the process by which readers of comics connect words and images within individual panels, and connect panels to each other.

CODE. As defined by John Fiske, a rule-governed system of signs, whose rules and conventions are shared by members of a culture, and which is used to generate and circulate meanings in and for that culture. See also **Ideological Codes**, **Social Codes**, **Technical Codes**, and **Conventional Representational Codes**.

CODE SWITCHING. The practice of alternating between two or more languages or language variants in conversation.

COLLECTIVE INTELLIGENCE. Associated with **participatory culture**, the ways in which consumers of media interact with one another by discussing the media they've consumed and collectively arriving at shared understandings.

COMMODIFICATION. The process of transforming something into a **commodity**.

COMMODITY. Anything that can be bought and sold.

COMMUNISM. An economic system in which the **means of production** are collectively owned and private property does not exist.

COMPROMISE EQUILIBRIUM. From **hegemony theory**, the ways dominant groups defuse resistance by incorporating and redeploying it in a way that serves the interests of the **dominant culture**.

CONFIRMATION BIAS. The tendency to favor or accept information that supports one's already-held beliefs or values.

CONGEALED IDEOLOGY. A way of expressing how **material practices** and objects reflect and participate in reinforcing **ideological** beliefs.

CONNOTATION. A sign's secondary, culturally specific relations or associations; contrasted with **denotative** (literal) meaning.

CONSTRUCTIVISM. The position in relation to the **sex / gender** debate that states how biological sex is expressed is directed entirely by cultural assumptions and expectations rather than some essence of masculinity or femininity.

CONVENTIONAL REPRESENTATIONAL CODES. As discussed by John Fiske, familiar conventions of narrative shaped by elements such as character, narrative, dialogue, action, and setting.

CONVERGENCE CULTURE. The way twenty-first-century technologies combine tasks and activities that previously were distributed among discrete systems, and the ways consumers of media content interact with that content and each other.

COSPLAY. Short for costume play and associated with **fandom**; the practice of dressing up as a character from a **source text**, such as a movie, novel, or video game.

CRITICAL RACE THEORY. An approach to culture that focuses on the ways in which racism is deeply entrenched in social structures including the law.

CRITICAL THEORY. Reflective approaches to cultural practices and artifacts that seek to unmask **ideology** that naturalizes oppression.

CRITICISM. The application of a form of critical theory to a specific object of inquiry.

CULTURAL APPROPRIATION. The adoption of the practices or customs of one group by members of another. Often, but not always, the appropriator is part of the **dominant culture**.

CULTURAL STUDIES. An expansive interdisciplinary field of study that investigates the things that people make and do in particular times and places in relation to broader systems of power.

CULTURE. The things that people make and do that convey meaning in a particular time and place.

CULTURE INDUSTRY. The way in which members of the **Frankfurt School** described popular culture, presenting it as a kind of factory producing standardized **commodities**.

DECODING. The process of interpreting a **message**.

DEEPFAKE. The convincing manipulation of images, audio, and/or video content using sophisticated technology.

DENOTATION. The most basic or literal meaning of a **sign**; a sign's dictionary definition.

DIACHRONIC. Literally "across time"; a study that traces the evolution or development of something across a period of time.

DIEGETIC SOUND. Sound that exists within the world of a fictional work; contrasted with **non-diegetic sound**.

DISABILITY STUDIES. An interdisciplinary field of study that focuses on the definitions and consequences of disability.

DOMINANT CULTURE. The ideological beliefs that prevail in a particular time and place and those who subscribe to and benefit from those beliefs.

DOMINANT / HEGEMONIC POSITION. The **decoding** of a **message** as intended and adoption of the intended attitude in relation to the message.

ELITE CULTURE. Also referred to as **high culture**, the **material practices** of the upper class within a given culture.

ENCODING. The process of packaging a **message** to send to a recipient making use of the **affordances** of a particular medium.

ESSENTIALISM. The assumption that people naturally think and act in particular ways and are better or worse suited to particular avocations and activities because of their biological sex. Such thinking attributes an "essence" to men and women—something universal that defines what it means to be a man or woman; contrasted with **constructivism**.

ETHNIC STUDIES. An interdisciplinary field of study that focuses on race, ethnicity, and indigeneity.

FALSE NEEDS. Associated with the **Frankfurt School**'s critique of **capitalism**, desires created by the **culture industry** for commodities that suppress **real needs**.

FAN FICTION (or FanFic). Fiction written by fans of a particular **source text** involving aspects of that source text such as the characters or aspects of the source text's fictional world.

FANDOM. A collective term for the fans of a particular media property, e.g., *Star Trek* fandom or *Harry Potter* fandom.

FEMINIST THEORY AND CRITICISM. An interdisciplinary field of study that seeks to understand the nature of gender inequality through a focus on the social roles played by women in relation to men, how those roles have developed, and the forces that maintain them. Feminist theory and criticism attempts to identify and critique the mechanisms through which women have been discriminated against and controlled in **patriarchal** culture.

FILK. A **genre** of folk music generated by fans of fantasy, science fiction, and horror. Filk can be playful and bawdy, offering light-hearted send-ups of its **source texts**, fans, and even of filk itself; however, it can also treat its subject seriously.

FOLK CULTURE. The traditional practices and customs of a specific geographic region.

FRANKFURT SCHOOL. Associated initially with the Institute for Social Research at Goethe University in Frankfurt, a group of intellectuals who combined **Marxist theory** with other approaches to analyze culture with a focus on forms of social stratification and inequity.

FUZZY SET. A class or **paradigm** of objects with degrees or grades of membership. Objects plotted at the center of the fuzzy set most fully embody the character or essence of the paradigm.

GENDER. The cultural assumptions and expectations overlaid upon **sexed** bodies.

GENDER STUDIES. An interdisciplinary field of study that focuses on society. Gender studies serves as an umbrella category that can encompass women's studies, men's / masculinity studies, and sexuality studies.

GENRE. A category of artistic expression characterized by a particular content, form, or style such as folk music, detective novels, or action films.

GRAPHIC NOVEL. A novel presented in a comic-strip format.

HEADCANON. In **fan fiction**, a fan's personal contribution to **canon**. Headcanon can evolve into *fanon*: commonly accepted traits or beliefs that started in fanfic.

HEGEMONY. The ways a dominant group secures the consent of subordinate groups by making the ruling class's values and beliefs the norm for that society. **Ideological state apparatuses (ISAs)** play a central role in this process.

HIGH CULTURE. See **elite culture**.

HISTORICAL MATERIALISM. A philosophy of history associated with **Marxist theory** proposing that the material conditions of human society provide the impetus for social change. History from this perspective is not driven by ideals but the material conditions of people's existence.

ICONIC SIGN. A **sign** for which the **signifier** resembles the **signified**, e.g., a picture.

IDEOLOGICAL CODES. As discussed by John Fiske, rule-governed systems of signs, whose rules and conventions are shared by members of a culture, and which are used to generate and circulate beliefs and principles for that culture.

IDEOLOGICAL STATE APPARATUSES (ISAs). Developed by Marxist theorist Louis Althusser, institutions such as the family, the church, the media, and educational systems that convey and naturalize prevailing **ideological** beliefs; contrasted against **repressive state apparatuses (RSAs)**.

IDEOLOGY. The ideas, beliefs, and principles that structure a particular world view.

INDEXICAL SIGN. A **sign** in which the **signifier** is caused by the **signified**, e.g., smoke signifying fire.

INTERPELLATION. Within **Marxist critical theory**, the process by which **ideology**, reflected in and conveyed through **ideological state apparatuses** and **repressive state apparatuses**, constructs subjectivity.

INTERSECTIONALITY. The idea that forms of social stratification such as race, class, sexual orientation, age, disability, and gender do not exist separately but are interwoven together.

INTERTEXTUALITY. Literally "between texts," or the ways texts interact; how one text acquires meaning in light of its relations with other texts.

MARXIST THEORY AND CRITICISM. Based on the writings of Karl Marx, an approach to culture that focuses on social class and class struggle.

MASH-UP. A **text** that combines elements of several other texts, e.g., a work that combines Dracula, Frankenstein, and the Wolfman.

MASS CULTURE. Associated with the **Frankfurt School**, a dismissive way to refer to the **material practices** of the lower classes.

MATERIAL PRACTICES. The things that people make and do.

MEANS OF PRODUCTION. The raw materials, machines, and factories needed to produce goods and services.

MEME. In relation to the Internet, a picture, video, and/or phrase that spreads rapidly and can often be altered by Internet users in creative and humorous ways.

MESSAGE. An idea a sender wishes to convey to a recipient.

METATEXTUALITY. The ways in which a **text** refers to itself or the conventions of its genre.

MODE OF PRODUCTION. From **Marxist theory**, the way a society is organized to produce goods and services.

MOTIF. A recurring element in an artistic work.

MYTH. In the **semiotic** sense, a process whereby history is presented as nature. More specifically, myth is a second-order semiological system in which an existing **sign** becomes the **signifier** for a new sign.

NEGOTIATED POSITION. The **decoding** of a **message** as intended and then mixed acceptance and rejection of it.

NON-DIEGETIC SOUND. Sound represented as coming from a source outside the represented fictional world, such as a soundtrack; contrasted with **diegetic sound**.

OPPOSITIONAL POSITION. The **decoding** of a **message** as intended, but a rejection of the intended attitude toward it.

PARADIGM. A category of related **signs**.

PARODY. A work of art that imitates the style of another work, artist, or genre using exaggeration for comic effect.

PARTICIPATORY CULTURE. A model of media production and consumption in which private individuals play both roles.

PASTICHE. A work of art that imitates another work, artist, or period. Pastiche can also refer to a work of art composed of selections from several different works.

PATRIARCHAL CULTURE. Culture governed by a social system in which power is held by men by law and custom.

POLYSEMIC. Having multiple meanings.

POP CULTURE PARADOX. The tendency to dismiss the popular culture objects and practices central to our lives as trivial or meaningless.

POPULAR PRESS. Material written for the general public, as opposed to specialists.

POSTCOLONIAL THEORY AND CRITICISM. An interdisciplinary field of study that explores the influence of colonialism and its aftermath on both colonized people and colonizers.

PRIMARY TEXT. A direct source of original information that, in popular culture studies, is generally the focus of analysis; primary **texts** may be objects, events, or practices.

PROLETARIAT. From **Marxist theory**, the working class.

PSEUDO-INDIVIDUALIZATION. Associated most directly with Theodor Adorno's critique of popular music, refers to pop songs that differ from one another only in minor ways.

QUEER THEORY. An approach to literary and cultural studies that emphasizes the social construction and maintenance of ideas of normalcy and deviancy, especially in relation to **gender** and sexuality.

QUEERING. When used as a verb, to look at something in such a way that it become strange; often this involves questioning the foundations on which a belief or idea rests or reading a text or practice "against the grain."

REAL NEEDS. Associated with the **Frankfurt School**'s critique of the **culture industry**, real needs are psychological needs to be creative, independent, and autonomous. According to the Frankfurt School, **capitalism** substitutes **false needs** for real ones.

REBOOT. A new version of an established fictional universe.

REFERENT. The specific thing—object, idea, event, and so on—that a **sign** stands for or gestures toward.

REIMAGINING. A **remake** that alters the plot of the **source text** in substantial ways.

REMAKE. A new version of an older **text**.

REMIX. In reference to narrative, a **remake** from a different perspective, as in a familiar story told by a different character.

REPRESSIVE STATE APPARATUSES (RSAs). Means employed by the state, such as the police, military, and legal system, to compel adherence to existing rules directly through force or the threat of it; contrasted with **ideological state apparatuses (ISAs)**.

SEMIOTICS. The study of **signifying systems**.

SEX. Categorization based on anatomy and genetics; see also **gender**.

SIGN. A basic unit of meaning consisting of a **signifier** and a **signified**.

SIGNIFIED. A concept or idea; see also **signifier**.

SIGNIFIER. The way in which a particular concept or idea—the **signified**—is expressed.

SIGNIFYING PRACTICES. The things that people make and do that convey meaning.

SIGNIFYING SYSTEMS. Rule-governed systems of meaning production.

SOCIAL CODES. As defined by John Fiske, **codes** that circulate in "real life" in a particular time and place.

SOCIALISM. An economic **mode of production** in which private property is still permitted; however, the **means of production** are owned communally and managed by a democratically elected government.

SOURCE TEXT. Either a work being **adapted** into another medium or a focal point of a **fandom**; e.g., *Star Trek* is the source text for *Star Trek* fandom.

STATUS QUO. The existing social structure and state of affairs.

STRUCTURE OF FEELING. The ways in which shared generational experiences and common values shape subjective experience; the felt sense of what it means to exist in a particular time or place.

SUBCULTURAL CAPITAL. The resources a member of a **subculture** possesses that afford that person status within the subculture.

SUBCULTURE. A group that differentiates itself within the broader culture by having a set of beliefs and/or practices that are to some extent at variance with prevailing norms or beliefs.

SUPERSTRUCTURE. In **Marxist theory**, everything not directly having to do with production, including culture, ideology, and social and political institutions; contrasted with **base**.

SURPLUS VALUE. The difference between the amount raised through a sale of a **commodity** and the amount it cost the owner of that product to produce it; e.g., if it costs $1 to produce a commodity and it is sold for $10, the surplus value is $9.

SYMBOLIC SIGN. A **sign** in which the relationship between the **signified** and **signifier** is arbitrary and cemented by convention.

SYNCHRONIC. Meaning "at the same time"; focuses on something at a particular moment in time.

SYNTAGM. **Signifiers** connected by proximity.

TECHNICAL CODES. As discussed by John Fiske, how **messages** are packaged in relation to the **affordances** of a communicative medium. For film and television, this would include how camera shots and angles, lighting, editing, music, and sound shape messages.

TEXT. Anything that requires interpretation to be understood. This includes written works, but also objects, both natural and manmade, as well as practices.

TEXTUAL NOMADISM. As coined by Henry Jenkins, a process of interpretation in which meaning is shaped by **intertextual** associations.

TEXTUAL POACHING. As coined by Henry Jenkins, the process of appropriating aspects of a published work and redeploying them in new creative contexts. Textual poaching is associated in particular with **fandom** practices.

THEME. An important idea or **motif** in a work of art.

TOXIC MASCULINITY. The idea that certain cultural norms associated with being masculine such as the need to dominate others, the refusal to compromise, and the resolution of conflict through violence, have been harmful to women, children, society, and, indeed, men themselves.

TRANSMEDIALITY. The process of **adapting** content presented in one medium into others, as in the novelization of a film that itself is adapted from a videogame.

TROPE. A word or expression used in a figurative or metaphorical sense.

PERMISSIONS ACKNOWLEDGMENTS AND IMAGE CREDITS

Payne, Matthew Thomas, and Michael Fleisch. Chapter 20: "Borderlands: Capitalism" from *How to Play Video Games*, eds. Matthew Thomas Payne and Nina B. Huntemann. NY: New York University Press, 2019. Copyright © 2019 by New York University. All rights reserved. Reproduced with permission.

Fiske, John. Figure 1.1, "The codes of television," *Television Culture*. 2nd ed. Routledge, 2011. Copyright © 1987, 2011 John Fiske. p. 4. Reproduced by permission of Taylor and Francis Group, LLC, a division of Informa PLC, conveyed through Copyright Clearance Center, Inc.

Images

Page ix: iStock.com/drante

Page xi: iStock.com/Katya_Havok

Page xii: Top right: "Nude Descending a Staircase, no. 2," 1912, by Marcel Duchamp, Philadelphia Museum of Art. Top left: 18th century portrait, artist unknown. iStock.com/PhilipCacka

Page xv: Image by Jeffrey Weinstock.

Page xx: iStock.com/skynesher

Page 3: iStock.com/deagreez

Page 4: Mr. B, The Gentleman Rhymer. Used by permission.

Page 8: iStock.com/inarik

Page 11: iStock.com/chris-mueller

Page 12: iStock.com/LoweStock

Page 15: iStock.com/dmitryzubarev

Page 21: iStock.com/monkeybusinessimages

Page 25: iStock.com/Cesare Ferrari

Page 31: iStock.com/svengine

Page 35: iStock.com/RichardVandenberg

Page 36: Bottom left: iStock.com/terryj; Bottom right: iStock.com/vm

Page 37, top to bottom: iStock.com/YakobchukHelena; iStock.com/KHellon; iStock.com/johnnyscriv

Page 38, left to right: iStock.com/isuzek; iStock.com/ljupco; iStock.com/vadimguzhva

Page 41: iStock.com/GeorgeRudy

Page 45: iStock.com/Chris Ryan

Page 46: Figure 2.14: iStock.com/Denise Erickson; Figure 2.15: kali9; Figure 2.16: iStock.com/anopdesignstock

Page 49: iStock.com/borchee

Page 50: Figure 2.18: iStock.com/Spauln; Figure 2.19: iStock.com/Rouzes

Page 52: Figure 2.20: iStock.com/fstop123; Figure 2.21: iStock.com/Corr

Page 54: iStock.com/klebercordeiro

Page 55: Lakeith Stanfield in *Sorry to Bother You*. Alamy/ © Annapurna Pictures/Entertainment Pictures.

Page 59: iStock.com/Ildar Abulkhanov

Page 65: iStock.com/Casarsa

Page 68: Figure 3.1: iStock.com/cyano66; Figure 3.2: iStock.com/sturti

Page 72: iStock.com/rvimages

Page 85: iStock.com/wacomca

Page 86: iStock.com/recep-bg

Page 92: iStock.com/oatawa

Page 93: FOX/Getty Images

Page 98: Screen capture from the White House Correspondents' Dinner, 2013.

Page 104: iStock.com/Uncleroo

Page 106: iStock.com/SeanPavonePhoto

Page 111: iStock.com/BetNoire

Page 118: iStock.com/firemanYU

Page 119: iStock.com/RyanJLane

Page 121: iStock.com/elwynn1130

Pages 123–24: Universal Pictures. Still images from *Get Out* (2017), directed by Jordan Peele. Courtesy of Universal Studios Licensing LLC.

Page 131: Netflix Studios. Still image from "Chapter One: The Vanishing of Will Byers," *Stranger Things* (2016), Season 1, Episode 1. Courtesy of Netflix US, LLC.

Page 137: iStock.com/EnolaBrain

Page 140: iStock.com/LesByerly

Page 149: Getty Images/David A. Smith

Page 157: Getty Images/Joseph Okpako

Page 165: iStock.com/ratpack223

Page 169: Figure 7.4: iStock.com/CSA images; Figure 7.5: IconicBestiary

Page 170: McCloud, Scott. From *Understanding Comics*, William Morrow, 1994. Copyright © 1993, 1994 Scott McCloud. Used by permission of HarperCollins Publishers.

Page 174: Hulton Archive/Getty Images

Page 189: Screen capture from *Wargames* (1983).

Page 190: Getty Images/Mondadori Portfolio

Page 195: Screen capture from *Red Dead Redemption 2*, Rockstar Games.

Page 201: Stephen Chernin/Getty Images

Page 203: iStock.com/South_agency

Page 205: Used by permission of the photographer.

Page 207: Top left: Screen capture from *Tomb Raider*, Core Design; Top right: Screen capture from *God of War*, Sony.

Page 208: Screen capture from *America's Army* game, U.S. Army.

Page 229: iStock.com/alexsl

Page 236: Dog meme; author unknown.

Page 237: *Weekly World News*. "Bat Child Escapes!" October 6, 1992. Copyright 2021 Bat Boy LLC - Weekly World News, Bat Boy and related marks are trademarks of Bat Boy LLC. Weekly

World News bridles at the suggestion its reliable reporting is "fake news." Reproduced with permission.

Page 239: Screen capture from "*The Shining* starring Jim Carrey: Episode 1 - Concentration [DeepFake]," *Ctrl Shift Face* YouTube channel.

Page 253: iStock.com/joeygil

Page 258: Harry Potter fanart by Kate Carleton. Used by permission.

Page 259: Photo by Greyloch, DragonCon 2019. Used by permission.

Page 261: Photo by David Samsky, DragonCon 2019. Used by permission.

INDEX

Note: Italicized page numbers indicate figures.

INDEX

FROM THE PUBLISHER

A name never says it all, but the word "Broadview" expresses a good deal of the philosophy behind our company. We are open to a broad range of academic approaches and political viewpoints. We pay attention to the broad impact book publishing and book printing has in the wider world; for some years now we have used 100% recycled paper for most titles. Our publishing program is internationally oriented and broad-ranging. Our individual titles often appeal to a broad readership too; many are of interest as much to general readers as to academics and students.

Founded in 1985, Broadview remains a fully independent company owned by its shareholders—not an imprint or subsidiary of a larger multinational.

For the most accurate information on our books (including information on pricing, editions, and formats) please visit our website at www.broadviewpress.com. Our print books and ebooks are also available for sale on our site.

broadview press
www.broadviewpress.com

This book is made of paper from well-managed FSC® - certified
forests, recycled materials, and other controlled sources.